Life
After
College

WARNING:

This guide contains differing opinions. Hundreds of heads will not always agree. Advice taken in combination may cause unwanted side effects. Use your head when selecting advice.

Life After College

The New Graduate's Guide

NADIA BILCHIK, SPECIAL EDITOR

WITH RICKI FRANKEL

Hundreds of Heads Books, LLC

ATLANTA, GEORGIA

Copyright © 2010 by Hundreds of Heads Books, LLC, Atlanta, Georgia

The articles "How to Pick Up at a Party," "5 Don'ts of Dumping," and "20 Dates for Under $20" © 2010 by Andrea Syrtash.

Start Here: Getting Your Financial Life on Track © American Institute for Economic Research 2009, excerpted and reprinted with permission.

Illustrations © 2009 by Image Club
Cover Photograph ©Istockphoto/Yuri Arcurs
Cover design by The Cadence Group
Book design by Elizabeth Johnsboen

Library of Congress Cataloging-in-Publication Data

Life after college : the new graduate's guide / Nadia Bilchik, special editor.

 p. cm.

ISBN 978-1-933512-90-7

1. Young adults--Life skills guides. 2. College graduates--Life skills guides. 3. College graduates--Employment. I. Bilchik, Nadia.

HQ799.5.L57 2010

646.70084'2--dc22

2010000965

See page 400 for credits and permissions.

HUNDREDS OF HEADS® books are available at special discounts when purchased in bulk for premiums or institutional or educational use. Excerpts and custom editions can be created for specific uses. For more information, please e-mail sales@hundredsofheads.com or write to:

HUNDREDS OF HEADS BOOKS, LLC
#230
2221 Peachtree Road, Suite D
Atlanta, Georgia 30309

ISBN-13: 978-1-933512-90-7

Printed in Canada
10 9 8 7 6 5 4 3

CONTENTS

THE HEADS EXPLAINED

With hundreds of tips, stories, and pieces of advice in this book, how can you quickly find those golden nuggets of wisdom? We recommend reading the entire book, of course, but you can also look for these special symbols:

 Remember this significant story or bit of advice.

 This may be something to explore in more detail.

 Watch out! Be careful!

 We are astounded, thrilled, or delighted by this one.

 Here's something to think about.

—*THE EDITORS*
AND HUNDREDS OF HEADS BOOKS

Introduction

What do you want to be when you grow up?

From the time we are children, the question fuels our curiosity, our activities, our dreams. Some seem to know exactly what they want to do from the time they are born. Others spend half of their lives searching before finally discovering their true calling.

And now, upon sitting through a commencement ceremony and receiving a piece of paper to be framed at a later date, you, as a college graduate (and reader of this book), are "grown up." What do you want to *be*?

The potential of your life is thrilling. It also weighs heavily. Is there any other transitional time of your life when you're faced with so many questions, doubts, and challenges?

That's why we created *Life After College*, which builds on other books of ours about the college and post-college experience. We interviewed hundreds of recent college graduates (as well as several experts on relevant subjects) to find out what advice they would pass along to you, as you embark on the first steps of your adult life – the journey to what you want to be.

Among the topics covered:

- What exactly does it mean to be an adult, and what is expected of you?
- Where should you live?
- What kind of career will you pursue?
- Where (and how) will you find your first job?
- What should you know about résumés and interviewing?
- How will you excel in the work place?
- What changes should you make to your social networking, email and technology habits?
- What do you need to know about cars, insurance and finances?
- Should you consider grad school?

- What about survival skills like cooking, wardrobe and adult etiquette?
- How should you find balance between work life, spiritual pursuits, and plain fun?
- And what about dating and finding love (or maybe just a one-night stand)?

Designed to be the "bible" for college graduates, *Life After College* answers these questions and more. It also features a special excerpt on finances for 20-somethings from the book *Start Here: Getting Your Financial Life on Track*, by R.D. Norton, Ph.D. – and some of the best advice from our books on jobs, moving, and dating.

This is a remarkable time in your life. It's filled with moments that will make you want to reconsider why you left college; it also comes with considerable self-fulfillment and happiness. This book just might help tip the balance in your favor.

As you read this book, remember: Every successful person you see, was once standing in your college-graduate shoes, wondering what they wanted to be, and how they would get there. So, now that you are grown up, what do you want to *be*? Read on to find your way to the fulfillment of your dreams - and don't forget to enjoy the journey along the way.

—THE EDITORS

Your first job out of college is often very different from what you had in mind. Indeed, your dreams and ideals can be temporarily thwarted by your first post-college position. That's why it's important to approach the reality of that first job with the right attitude.

This was certainly what I experienced when I graduated with a degree in drama from a prestigious South African university. Fresh out of college and bursting with self-confidence, I truly believed that I would soon become a famous actress. Or, that is what I *thought* would happen as soon as I started my first job as an assistant casting director for a South African film company. Imagine the horror when I found myself being asked to photocopy scripts for an upcoming production! I remember feeling humiliated and indignant and somewhat betrayed that a four-year degree at a top university had led to this.

"Surely I deserve more," I pouted. "Surely I should be sitting in on casting sessions and reading scripts."

Fortunately I had staying power and a sense of humor, surviving what seemed like an endless succession of pointless and menial tasks. I also got to sit in on the casting sessions, and – the big break! – I was fortunate enough to actually get a part.

This was how I ended up as a Nicaraguan terrorist opposite Gary Busey in a rather awful action movie called "*Act of Piracy*" (1990). What followed were eight other leading parts in a series of low-budget action movies. I was fated to die a violent death in each movie. Turns out I wasn't meant to be a movie star. But this experience set me on a career path. It led to my part in a series of "Candid Camera" films, which cultivated my interest in interviewing people.

I soon auditioned for MNET, a South African television station, and became a prime-time anchor. When I moved to America in 1997, I pursued both my TV anchoring career and that of a media and presentation skills coach. I have anchored for CNN Airport Network and various feature programs for CNN International. I also founded Greater Impact Communication, a media and presentation skills training company, and I wrote a book on networking.

So, I'm still ambitious. My career path could not have been predicted by that indignant version of me working on a movie set. But it has been a thrilling ride, and I'm deeply satisfied with my career. You see, so often we have an image of how it's supposed to be, but events transpire in unexpected and surprising ways. That is why it is important to always remain open to the possibilities that present themselves along the way.

It also helps to have some guidance, which is why I've helped edit this book. The advice you'll find in here from other recent college grads is real, helpful, and inspiring. We've also included expert advice on specific topics, including my own tips on networking, dealing with personality types, dinner with the boss, and more.

I wish I could hand it to that younger, pouting version of myself – and tell her that everything would work out fine! And I hope it does for you, too!

—NADIA BILCHIK

Adult Life: What's That?

t might not get the attention of a midlife crisis, but the age when you leave behind your schooling and enter the real world is certainly rife with anxiety. And where there is a personal crisis, there are meaning-of-life questions: Are you really an adult now? Will you ever feel like an adult? What is an adult? What are you going to do with your life? What is life all about? Does it have good benefits? More than two million college grads consider these questions every year. As you take your first steps into adulthood, we provide answers and personal stories.

I WAS STUNNED when I finished college. I literally sat around, staring ahead of me, saying, "What am I going to do?!"

—*A.C.*
TORONTO, ONTARIO, CANADA

I NEVER WANTED TO LEAVE COLLEGE. I WANTED TO BE A STUDENT FOREVER.

—*LEANNE*
ATLANTA, GEORGIA

HEAD LINES
Best Advice and Top Tips

- Finding your way in the world takes time—be patient.
- The first step to becoming an adult is to realize your parents will no longer bail you out of everything.
- Your 20s are the perfect time to think about what you want out of life and what's important to you.
- Being 21 may make you legally an adult, but maturity comes much later.
- Take your time—it's OK if you don't have a spouse, a house, a career, and kids by the time you're 25.

I don't go out during the week anymore, but my weekends are just the same: pure debauchery.

—JIM
HOBOKEN,
NEW JERSEY

UPON GRADUATING COLLEGE, I employed a reliable, time-honored strategy: stalling. I convinced my financial benefactors—my parents—to support my indolent lifestyle for a few extra years by floating ambitious career plans without making too much headway. This approach works. Irresponsibility, bad behavior, and fun should not end with college. You do have to work and pay back loans, but at the same time you can screw up, try a few different things and find out what works best for you. If you are 25, without a marriage, career, mortgage, and kids, that's just fine. It is probably all for the better.

—A.F.
NEW YORK, NEW YORK

ADULT LIFE MEANS THAT THERE IS NO ONE there to wake you up in the morning if you oversleep, no one there to make sure you eat right, no one there to remind you to take your medication, and no one there to turn off the television if you leave it on when you go to sleep. Adult life means you have to do for yourself.

—*KELLEY FREID*
POLAND, OHIO

• • • • • • • •

" Your 20s are this golden period of opportunity; don't waste it. Think hard about what you might regret. What is really important to you? Money? Love? Security? Adventure? It's different things for different people. "

—*GRACE*
CHAPEL HILL, NORTH CAROLINA

• • • • • • • •

WE'RE INUNDATED WITH HOLLYWOOD images about how our first love, our first job, and our life will look as adults. In a way, we're set up to reach for things that may not be realistic. Finding your way takes time, and it helps to know others feel this way, too.

—*J.B.*
TRURO, NOVA SCOTIA, CANADA

NEED A LIFE COACH?

Life coaching: Used by a growing number of psychologists to aid clients with transitions in their personal life, and in the process of self-actualization. Life coaching draws from a number of disciplines, including sociology, psychology, career counseling, and other types of counseling. The coach, or counselor, applies mentoring, values assessment, behavior modification, behavior modeling, goal setting, and other techniques in assisting clients.

I recall Dean Wormer's advice from *Animal House*: "Fat, drunk and stupid is no way to go through life, son."

—*ANONYMOUS*
GENEVA, OHIO

I LOST A LOT OF SLEEP AFTER GRADUATION and had a few panic attacks. Men and women in my generation feel a great amount of pressure to succeed at a young age. It is more important to travel, continue school (i.e., graduate school, if possible), find yourself, and feel happy and strong on your own before entering the workforce. The real world will always be waiting, so make sure that you see and experience everything before you are tied down to a certain amount of vacation days and time constraints.

—*STEPH MATHEWS*
ST. LOUIS, MISSOURI

• • • • • • • •

I STILL DON'T FEEL LIKE MY OWN PERSON. At 22 years old, I feel like I borrowed bits of other people's personalities. I don't know if that makes sense, but I just don't really understand who I am yet. But I understand others and what I like about them, so I adopt those traits. Maybe this is what it's all about. Hopefully I will become more than just the cool things about other people as I get older.

—*JESSICA*
SEATTLE, WASHINGTON

MY PARENTS FUNDED EVERYTHING IN COLLEGE. Maybe I was spoiled. But there's none of that in the "real world." You're not working a part-time job so you have some bar money on the weekends. You're working full time so you can pay rent, cable, phone, and electricity bills; you work to live. If you don't do your laundry, you can't put on dirty clothes and stroll to class. You have to have ironed clothes for client meetings. In the "real world," you're more accountable for all of your actions, and you're truly independent.

> —JIM
> HOBOKEN, NEW JERSEY

• • • • • • • •

I FELT LIKE A GROWN-UP WHEN I realized that I and my space—the space I take up on this earth—are just as important as anyone else and the space they take up. Once you realize that, you can stand there and not be intimidated by anybody else. That's when I started feeling like an adult.

> —JOEY
> CAPE COD, MASSACHUSETTS

• • • • • • • •

WHEN YOU GRADUATE, don't have a nervous breakdown over your career choice; you will probably change careers somewhere along the line. Lots of people start out in one career and then move into another one. Even specialized careers like medicine and law have some latitude within them. I know lawyers who went from corporate law to criminal defense, and massage therapists who later became teachers.

> —ANONYMOUS
> SOUTH BEND, INDIANA

YOU'RE FREE! CELEBRATING YOUR GRADUATION

I WENT SKINNY-DIPPING WITH THREE FRIENDS at Table Rock Lake—totally impromptu and totally awesome. It was the most invigorating, timeless afternoon I have ever experienced. I felt so free and unguarded. It's like shedding the bathing suit also shed my insecurities, my need for self-preservation. It sounds corny, but it's totally true. Everyone should do this at least once in his or her life. But look out, because it can become addictive!

> —*ANGELA WILSON*
> *SPRINGFIELD, MISSOURI*

FORGET A PARTY. Get the hell out of town (on your parents' dime) and enjoy every last bit of irresponsible behavior you can possibly stand. I went to Aruba for a week after I graduated and absorbed every last second of the comforts of the family benefit plan.

> —*KRISTI KAMERMAN*
> *BATON ROUGE, LOUISIANA*

MY MOM AND I WENT TO A DUDE RANCH IN COLORADO for a week and a half to celebrate my graduation. I love horses, and it was something I had always wanted to do. It was great because we got to spend some quality time together. She told me how proud she was of me for getting my degree. It was really special. I'm glad that I had the opportunity to celebrate with my mom, especially now that I'm starting my career and don't have as much free time.

> —*JACKIE MOORE*
> *OZARK, MISSOURI*

I CELEBRATED ONE NIGHT AT OUR FAVORITE COLLEGE BAR with my friends and family, then woke up the next morning and started my job as a meat cutter at a barbecue joint to pay the bills until I found a "real job." I got 50 cents more an hour than anyone else because I was the only meat cutter with a college degree.

—JAMES RINEY
FORT WORTH, TEXAS

THE DAY AFTER MY GRADUATION, my mom and I went out and I bought a brand-new Honda Civic. There were only six miles on that baby, and that was after my test drive. I felt like I was signing my life away.

—K.R.
BELLEVILLE, ILLINOIS

GRADUATION FROM COLLEGE WAS one of the most surreal times of my life. Be sure to make time for everyone that meant something to you during that magical time of your undergrad. Eat at all your favorite places. Have a drink at your favorite bar. Spend time at the fountain where you and your roommate would eat pints of ice cream and talk about boys. Celebrate all of your recent successes and all those that are waiting ahead of you. Even if you can't get everyone together at once, figure out a way to see them. You never know when you'll see them again.

—ERIN HUDAK
AUSTIN, TEXAS

BE PREPARED FOR YOUR RELATIONSHIP with your parents to do a complete 180. My parents and I were never friends when I was in my teens. We battled out every issue in a full-on war. But as I progressed into my 20s and became more independent and more able to financially support myself, our relationship changed. We are now good friends. I call my mom every week just to hear how things are going.

—HEATHER POLLOCK
ORANGE COUNTY, CALIFORNIA

YOU HAVE (OTHER) OPTIONS ...

I didn't consider graduate school because I always thought that you could learn more at a minimum wage job than you could getting an silly degree. Plus, you'd probably be in a lot less debt. I did learn quite a bit working at a hardware store for $7.50 an hour in rural Connecticut. Say what you will about a liberal arts education, but it often does not cover the ability to remember the difference between a carriage bolt and a lag bolt, or if this pesticide will accidentally poison your dog. By all means, I'd recommend that a college graduate get a job like this. Not only do you learn the value of a dollar, but retail jobs in general afford you the opportunity to see the best and worst of people. It's a great chance to observe what life is like away from the quad, which is something your buddies with, say, consulting gigs in big cities, don't get a chance to do. For most college grads, those bland, white-collar opportunities will always be there for you. But the opportunity to do something random or unique for a short period of time will not always be there, especially once you find yourself established in the real world.

—*ANONYMOUS*
ATLANTA, GEORGIA

FOR THE PAST FEW YEARS since graduating college, I haven't been as social. I wanted to figure out what was important to me by figuring it out on my own, not by joining a larger community and figuring it out by what others deemed to be important. This was my intuition, and I followed it. Instead of trying A, B, and C, I opted for X, Y, Z. Be open to listening to your instincts; they come from a deep place. Post-college is a time of change, and it's very personal.

—*NICHOLAS WEISS*
SAN FRANCISCO, CALIFORNIA

ADULT LIFE TO ME: NO MORE COLLEGE BREAKS!
This meant no more spring break and no more
month-long Christmas breaks. This was the hardest part for me.

—*MICAH KARBER*
SILVERTON, TEXAS

• • • • • • • •

MOVING AWAY TO COLLEGE is much different than
moving to a new city once you graduate. When
you're still in college, you might be far from
home, like I was, but you're still connected to
your family—through money, through visits,
through the way you are seen in your parents'
eyes. Out of college, I moved away to a big city,
and that's when I finally cut the apron strings and
did whatever I wanted. It was freeing and frightening at the same time.

—*MICHELE*
HOLLY, MICHIGAN

Consider

BEFORE YOU TURN 25 …

… Enjoy your free time! According to a U.S.
Department of Labor survey, here's how
Americans between the ages of 25 and 54 spend
their day:

Working – 8.7
Sleeping – 7.6
Leisure – 2.6
Other – 1.7
Caring for others – 1.2
Eating and drinking – 1.1
Household activities – 1.1

WHAT ARE YOU?

Main entry: adult
Function: noun
1: one that has arrived at full development or maturity especially in size, strength, or intellectual capacity
2: a human male or female after a specific age (as 18 or 21)

BEING AN ADULT MEANS that when you create a problem for yourself, you have to solve it yourself. It's the point in your life where you can't turn to Mom and Dad to bail you out. It means being personally responsible for yourself and your actions. If you find yourself still looking around for someone else to clean up things that you did wrong, you are not yet an adult.

—*SUZANNE EDENHART*
WILLIAMSTOWN, KENTUCKY

• • • • • • • •

IF YOU STOP ASKING THE QUESTION "What should I do with my life?" life will hold little meaning, and your talents could be left undiscovered. I face this question every day. No matter how "successful" I have become or how comfortable I feel with my current situation—job or no job, relationship or not—I find myself asking questions: What is my purpose? Why am I here? So far, I haven't been able to answer. But the fact that I have asked in the first place is progress in itself.

—*JERALYN*
AUSTIN, TEXAS

• • • • • • • •

BEING AN ADULT MEANS being content with the unknowns in life and feeling confident that you can handle them when they catch you by surprise. If you're still feeling some "angst," restlessness, insecurity, or confusion about where you fit in the world, then you're probably not an adult yet. But if you're willing to go through these restless experiences with an open mind and some courage and patience, then you're one HUGE step closer to being an "adult."

—*KATRINA*
NEW YORK, NEW YORK

TOP 5 COMMENCEMENT SPEECHES

The Huffington Post had readers vote on their favorite commencement speeches of all time. With your commencement speech still fresh in your mind, here are the top five. Google them and get inspired:

1. Stephen Colbert at Knox College
2. Jon Stewart at William & Mary
3. Steve Jobs at Stanford
4. Oprah Winfrey at Howard University
5. President John F. Kennedy at American University

I KNEW I WAS AN ADULT when I filled out the tax forms for my new job and didn't claim dependency on my father. Oh, and that first round of utility bills did it too.

—*LACEY CONNELLY*
CHICAGO, ILLINOIS

• • • • • • • •

I'm not really clear on what path to take now, but I don't think the path needs to be clear. I've spent 17 years in school preparing for being an adult, and now I finally have the freedom to see what's out there and to do what I want.

—*CLAIRE LEVY*
BERKELEY, CALIFORNIA

> You really don't have to be good at everything. Find the one thing you like to do and explore that!
>
> —*NADIA*

SO, WHAT ARE YOU GOING TO DO WITH YOUR LIFE?

CONGRATULATIONS! You are entering a period of your life when you are finally, finally on your own and can make your own decisions. This doesn't come, however, without one final flurry of in-your-business questions from your parents (as well as aunts and uncles, neighbors, friends of your parents, the family doctor, etc.). Here are some questions to expect, and how you can stealthily avoid them (and buy a bit more time away from the real world). Note: It doesn't matter if any of these answers are true, only that you deliver them in convincing fashion.

Q. So, what are you going to do with your life?

A. I'm exploring options right now. I majored in _____, so I'm hoping to use my degree in a positive way. I have a few leads, and I want to make sure I get started on the right foot. I've given myself a three-month timeframe, and after that I'm diving in.

Q. When are you going to move out of your parents' house?

A. Trust me, as soon as I can. Of course, I love my parents and am grateful for their generosity. I don't want it to go to waste! In fact, I was just recently talking with a few friends about getting a place together.

Q. What careers interest you?

A. You know, I have a lot of interests. Based on what you know about me, what do you see me doing?

Q. How are you going about looking for a job?

A. I've been doing a lot of networking through my friends as well as online research. In fact, if you know anyone who has connections to the fields I'm interested in, I'd be grateful for an introduction.

Q. Why don't you just go to Mexico and live on the beach for the summer?

A. Great idea! Do you have some cash handy?

—*The Editors*

DON'T GROW OLD TOO FAST by worrying prematurely about a career, family, and so on. The opportunity for trying out all kinds of work, even experimenting with not working at all (spare change, food stamps, selling all your belongings and living in the woods) is not to be missed. Follow your whims: pump gas, preach the apocalypse, worship the devil, volunteer in a nursing home, and get to know the joys and regrets of people at the other end of the road. It's impossible to screw up your life so much at this stage that it can't be repaired with a little dedication and hard work somewhere down the line. One of the most freeing verses I've ever heard was Bob Dylan's: "It's alright, Ma: it's life and life only."

—*JOE*
BOSTON, MASSACHUSETTS

· · · · · · · ·

I KNEW I WAS AN ADULT when others started to view me as one. Example: Once I stayed out way too late and did something I probably shouldn't have been doing. The next day I got a call from a friend and I told him what I did. He said, "Hey man, you're grown up now. You've got a real job. You can't act like that anymore."

—*BRANDON*
DALLAS, TEXAS

· · · · · · · ·

THERE WAS CERTAINLY A POINT when I thought, "Oh, shit. My parents are not going to bail me out of this anymore." It is a powerful feeling.

—*J.G.*
CHAPEL HILL, NORTH CAROLINA

One of my favorite Nelson Mandela quotes: "Our deepest fear is not that we are inadequate. Our deepest fear is that we are powerful beyond measure."
—*NADIA*

THE REAL WORLD – OR THE TV SHOW?

The Apartment: On *The Real World*, the palatial apartments are exquisitely furnished and decorated by IKEA. The roommates always play pool, always congregate in the hot tub, and always have their cupboards magically stocked with delicious food upon their arrival. I have lived in several apartments in the real world and, I am sorry to say, none of this ever happened.

The Cameras: This is an obvious one. On *The Real World*, there is a camera in your face nearly every second of every day, except when you use the restroom. In the real world, you can lounge in your pajamas, examine your pores, put on a mud mask, eat cereal for dinner, or fight with your significant other, and nobody has to know!

The Sexuality: "Are you gay? Are you straight? Wait, wait, don't tell me. You're bi! Aren't you? Huh, huh? Tell me, please!" Few people in the real world are this obnoxious about whether you date men, women, or both. Thank goodness.

The Roommates: Imagine living with 7 other people whom you neither know nor have chosen. It boggles the mind. In the real world, you will probably live with no more than 4 other people. Best of all, you will get to screen out the Loud, Messy, Insomiac-types from your enclave of Clean, Quiet, In-bed-before-11-types.

The Confessional: On *The Real World*, everyone must confess. In the real world, only Catholics must confess.

The Drama: *Jolene, who is really in love with Dwight, hooked up with David. Sandy and Kelly kissed. Now, Sandy is concerned how her girlfriend back home is going to react. Wendy is upsetting everyone in the house because she leaves her toenail clippings on the coffee table. The angry tension between Michelle* *and Keegan came to a head when she threw a marble statue at his head, but ended up smashing the enormous fish tank instead. Will Michelle be kicked out of the house?*

While these sorts of things *do* happen in the real world, they probably won't *all* happen to you. At once.

—*Sarah Franco*

DO WHAT MAKES YOU HAPPY. I spent five years working for our family business. I realized I was on my way to becoming an adult just recently, when I told my family that I wanted to work elsewhere. I just landed my first job on my own, doing something totally different. I love my family, but I want to make it on my own.
— *TAWNY WHITE*
SPRINGFIELD, MISSOURI

• • • • • • • •

WHEN I FIRST HIT THE ADULT AGE OF 21, it meant I was old enough to do adult things. I could live where I wanted and drink what I wanted. Being a *mature adult* came a lot later, and proved to be a learn-as-you-go process. I wanted people to take me seriously, and it took a lot of falling down. There was still a part of me that wanted to be young and carefree. It took a lot of practice.
— *CHRISTOPHER*
HAVERTOWN, PENNSYLVANIA

You only live once. Go with the flow ... or paddle like hell.
—*JOE*
BOSTON,
MASSACHUSETTS

A PLACE TO START WHEN YOU DON'T HAVE A CLUE

Many people come to me not knowing what they want to do. I suggest we start by looking for clues throughout their lives. For example, I ask them to start with a basic question: "What do I like to talk about?" I call it the "conversations" homework: Begin to observe and keep a record of the conversations that you enjoy and those you do not. Notice what piques your curiosity, what engages you, whom you enjoy talking to, and what makes your eyes glaze over. Do you like to talk about sports, fashion, real estate, or gardening? Just paying attention to which conversations excite you and which do not will give you insights about where you want to go. Record what catches your interest. With some reflection, some answers and themes will emerge.

—*Ricki Frankel*

The transition from college to the real world is all about maturity.

—*S.K.*
WICHITA, KANSAS

ESTABLISHING REASONABLE BOUNDARIES in your relationship with your parents is the key to being an adult. People do this at all different ages. But it is only through this process that you understand how to cope in the world.

—*L.F.*
NEW YORK, NEW YORK

• • • • • • • •

BEING AN ADULT MEANS you no longer have any financial and decision-making strings attached to your parents. You have carved your own career and life path, learned a lot in the process, and no longer have to depend on anyone else to assist you. It's not an age; it's a degree of responsibility.

—*KATIE*
ATLANTA, GEORGIA

A GOALS LIST FOR YOUR 20s

The journey is not the map. But it helps to have a map for your journey. Otherwise, you might get lost. Which is why you should write up a Goals List for your 20s. It doesn't have to be in-depth. It doesn't have to accurately predict the future. It should merely offer direction and be realistic. Review the list every year or so to update it and admire anything you have accomplished. Here are the main topics to cover:

Career Goals. Try to think big-picture *and* small-picture here. Big picture: What do you want to accomplish, and by what age? Small picture: What steps will you take each year to get there? You might also include a list of five realistic goals you'd like to reach at your current job. And a line that says, "Spend 30 extra minutes at work each evening."

Financial Goals. Everyone is different. If you're horrible at finances, work on becoming better at budgeting. And always include an entry like, "Pay off debt" or put an annual spending limit on credit cards. Once you reach 25, you should visit a financial advisor for more in-depth direction.

Relationship Goals. You can't predict when love will find you, but you can think about when you might want to settle down (if ever). Your thoughts on this can inform all of your dating experiences – even if you fall in love. For instance, if you don't want to settle down and start a family until your mid-30s, a love affair at 25 might be less burdened by those expectations.

Fun Goals. Visit Bora Bora? Run an adventure race? Learn guitar? What do you want to accomplish before you get, ahem, *old* and start a family? Make a list, and try not to put more than one fun goal a year. If you can accomplish more than one, more power to you. But there's no need to turn "fun" into another responsibility that needs to be tended to.

—The Editors

5 TIPS FOR CONQUERING POST-COLLEGE BLUES

Does it suck to be you? College is over; career options are limited; friends are scattered; and things just seem *different*?

You might be suffering from a very common case of post-college depression. It's brought on by one of the most turbulent life changes you will experience: One moment, your days are scheduled with classes, graded achievement, friends, extracurriculars and parties; the next, you're on your own and no one is telling you where to go or what to do.

Here are five tips to help you overcome the "quarter-life crisis."

Make an effort to meet new people. One of the biggest benefits of school life, from grade school to college, was the built-in social calendar. That's absent now. But don't let that be your excuse to crawl into a hole or settle for a night of drink specials at the local watering hole. Reach out to new people. Join groups and organizations. Remember: There are many others in your shoes, looking for new people to meet and cool things to do.

Find a new hobby. The learning never stops – even, *especially,* after college. You're still growing and maturing and learning what you want out of life. Explore. Take a class or two. Join a sports league. Discover the great outdoors. It will give you something to look forward to and focus extra energy on.

Create career goals. Whether you love your first post-college job or hate it, you're not going to be there forever. Where will you go next? What do you want to accomplish in five years? Write down specific (and doable) goals, and check in with them often to make sure you're on target.

Travel. You're young. You don't have a lot of money, but you can travel cheaply. Use vacation time to explore new places and take new adventures. You might find the next city you want to call home; you might experience a memorable week on the rails of Europe. These experiences will fuel your work and life.

Let go of your student identity. It's fine to cheer for your college and wear your colors now and then. But it's also important to embrace your new self. What new person do you want to become in your 20s? How will you get there? A clear picture of who you are and want to be is important in your continuing development.

—*The Editors*

DO WHAT MAKES YOU HAPPY. I spent five years working for our family business. I realized I was on my way to becoming an adult just recently, when I told my family that I wanted to work elsewhere. I just landed my first job on my own, doing something totally different. I love my family, but I want to make it on my own.

—*TAWNY WHITE*
SPRINGFIELD, MISSOURI

• • • • • • • •

WHEN I FIRST HIT THE ADULT AGE OF 21, it meant I was old enough to do adult things. I could live where I wanted and drink what I wanted. Being a *mature adult* came a lot later, and proved to be a learn-as-you-go process. I wanted people to take me seriously, and it took a lot of falling down. There was still a part of me that wanted to be young and carefree. It took a lot of practice.

—*CHRISTOPHER*
HAVERTOWN, PENNSYLVANIA

HERE ARE THE THINGS YOU MUST STOP doing as an adult: 1. Drinking directly out of the milk carton. 2. Forgetting to flush the toilet. 3. Leaving your underwear lying around. 4. Spending all your money on beer and cheeseburgers. 5. Sleeping until noon on days off.

—*VIGGY FAIRFIELD*
HARRISONBURG, VIRGINIA

• • • • • • • •

66 I recommend that, before you settle down with a real job, you become a lobster fisherman in Maine. I did that for a few months, and it was a great experience. You live in a small cabin with other fishermen, get up early, and spend hours at sea. It changed me. 99

—*AARON*
DULUTH, GEORGIA

• • • • • • • •

ADULT LIFE MEANS PAYING for everything yourself, not being able to blame others for your mistakes, gaining weight, and having to move heavy objects on your own.

—*ELIZABETH*
PHILADELPHIA, PENNSYLVANIA

ONE STEP AT A TIME

People sometimes believe they need to figure out what they want to do for the rest of their lives. The words *for the rest of my life* add an awful lot of pressure—that's a long time! No wonder people feel stuck; the problem simply becomes too big. Keep in mind that you are not locked into any one career path for the rest of your life. Frame the problem in a smaller way: Figure out what you want to do *next*. That's a smaller, more manageable task. Based on what you know about yourself, and the various career paths and companies you know about, what seems to make sense *today*? You cannot possibly know exactly what career you will love forever. If you define the problem in a smaller way, you'll make a lot more progress more quickly.

—Ricki Frankel

TAKE TIME TO DECIDE WHAT you really want to do, but also be responsible. Take a job so you can earn money while you research other careers. I worked in an administrative office while I decided on my career path. As it turned out, I really enjoyed my work. I eventually became the manager in the office, which gave me more flexibility in deciding how to run the office. It turned into my dream job.

—LORAINE BRANCATTO BOERSMA
TOLEDO, OHIO

YOU DON'T FIND WHAT YOU WANT TO DO; it finds you. I've watched people try to find out exactly what they're supposed to be and what they want to do, and it just stresses them out. I always tell people not to worry about it. You just figure it out one day without even realizing you're thinking about it.

—*DIRK*
ATLANTA, GEORGIA

• • • • • • • •

" Finding a career you love is like dating: You have to meet many people in your life before you can decide what you want. "

—*DEBS*
SAN DIEGO, CALIFORNIA

• • • • • • • •

WHEN DID I KNOW I WAS AN ADULT? I had been out of college for about a year, lost my job, and was about to get kicked out of my apartment because I was a month late with the rent. I went home to talk to my dad about it, subconsciously thinking he'd say I could move back home if it came down to it. But he told me the exact opposite. Without saying it in so many words, he told me that I'd have to find a way to get through it on my own. I knew then that I was welcome to visit, but that my days living there were over.

—*CAM THORNTON*
JAMESTOWN, NEW YORK

Oh, the Places You'll Go! On Traveling & Adventure

Have you watched The Graduate *yet? You should! But in case you haven't, allow us to spoil a very important part. In a particular scene, the "graduate," played by Dustin Hoffman, is riding on a bus with his love, played by Katharine Ross. It's not clear where they're headed – just that they're going somewhere else. The scene encapsulates the mood of young people not just the 1960s (as some would have us believe) but every graduate leaving college behind. The world is out there, and for the first time in your adult life, it's time to really explore it. We asked grads: Where did you go once you got out? What adventure did you find?*

CAP YOUR COLLEGE EXPERIENCE with a summer trip with your best friends. It's pretty painful to graduate and leave "the best years of your life," so I recommend something fun to ease the transition.

—DENISE
BOSTON, MASSACHUSETTS

DON'T BE AFRAID TO EXPLORE THE WORLD!

—M.B.
WEEHAWKEN,
NEW JERSEY

HEADLINES
Best Advice and Top Tips

- Get out and see the world while you still can.
- Move to a new city. Experience life away from your family and friends.
- Don't move someplace just because you're in love—unless you think you'll be happy there even if the relationship ends.

READY TO SEE THE WORLD?

Check out the State Department site for passport and visa requirements for each country: travel.state.gov.

IF YOU WENT TO SCHOOL in a college town, move away once you graduate. College towns have this strange thing about them where people who stay there after school think it's OK to act like they are still in school but without the learning part. I know so many bright people who graduated and then just hung around, drinking and playing in bands and working in restaurants. The same thing could have happened to me, but I moved to New York and went to grad school. Being in a city like that made me really understand the value of ambition.

—*LIZ*
GREENVILLE, NORTH CAROLINA

• • • • • • • •

IF YOU'VE NEVER BEEN TO EUROPE, you can get yourself a Eurail pass and see some of the world's most famous places. Do it before you're 26, because that's the age when you can longer get "youth" discounts. I saw places that everybody talks about, like Paris and Rome. It makes me feel more like a part of the adult world.

—*CLARE*
SEATTLE, WASHINGTON

MY TRAVEL EXCURSIONS so far have mostly involved breathtaking drives along the country's interstate system, cuisine at the nation's finest convenience stores and fast-food outlets, and luxurious stays at the Super 8 Motel's most exotic franchises. Weekends in the Caribbean are still just something I see footage of on the E! network.

—*JESSE AMMERMAN*
CHICAGO, ILLINOIS

· · · · · · · ·

AFTER COLLEGE, I BACKPACKED around Asia for almost a year. Even though I started out alone, I met up with great people and had travel partners when I wanted them. I did beaches, temples, great natural sites, and partied like a rock star, all in places that are way off the map and cheap, cheap, cheap. My favorite countries were Vietnam and Indonesia, but everybody loves someplace different. Take a trip like this while you've got the time and energy.

—*J.R.*
CHICAGO, ILLINOIS

· · · · · · · ·

IN THE PAST, VACATION MEANT paying for transportation to a place where I knew someone. This way, lodging was always free, and I got to see old friends. Now that I've been out of school for four years, I can finally afford to take a real vacation, to a city where I don't know anyone, and stay in a hotel. I can't afford a luxury vacation and have to take the time to search online to find the best deals, but it still feels very grown-up.

—*M.B.*
WEEHAWKEN, NEW JERSEY

SEEK ADVENTURE NOW. As soon as I graduated, I climbed Mount Popocatepetl in Mexico and Mount Washington in New Hampshire. They were both very challenging and both very different, but I summited both of them. I'm glad I did it before falling into a career. I'd love to go to Mount Everest sometime, but how do you tell your boss you need a month off work to go climb a big hill?

—*ALISHA HIPWELL*
FRANKFORT, KENTUCKY

" Register for automatic email updates on super-saver fares from airlines. I get weekly emails from Delta, American, United—you name it. I once saved $200 on a flight that way. "

—*STEVE GEHN*
GERRY, NEW YORK

TAKE TIME TO LIVE IT UP. I traveled to random cities in the United States where I knew somebody. I didn't even have to know the person well; I just had to make sure that they extended the invitation to visit them at some point, and I took them up on the offer. My goal was to experience the nightlife in various cities around the country with new people.

—*JEFF MALTZ*
SAN FRANCISCO, CALIFORNIA

TAKING A 'GAP YEAR'

There is great achievement in graduation. But for many, even as their mortarboards fly into the air, the future looms as a great and amorphous unknown. They still don't know what they want to be when they grow up; there is no magic epiphany, and, for many, self-doubt and depression set in.

It is at this point that you have a choice, and going back to college for a graduate degree is not the only one. Another idea, if you can afford it, is to take a gap year or two to explore your options. Then you can go back to college or into the work force with more direction and commitment. Indeed, you will find that graduate admissions officers and human resources departments will look kindly upon students who take productive gap years. Both are looking for well-rounded people who have a clear idea of the direction they want to follow.

But before you take a gap year, you need to understand that taking a break like this does not mean spending the year on the couch eating potato chips and feeling sorry for yourself. Rather, the purpose of a gap year is to go out into the world to learn, grow and gain personal insight – and to do this without parents. In essence, this is a time to gain life skills and maturity, and bring them back to commit to the development of a successful post-graduate career.

Travel, volunteer, or get a part-time job – particularly if your gap year includes going to another country. There are many programs, Peace Corps among them, that employ recent grads to travel abroad and provide services in another country. Ultimately, you should take care that your travels do not devolve into a glorified (and essentially unproductive) vacation.

If you take a gap year, it should be a time where you are socially useful and engaged in some way. If you take full advantage of it, you could land a better job, get in to a better grad school program, and takes steps that could pay off for a lifetime.

—*Nadia Bilchik*

DON'T FOLLOW SOMEONE BECAUSE you're in love with them. When I graduated college, I followed my boyfriend to this town because he wanted to be a musician, and he thought it was the right place for him to be. Of course there was nothing there for me, and I ended up waiting tables in that town for 10 years. No man is worth that.

—*J.*
BINGHAMTON, NEW YORK

* * * * * * * *

❝Do you actually think your future boss or spouse is going to let you take three months off to hit Eurail? Go now, while you're free from obligations. ❞

—*J.A.*
ATLANTA, GEORGIA

* * * * * * * *

IF YOU CAN FIGURE OUT A WAY TO GO ABROAD, do it. You will experience things that will never happen to you in the States. I went to Spain with some friends and we wanted to go to Pamplona to see the running of the bulls. We needed a ride there. We were about two hours away, and we caught a ride with this guy with an 18-wheeler. I wouldn't be caught dead riding in an 18-wheeler in the United States. You'd be chopped up into little pieces. But for some reason, it was OK in Spain.

—*LEANNE*
ATLANTA, GEORGIA

SPEND THIS TIME REALIZING PERSONAL GOALS. After I was out on my own, I spent one year living away from home with no boyfriend and nothing to tie me down. After that, I was always in a relationship. I got pets. I let my world become very domestic very quickly. Because of this, I never did a lot of the traveling I wanted to do, I didn't apply to a few fellowships and writing retreats that I wanted to, I never took the time to learn Spanish—so many things that I now regret pushing aside for relationships and work.

—*B.*
CHAPEL HILL, NORTH CAROLINA

• • • • • • • •

WHEN YOU ARE IN YOUR NEW CITY, find all the old constellations you knew from your old city. That's very reassuring. It's something you were used to seeing before, and there it is again, right above your house. It makes the whole world seem smaller, because the people that you miss are not that far away. You're both looking at the same sky.

—*KAMI*
CAPE COD, MASSACHUSETTS

• • • • • • • •

I THUMBED MY WAY ACROSS EUROPE with practically no money in my pockets. Looking back, it's a miracle that I wasn't killed. I'd take rides with anyone and sleep wherever I could. When I got desperate for money, I'd take some little job for a week and then move on. I know other people do this, but they usually have some money. I spent all I had on the flight. It was a lot of fun—the experience of a lifetime.

—*CHARLENE WHITTED*
JAMESTOWN, NEW YORK

DO IT WHILE YOU'RE YOUNG

Eurailpasses are significantly cheaper for people who are under 26 years old. Check out www.raileurope.com for details.

CARPE ANNUM! (SEIZE THE YEAR!)

One of the best ways to make living in the real world easier later on is to use at least one year (two at max) after college to live in total fantasy. This does not mean snorting coke off hookers' backs every night (you won't be able to afford it yet), or not paying your bills, but rather allowing yourself one year to do what you have always dreamed of doing. If you have always wanted to work on a cowboy ranch, do it. If you have always wanted to teach English in a foreign country, do it. Always wanted to live in Seattle? Pack your duffel and go. Seriously. Do not worry about what will happen to you or whether this choice is directly contributing to your future. Because it definitely is, even if you can't see the connections right now.

One of the best things I did for myself was to pack a couple of suitcases and move to San Francisco a year after college graduation. I had no job there, but I found one quickly at an expensive art store, and then as a receptionist at a software company. I had no apartment, so I stayed with my aunt in Sausalito for a month until a high school friend moved out there and we found a kick-ass place. I was in a Vespa scooter club, took a creative writing class, dated some hot Buddy Holly–looking programmers. It felt crazy and aimless at the time, but it was the best thing I ever did, because A. Now I never have to say, "Gosh, I wonder what my life would be like if I lived in San Francisco"; B. Now I know some awesome restaurants and places to go whenever I visit; and C. Now I know that I actually have the fortitude and wherewithal to just move across the country with nothing and make it for at least a year. This is perhaps the most important thing of all.

—*T.M.*
ATLANTA, GEORGIA

BEFORE YOU GET INVOLVED WITH SOMEONE, when you can go where *you* want to go, pick a location you have never seen and will be unlikely to see again. The only trip like this that I ever got to take was to Grand Teton National Park. I had seen a PBS special on it and couldn't get the images out of my mind. It was a spur-of-the-moment decision to go, and one I figured I'd never have the chance to do again. It was the most memorable trip I've ever taken. And I think part of that is because it was *my* trip and mine alone.

—JAKE ELIAS
HARRISONBURG, VIRGINIA

• • • • • • • •

I TOOK A LEFT TURN OUT OF COLLEGE. I was meant to go to law school and went over to England instead, working in advertising. I learned more in the first five years out of school than I did during my 80,000 college experiences. When you go through something like that, it becomes not just a book you read; you understand it. Not everyone can afford to take a year to travel overseas. But take it. It's invaluable.

—STEFANIE
NEW YORK, NEW YORK

• • • • • • • •

YOU COULD GO TO A MILLION PLACES that cost a ton of money. Or you could do something that's perfect for a college grad—cheap, adventurous, and best done before you have major responsibilities. I'm talking about the great U.S. national parks. I went camping and hiking for a whole summer with my best college buddies through Bryce, Arches, Zion, and the Grand Canyon, and it is still one of the greatest memories.

—SAM
SANTA MONICA, CALIFORNIA

Americans think it's a big deal to move to a foreign country, but people who live outside of the United States think nothing of it.

—BILLIE
CHICAGO, ILLINOIS

IT'S A GOOD EXPERIENCE FOR EVERYONE to have to adapt to a new place. When I graduated college, I went to Japan to teach English. I thought it would be a good move professionally, but looking back now, the biggest growth occurred personally. I learned a lot about myself by being in a different culture. It's like that old Zen expression, "If you don't bend, you'll break."

—*DARCY BELANGER*
SHERWOOD PARK, ALBERTA, CANADA

WHEN I GRADUATED COLLEGE, I drove across the country with this boy I hardly knew. I took my graduation money and blew it. I had a wonderful time. It makes my hair stand up to think of some of the situations I got into. But I had done the right things: I went straight from high school to college; I got good grades. I needed that time to find out who I was.

—*LAUREN*
CHAPEL HILL, NORTH CAROLINA

I THINK THIS IS A PERFECT TIME in your life to just leave the country. GO! The best thing I've ever done for myself: I just packed up and left the country. I exhaled. For a year. I fell in love. With a man, with a city, with the simple things in life. Experience that before you experience any other "real-world" nonsense. Stop time. Just for once. And ... live.

—*AMBREEN HUSSAIN*
NEW YORK, NEW YORK

NEW YORK CITY! Coming from the West Coast— Seattle and the Bay Area—New York is a whirlwind where you can learn and be anonymous if you need to. Check out craigslist.org or other boards, and try to line up a job before moving out. Then try to crash for a few weeks with your brother's friend's cousin, or someone like that, while you find a place to live. Search for digs downtown and don't rule out Brooklyn. You might get a better deal on a place and still have incredible access to the energy of the Big Apple.

—*JENNIFER*
SEATTLE, WASHINGTON

• • • • • • • • •

DO SOMETHING CRAZY. Once, my friends and I bought these supercheap airline tickets from Southwest. We flew down to San Diego and then rented a car and drove down to Mexico. We only bought the plane tickets one way, and then we didn't have enough money to fly back, so we had to take the rental car and drive it from Mexico the whole way to Kentucky. We almost didn't even have enough money to do that. When we got back, I think we had about $17 left between us. But it was a superfun trip. When you are 21 years old, I can't think of a better place to go.

—*CARLOS ZAHIR*
INDEPENDENCE, KENTUCKY

Home Away From Home: Finding Your First Post-College Pad

How's that plan to land a trust fund working out for you? Well, assuming you're not A) already rich, or B) The Talented Mr. Ripley (and let's hope you're not), you're just going to have to leave behind your plans to travel Europe for your entire life. At least, temporarily. That means getting a job, and finding a place to live. Let's explore the living arrangements first. Where will you start your new post-graduate life? At mom's house? Around the corner with a roommate? A distant, thriving metropolis? We asked others how they handled this transition. Read on for the keys to your new place.

FIRST AND FOREMOST, I would not have moved in with my college sweetheart. If you're in a serious relationship at the end of your college career, give it some thought before you decide to move in with him or her.

—ALEX
ATLANTA, GEORGIA

ONE DAY YOU'RE GOING TO TELL FUNNY STORIES ABOUT YOUR AWFUL FIRST APARTMENT.

—J.A.
ATLANTA, GA

HEAD LINES
Best Advice and Top Tips

- Pick a city you want to live in and then find a job. Don't let the work dictate where you live.

- Find a place you can afford. You want to have extra cash to do a few fun things each month.

- Many things in your lease are negotiable – including the monthly rent.

- Don't move somewhere else because you're in love – unless you think you'll be happy there if/when the relationship ends.

THE BEST ADVICE MY DAD ever gave me was "Once you graduate from college, move to the place you want to live and then find a job. Don't let your job dictate where you live, if you can afford it." I wanted to live in California, so I moved there out of college. My first apartment was a 400-square-foot studio that only had room for a minifridge, not even a real freezer. I lived there for four years, but eventually I moved into a two-bedroom apartment. And now, I actually own my own condo in Southern California, so I'm finally "in." I never could have done it if I had taken a job in Chicago (where I went to college) and then tried to move to San Diego. It's the best advice my dad could have given me, and I love every minute of it!

—*ANONYMOUS*
SAN DIEGO, CALIFORNIA

· · · · · · · · ·

WHEN LOOKING FOR AN APARTMENT, the phrase you should look for is "All utilities included."

—*DOMINIQUE COLEMAN*
SYRACUSE, NEW YORK

THE TWO MOST IMPORTANT FACTORS in choosing a place to live out of college are price and location relative to activity. It is tempting to look at that five-figure salary on your offer letter and then go shopping for the apartment you always wanted but couldn't afford. Don't make a move until you put pen to paper. Research the cost of utilities, phone, cell phone, Internet access, cable, renter's insurance, car payment, vehicle insurance, and so on. Create a budget and decide what is reasonable for monthly rent. After that, try to find a place in your budget where you'll find activities for young people. Usually, it's closer to the center of the metropolitan area rather than way out in the suburbs, where families mostly live.

—*JAMES RINEY*
FORT WORTH, TEXAS

• • • • • • • •

MY FIRST POSTCOLLEGE HOUSE was a little rental on the south side—the poor side—of Ottumwa, Iowa. I paid $300 a month for this place, and that was actually a huge chunk of my monthly income. My first job as a copy editor for the local newspaper didn't pay all that much. I remember telling myself that to be able to enjoy the other parts of my life, I'd have to live in a cheaper part of town. That ended up being a great decision. My little blue one-bedroom house eventually became somewhat of a party place. I made it my own and people loved to come over for barbecues, ice-cold beer, and my famous Bloody Marys. Even though I didn't have much, I made the best of it, and I learned many valuable lessons just by sacrificing a little bit of comfort and style to live within my means.

—*E.E.*
ST. LOUIS, MISSOURI

HOME COOKING

Five million Americans aged 25 to 35 are living with their parents.

LIVE SOMEWHERE IN THE MIDDLE. Not too big, not too small. This is especially important if you are venturing out into the real world for the first time. Too big will equal a very thin wallet, a large insecurity about the friends you've acquired, and a constant yearning to fit in. Too small will equal a scarce social life, a longing to do greater things, and a head full of regrets on where you haven't been and what you haven't done.

—*KRISTI KAMERMAN*
BATON ROUGE, LOUISIANA

• • • • • • • •

AUSTIN, TEXAS, IS BY FAR THE BEST PLACE to live out of college. While it is not a giant city like Dallas or Houston, it offers all the draws of big-city life. However, you can drive from one side to the other in 20 minutes. It is a very eclectic town with friendly people and a unique personality. And, given that it has a huge university in the middle of it, the transition from one's college experience to the real world is easier, as the city is chock full of students and activities for young graduates.

—*ERIN HUDAK*
AUSTIN, TEXAS

• • • • • • • •

LIVE NEAR YOUR FRIENDS. That way, you instantly know your neighbors. Every Saturday night, my friends and I ate chicken fajitas and hamburgers and played board games. I could go "out" by only moving 20 feet. It made me feel like part of a community and part of a family.

—*SHAWN W. HARWARD*
SAN ANTONIO, TEXAS

EASY AS 1, 2, 3

Most people totally freak out after graduating from college; many to the point where they end up moving back in with their parents. I don't get it. It's really not that bad.

Step One: Decide what you want—to be close to family or friends, to meet new people, to have nice weather or specific job opportunities.

Step Two: Move to the place where you can get that. Get a job. It doesn't matter what kind. Anyone can find enough work to pay the bills, especially if you have a college education. If the job sucks, work until you find something better.

Step Three: Work your way up until you have the career you want, or enough money to go back to school or to travel or whatever.

It's really that simple. Set some goals; *do* things. It's better than hanging out in your mom's basement.

—*Fred*
   Washington, D.C.

Do your research. I moved to Los Angeles from Iowa shortly after I graduated, along with thousands of other recent grads. I met more than a few people my age in L.A. who were just biding time and hoping to be discovered as an actor. But if you don't do your research beforehand, set up a few job connections, and find a place to live, you're more likely to end up as the next night shift manager at Taco Bell than the next Brad Pitt.

—*Jesse Ammerman*
   Chicago, Illinois

APARTMENT HUNTING 101

You can't take road trips forever. Sooner or later, you'll have to settle down in one place, and for the recently graduated that usually means finding an apartment. Here are some proven tips to help you along.

BEFORE YOU SIGN A LEASE ON AN APARTMENT, find out how flexible the landlord will be on the length of the lease. Most leases are for one year, but the attitudes of landlords vary. If you are planning to buy a home in six months and your rental lease is for one year, you will likely lose your security deposit if you break the lease. My landlord agreed on a month-to-month lease agreement after the first six months. I think he was agreeable to it because I was up front with him about my plans and didn't just sneak out in the middle of the night.

—ANONYMOUS
STRONGSVILLE, OHIO

. . . .

ON APARTMENTRATINGS.COM, current and former tenants of complexes nationwide share their experiences living in particular places. The site is pretty accurate, too. When I logged on to check out a complex I'd just moved out of, I saw their satisfaction rating was only 25 percent. This was completely fitting, considering that, after I broke my lease, they chose to withhold my security deposit (even though there was no damage) and about $2,500 extra.

—R.W.
FORT COLLINS, COLORADO

. . . .

JUST BECAUSE A LANDLORD ASKS FOR A DEPOSIT or the lease says a deposit is required, don't feel that this item is non-negotiable. Everything, including the rent, is negotiable. It depends on how badly they need to rent the space out. Look for apartment complexes that have lots of vacancies. Those landlords will be more willing to work with you on some of those issues just to get you in there.

—BRETT DAVID
HARRISONBURG, VIRGINIA

CHECK OUT THE CARS IN THE NEIGHBORHOOD you are considering. Make sure that they all have tires on them, that the windows are not knocked out and covered with plastic and that they have no big locks on the steering wheel.

—*K.S.*
BALTIMORE, MARYLAND

• • • • • • • • •

WHILE INVESTIGATING A NEIGHBORHOOD or a particular building, ask the locals for their opinion. At an apartment building I was interested in, I pushed buttons until I found someone home. The guy who answered let me up into the building and answered all my questions about neighbors, rodents, and utilities. You can also ask people on the street. I stopped a woman and asked her if it was a safe area. She gave me good information. People usually tend to be helpful, and want to show what they know.

—*ANONYMOUS*
BUFFALO, NEW YORK

• • • • • • • • •

EVEN IF LIVING QUARTERS ARE HARD TO FIND, don't allow yourself to take a place too far from where you work. When I moved to New York City, I wound up in an apartment in Jamaica, Queens. By subway, it was 1 hour and 45 minutes to work. And I had 3 jobs! I was a mess; I was never home. I would finish work at 1 or 2 in the morning, then I had to take the train all the way back. As soon as possible, I moved closer.

—*BRANDON CUTRELL*
COLUMBUS, INDIANA

• • • • • • • • •

DON'T BE AFRAID TO MOVE OUT OF STATE for a job. My hometown had 6,000 people in it; I wanted something larger. I had a job offer from a place where I had interned, in Wisconsin, but I didn't want to stay there forever. I like big cities. So I turned it down and cast a wider net.

—*MARCELLE HENDRICKS*
WESTMINSTER, COLORADO

DON'T ASSUME that the monthly rent figure that you are quoted is set in stone. Feel free to try to negotiate it with the landlord. Why not? What have you got to lose? Ask them if they would take less; if they won't, ask them if you could get a discount for paying early each month. You never know if you don't ask.

—*TRINA AMAKER*
NIKEP, MARYLAND

• • • • • • • • •

USE YOUR ALUMNI NETWORKS (online groups and local alumni associations) to find recent grads with rooms for rent. You're more likely to find someone who's got something in common with you, and if you're moving to a far-off city, it's nice to have a room-mate who knows what you're going through.

—*JERRY*
NEW YORK, NEW YORK

• • • • • • • • •

WHEN LOOKING AT AN APARTMENT, don't get suckered in by fresh paint or carpet. Make sure you bring along somebody who knows about housing. I ended up in a freshly painted and carpeted rat-hole with major cockroaches, stopped-up toilets, and mildew everywhere. At the time, I was so proud of myself for finding it. Then the first time my Dad walked through, he pointed out all of those things that did, in fact, become huge problems for me.

—*C.C.*
RENO, NEVADA

• • • • • • • • •

A GOOD WAY TO FIND AN APARTMENT is to just drive to areas you'd like to live in and look for "For Rent" signs there. I did it, and it helped me learn my way around. This is better than reading the classified ads and then wasting your time going to a place only to find out it's somewhere you'd never want to live.

—*J.R.*
FREDERICK, MARYLAND

NEVER MOVE OUT ON YOUR OWN unless you have saved up *at least* $3,000. I moved from New York to Georgia after college. I thought it would be easy considering how much you get for your dollar in Georgia compared to New York. But even the low rent was something I could not afford. I also found out the hard way that public transportation in Georgia is darn near nonexistent. I am a city girl, and I found myself walking country dirt roads trying to get to work. So, two things: 1. Make sure you research a new town before your big move, and 2. *Stay away from Georgia!* Just kidding. But adequately prepare your finances, or you will find yourself in a bind and it'll be back to Mom and Dad's for you!

—*Q.S.*
NEW YORK, NEW YORK

TOP 5 YOUTH-MAGNET CITIES

The Wall Street Journal named the following cities as the ones that "will emerge as the hottest, hippest destinations for highly mobile, educated workers in their 20s."

1. Washington, D.C.
2. New York, NY
2. (tie) Seattle, WA
4. Portland, OR
5. Austin, TX

5 THINGS TO CONSIDER BEFORE MOVING TO A CITY

1. **Urban?** The bright city lights may be summoning you like a moth to a flame, but do you really want to live in an urban environment? If you're a country mouse, visit your city mouse friend for a weekend. Can you tolerate the noise, the people, and the unique scents of a city?

2. **Employment:** A few friends of mine have boldly gone to live in New York City and *they didn't even have jobs*! They decided they would move and just see what happens. If you're moving to a new place, consider your employment prospects. Do you have a job lined up? If not, is the industry in which you are qualified to work hiring a lot of people right now? Do you have enough in savings to live for several months in case you don't land your dream job right away?

3. **Housing:** Rent can be exorbitant in some cities. Can you afford to live in a safe, secure apartment in your intended destination? Will it be relatively close to your work? Do you mind having several roommates?

4. **Things to Do:** Ever since you were five years old, Aikido, a Japanese martial art, has been your passion. You absolutely must train 3 times a week, or your chi feels out of whack. Is Aikido (or whatever your passion may be) available in your city of choice? Or, perhaps you don't know what your passions are, but you're always game for trying new things. Are there lots of exciting and fun things to do where you plan to move?

5. **Lifestyle:** Are you a liberal, crunchy-granola, political activist? Are you a politically-apathetic rocker dude-cum-culinary genius? Are you a straight-laced, no-funny-business-but-all-business gay man working his way up the corporate ladder? In other words, think of who you are; think of how you want to live your life. Will the city you have in mind enable you to follow your lifestyle choices and help you to achieve your goals?

—Sarah Franco

I MOVED TO NEW YORK CITY in the same month that I graduated from college. I didn't know what to expect from living in the city, since I was moving from the suburbs of New Jersey, but I just went through with it. It all worked out in the end, but it was kind of tenuous for those first 3-4 weeks of adjustment. It's hard being in a new place where you're not familiar with how things work (public transit, grocery stores, libraries, parks), but after a while you start to get the hang of it.

—*JULIA*
NEW YORK, NEW YORK

• • • • • • • •

WHEN YOU MOVE TO A NEW CITY, live in a neighborhood where there are other young folks you can connect with – even if this means a longer commute to work. If you won't be happy socially, you won't be happy at work.

—*BARAK*
TEL AVIV, ISRAEL

Consider

• • • • • • • •

FIND OUT WHO YOU ARE, on your own. When my dad said I could start paying him some rent money, I told him, "I would rather pay rent to someone else than to you," and went and found an apartment. It was an old building with leaded-glass windows, glass doorknobs, wood floors, and arched entryways between rooms. The place was unique and had character. It was nice to have a neat place where friends could come hang out and party without bugging my parents.

—*BRETT*
CHICAGO, ILLINOIS

WHEN I GRADUATED FROM ART SCHOOL, it seemed like the natural thing to do was to move to New York. I resisted this idea for a long time prior to graduating, but then I realized that if I wanted the exposure to other people who were actually making art to support themselves, this was the place to be. I absolutely love it here. In the nearly five years I have lived here, I have had to shed a lot of the romantic ideas about starving artists eating raw noodles just long enough to make that one great painting that puts them on the map. It can be done that way, but more than likely you will want to live in a place that is semi-rodent-free and go out for the occasional cocktail with the thousands of other artists trying to make it in this city.

—*CHARLES*
  BROOKLYN, NEW YORK

KIPLINGER'S BEST CITIES TO LIVE IN

1: Houston, TX
2: Raleigh, NC
3: Omaha, NE
4: Boise, ID
5: Colorado Springs, CO
6: Austin, TX
7: Fayetteville, AR
8: Sacramento, CA
9: Des Moines, IA
10: Provo, UT

DORMING AT HOME

LIVE WITH YOUR PARENTS until you can live on your own. I lived with my parents for a couple of years because in my industry, television, you don't necessarily get a full-time job right away. It took me a few years to get comfortable and get a steady enough gig and income to justify getting my own place.

—JOSH TIZEL
TORONTO, ONTARIO, CANADA

· · · · · · · · ·

LIVE AT HOME. I didn't have a high-paying first job, so I needed to live at home with my parents for a year. But I think it helped make the transition from college to the "real world" a little easier. Plus, my mom is a good cook and I hate doing laundry.

—JIM
HOBOKEN, NEW JERSEY

I MOVED TO NEW YORK CITY in the same month that I graduated from college. I didn't know what to expect from living in the city, since I was moving from the suburbs of New Jersey, but I just went with it. It all worked out in the end, but it was kind of tenuous for those first 3-4 weeks of adjustment. It's hard being in a new place where you're not familiar with how things work (public transit, grocery stores, libraries, parks), but after a while you start to get the hang of it. It almost feels like you're back at the beginning of undergraduate since you have to get used to a new location and school all over again.

—JULIA
NEW YORK, NEW YORK

KNOW YOUR ROOMMATE

A FEW WEEKS AFTER MY NEW roommate moved in, I discovered that she was bulimic. The year we lived together was a long one. When looking for a roommate, don't be afraid to ask questions, even if you feel like you are prying a little. And you have to be forthcoming - with pet peeves, peculiar habits, etc. Making a first impression is important, but when you are going to be sharing personal space with someone, a good first impression isn't as important as an accurate one. If you aren't OK with having overnight guests frequently, you have to say that up front. Get really upset when people run the air conditioner too high? Much better to say those things when you first meet than to get in fights about it all the time later.

> —LESLEY
> ATLANTA, GEORGIA

THE BEST THING I DID A FEW MONTHS after finishing my degree was to move to a part of town that was cheaper, walk-able, full of nightlife, and friendly. I can actually afford my own apartment in my new neighborhood, and it has everything I need within biking distance. This saves enormously on gas and stretches a tiny starting salary to the point that it doesn't hurt to go out for happy hour once in a while. I stay fitter and healthier because I bike and walk everywhere, and I have a farmer's market with fresh produce right across the street on the weekend. If you have the freedom to move, get away from strip malls, suburbs, and overpriced neighborhoods that are hostile to young people, and move to a neighborhood that feels good to walk around in.

> —EMILY
> SAN DIEGO, CALIFORNIA

MY PET PEEVE IS with people who spend all that time and money getting a college education and then limit themselves in where they can work and live by wanting to stay close to home. What a bunch of nonsense. If you are afraid to move too far away from Mommy, then you are never going to amount to anything. Do a nationwide job search and just go. My first job was in upstate Montana. I had never been to that part of the world in my life. It was so beautiful up there. And cold. But it forced me to act and think for myself because I was thousands of miles from my parents. It really caused me to grow up much faster than I would have had I stayed close to home.

—*CANDACE MISTELLI*
   BOARDMAN, OHIO

* * * * * * * *

IT PAYS OFF TO PUSH OUTSIDE the comfort zone of home. After I finished my master's degree in communications, I was desperate to start my life. I didn't want to fall into the proverbial black hole in my hometown, where college grads came home to live at their parents' houses and work at Starbucks because they were too afraid to leave their safety zones. It is really hard at first, but sticking it out is worth it.

—*CHERYL*
   PHILADELPHIA, PENNSYLVANIA

Rolling Stone: Your First Move (As an Adult!)

Why, it was only a few years ago when your parents packed up all your belongings for you, bought you some new bedding and supplies, and sent you off to the magical Land of College. Now the Land of College has handed you an eviction notice, your parents are probably less helpful and generous, and you've got to move all your stuff to Your First Post-College Apartment. There's nothing like a first move to let you know just what the Real World is going to be like. As you embark on this journey, whether it's across town or across the country, heed the advice of other movers and shakers. Some of these tips are worth keeping in mind for future moves, too.

MOVING IS AN ADVENTURE—a chance to start over, meet new people, and see new places. It's a chance to set up a new house and make it your own, each time making changes and redefining yourself.

—JENNIFER PIKE
MONTICELLO, MINNESOTA

MOVING IS THE MOST EXCITING THING YOU CAN DO.

—SHARON LONDON
SAN FRANCISCO, CALIFORNIA

HEADLINES
Best Advice and Top Tips

- Pay all your bills in the place you're leaving. It's harder to keep track of them once you're in a new place.

- Change your address with the post office – you can do it online at usps.gov.

- Pack your stuff carefully in boxes, as early as possible, and label the boxes. Pack your moving truck carefully, too.

- Make sure you know exactly where you're putting your important documents and keys.

- Food and drink should be given to all who volunteer to help you on moving day.

- If you can avoid moving on the weekend, do.

CONTACT YOUR PHONE COMPANY AND ISP at least a month in advance with your new information. I gave them only a couple weeks last time and they royally messed things up. If I'd had some buffer time, I would have been golden when I arrived.

—ANNETTE C. YOUNG
VANCOUVER, WASHINGTON

START PREPARING NOW. No matter how far you're going, moving is a big deal. I've been sorting through my things, organizing, donating, and throwing things out. It's taking a long time, but I'm determined that by the time I'm ready to move, all of my belongings should fit in my Honda Civic!

—JUDY BECK
PERKASIE, PENNSYLVANIA

DO NOT LEAVE YOUR HAZARD LIGHTS in your U-Haul blinking as you move. When you try to start the engine and hear a clicking sound, it means that your battery has died. Trust me—you don't want to deal with this.

—*AMY HIROTAKA*
NEW YORK

• • • • • • • •

GET A LANYARD THAT YOU CAN PUT around your neck and attach all necessary keys to it. DO NOT TAKE IT OFF while moving. I once sealed my front door key into a moving box. Another friend locked the U-Haul key . . . in the U-Haul.

—*SARA CLEMENCE*
ALBANY, NEW YORK

• • • • • • • •

MAKE SURE YOU HAVE A GOOD, REAL REASON for moving—e.g. to be closer to family, move in with your fiancé, accept a great job or enter the witness protection program. Whether you move to Nowheresville or a fun, busy city, it helps to have a career to focus on or a relationship that provides you with support and a social outlet.

—*TINA MITRO*

• • • • • • • •

JUST IN CASE everything goes wrong with your move, pack an "emergency bag" and keep it with you, not in the truck. Fill it with a change of clothes, pajamas, toiletries, medicines.

—*ANONYMOUS*
CALIFON, NEW JERSEY

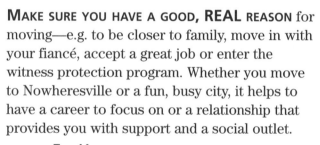

IT SOUNDS STUPID, but you need to pay all of your parking tickets in your old city before leaving for a new one. It's something that most people forget to do, but once you leave, it's harder to track down what you owe. I knew that I owed about $40 after I moved, but when I called to pay by phone, the lady on the other end said I owed $75. It wasn't worth it to argue, but I could have had I been there in person.

—M.S.
EVANSTON, ILLINOIS

• • • • • • • •

" Call a week ahead of time and make sure the electricity will be turned on and the High-Definition cable installer will be there the day you move in. Gas, water, garbage, and phone are all optional as long as you have ESPN in High Definition on Day One. "

—J.S.
EDINA, MINNESOTA

THE ART OF PACKING A TRUCK

First of all, make sure you've got a lot of rope. And get a lot of the big stuff out there first, especially the heavy pieces. Find whatever pieces fit as flush against the front wall as possible, and start putting them in. The whole process is like fitting the pieces of a puzzle together.

Fill the front overhang with boxes, chests, etc. Make sure the heavy pieces, like sofas, go near the front. Turn tables upside down and lay them on sofas. Pack boxes, pillows, cushions, etc., around table legs. Set one chair in the truck right-side up, the other one upside down on top of it. Put small boxes, lampshades, children's toys, odds and ends under the bottom chair and on top of the top chair.

Stand mattresses and box springs on their sides at either side of the truck and slide headboards, paintings and mirrors between them. Push sofas, tables, boxes, etc. against the mattresses to keep them upright.

Stack things up to the roof, if you can, putting lighter stuff on top, but make sure that everything is stable and solid. Then, every five or six feet, rope that section off. Tie the rope to a hook on one side of the truck and run it across the exposed end of the stack, wrapping it around sofa legs, chairs, boxes, anything that will restrain the load. Tie the rope to a hook on the other side, and you're ready to start the next section.

—J.C.
ATLANTA, GEORGIA

You Are Not Alone

Thirty-five percent of people in their 20s move in a given year.

DON'T FORGET TO BACK UP YOUR ADDRESSES and anything else from your computer on a disk. Our computer got damaged in the move, and we were just going to throw it away and get a new one, since it was pretty old. But then we realized it had all of our contacts on it, and we didn't know how to track down some of those people otherwise. We ended up paying a technician over a hundred bucks to retrieve the information from our damaged old computer.

—*J.D.*
BALTIMORE, MARYLAND

• • • • • • • •

TRASH BAGS ARE A HUGE HELP. You can throw anything into them: clothes, stuffed animals, books.

—*DAWN COLCLASURE-WILSON*
RANCHO MIRAGE, CALIFORNIA

ESSENTIALS FOR YOUR FIRST APARTMENT

1. Mattress/bed
2. Trash cans
3. Shower curtain and shower rings
4. Curtains or blinds
5. Chest of drawers or hanging closet organizers
6. Dishware, cups and utensils
7. Table and/or desk
8. Chair
9. Lamp
10. Bookshelf
11. Sofa or futon
12. Cleaning supplies
13. Bathroom supplies
14. Toilet paper

Do NOT MOVE INTO A FOURTH-FLOOR WALK-UP apartment with your girlfriend. You'll end up carrying everything up and down the stairs, including the laundry.

> *—J.P.*
> *NEW YORK, NEW YORK*

• • • • • • • •

MAKE A TIME-LINE OF EVENTS IN THE PROCESS to the finest detail. Make a list of address changes before leaving. Open a new bank account early. Organize your important papers in file folders. List important transfers: insurance, drivers license, medical. If moving out of state, get contacts early (i.e. utilities, medical, insurance contacts).

> *—SHARLANE BLAISE*
> *PORTLAND, OREGON*

• • • • • • • •

WHEN YOU'RE CONTEMPLATING RENTING a truck to drive across three states, the cost can be daunting, and it inevitably seems easier to ditch your stuff and plan to buy when you arrive in your new home. Sure, the furniture you have was bought on the cheap in college, so it seemingly makes sense to upgrade and leave the old behind. Don't! So many people spend insane amounts of money outfitting their new places in one fell swoop, or being depressed about their new home because it doesn't feel like it's theirs. Plus, it will cost FAR more to outfit a new place than to pay the moving cost. My advice is to suck it up, take a deep breath and pay the $500 for moving, take your futon with you, and buy a new couch five months later when your recent moving costs aren't still biting.

> *—AMELIA*
> *ATLANTA, GEORGIA*

Find a pace that's comfortable and always lift with your knees.

> *—DOMINIQUE*
> *COLEMAN*
> *SYRACUSE,*
> *NEW YORK*

THE POOR GIRL'S GUIDE TO MOVING

1) **PLAN AHEAD.** Make lists of tasks and deadlines, and post them.

2) **SEPARATE YOUR POSSESSIONS INTO TWO CATEGORIES:** things you can't live without and things you might be able to sell.

3) **START PACKING IMMEDIATELY.** You have twice as much stuff as you realize.

4) **EVERY SINGLE TIME YOU LEAVE YOUR APARTMENT,** take something out the door with you.

5) **EVERY TIME SOMEONE ELSE LEAVES YOUR APARTMENT,** they must have something of yours in their hands.

6) **PAY THE AIRLINE TO TAKE EXTRA SUITCASES.** You can cram a lot into a suitcase, and it costs much less than shipping.

7) **GIVE YOUR FRIENDS PACKED SUITCASES TO BRING** with them when they come to visit.

8) **KEEP YOUR HOUSE STOCKED WITH READY-MADE FOOD:** salad kits, deli slices, etc. It's easy to spend a fortune eating out when you are in the process of moving.

9) **TRY TO FINISH YOUR PACKING AND CLEANING EARLY.** Don't put yourself in the position of staying up late, night after night, the week before your move.

—HESTER KAMIN

SET ASIDE A BOX FOR YOUR REMOTE CONTROLS, a tool kit and a phone—anything you need right away. This should be the last box you pack and the first box you open at your new place. It's great because you don't waste time digging through a dozen boxes to find the important stuff.

—*ROB MCHARGUE*
SAN ANTONIO, TEXAS

• • • • • • • •

UPS HAS THESE REALLY COOL, clear plastic sleeve covers that you can order for free from their website; they make labeling moving boxes so much easier! Simply attach one of the sleeve covers to the outside of a box, write on a separate sheet of paper exactly what that box contains, and slip the paper inside the sleeve cover. The beauty of this system is you never have to ruin your original boxes by writing on them, so you can use them over and over again.

—*CARRIE K.*
CHICAGO, ILLINOIS

• • • • • • • •

KEEP EVERYBODY MOVING. Even if they're carrying small boxes, they're moving the rock. If you give people an excuse to stand around, they will.

—*EVAN*
ATLANTA, GEORGIA

• • • • • • • •

UNPACK ALL YOUR BOXES within a week of moving in. It's too easy to only unpack the necessities and leave everything else for later. But "later" becomes three months later, and you still have spare rooms full of boxes.

—*J.S.*
EDINA, MINNESOTA

Only keep what you actually need, or is stunningly beautiful. We all accumulate too bloody much stuff!

—*NADIA*

LIFE AFTER COLLEGE: THE NEW GRADUATE'S GUIDE

Consider

DON'T MAKE THE MISTAKE of unnecessarily pulling all of your clothes off of their hangers and packing them, only to hang them back up in your new home. Secure a bundle of clothes on hangers together with a rubber band, and then cover the bundle with a garbage bag to protect them. When you move in, you can just hang them up and tear off the bag.

—*J.H.*
CHICAGO, ILLINOIS

• • • • • • • •

I RECOMMEND LABELING YOUR electronic cords when disconnecting things for a move. I would put a piece of tape at the end of each cord and label it with a number or letter and then put a piece of tape near the outlet where the plug belongs and label it with the same symbol. That way, things won't be confusing when it's time to reconnect.

—*D.L.*
CHICAGO, ILLINOIS

• • • • • • • •

GET A VARIETY OF SIZES OF ZIPLOC BAGGIES and a Sharpie marker. Whenever you take apart a piece of furniture, put all of the nuts and bolts into one of the baggies and label it clearly. This prevents important pieces from getting lost.

—*STACY MCHARGUE*
SAN ANTONIO, TEXAS

3 THINGS 'U' SHOULD KNOW

1. Plan ahead.
2. Make your reservations as far in advance as possible.
3. Try moving on a weekday, when banks, utilities and government offices are open.

—*U-HAUL*

HOW NOT TO MAKE NEW FRIENDS

NOT THAT I HAVE EVER DONE THESE THINGS, of course, but if you have recently moved into a new place, you should avoid the following in order to comfortably settle into your new neighborhood:

- **PRACTICING NAKED YOGA** at night, in front of your window, with the blinds open

- **LEAVING YOUR TRASH CAN OUT** for three days following trash pick-up

- **LETTING YOUR DOG POOP** in the neighbor's yard . . . and leaving it there

- **WATCHING THE NEIGHBORS** through the permanent peephole in your blinds

- **LEAVING YOUR DOG** in the yard all day, letting him constantly bark at everything

—H.
OKLAHOMA CITY, OKLAHOMA

DON'T ALWAYS EXPECT TO FIND a career in your academic major. There is a lot of competition in the real world. After one too many rejections in the fashion design field, I knew it was time to move on. I fell in love with real estate, and now I am my own boss. Looking back, I am so happy I was rejected!

—ZAKIA SIPP
CHICAGO, ILLINOIS

TIPS FOR HIRING MOVERS

GET SEVERAL ESTIMATES AND GO WITH A FIXED ESTIMATE wherever possible. Check out the company's record with the Better Business Bureau. How many complaints have they had? Were they resolved amicably? The lowest price is not always the best service. Look for hidden charges, like insurance, travel, tolls and gas. Make sure there are enough guys—too few will up the costs considerably.

> —*LIZ SCHERER*
> *ANNAPOLIS, MARYLAND*

BEWARE OF HIDDEN CHARGES with moving companies. I once hired people to move a piano from a third floor apartment and it ended up costing me $400 extra because the workers had to disassemble the hallway and staircase since the piano couldn't be taken apart—and they were charging me by the hour.

> —*M.F.*
> *BUFFALO GROVE, ILLINOIS*

CHECK TO MAKE SURE MOVERS HAVE INSURANCE. Then, if something gets damaged, it's covered.

> —*SAMANTHA*
> *LOS ANGELES, CALIFORNIA*

IF YOU HAVE TO RELOCATE FOR WORK, ask the new company if they would consider paying for your move. If you don't ask, they probably aren't going to offer.

> —*ANONYMOUS*
> *READING, PENNSYLVANIA*

TAKE ALL OF YOUR T-SHIRTS AND USE THEM to pad your dishes and other breakable things. Then get a box of garbage bags. Leaf bags, to be precise. The heavy ones. Pack everything else that is soft in them (clothes, linens, pillows, whatever) and use them to pad your moving vehicle.

—*SARAH*
SEATTLE, WASHINGTON

❝Old clothes can be taken to the Salvation Army. Old pictures of your ex can be burned ceremonially in the living room.❞

—*R.G.*
CHICAGO, ILLINOIS

IF YOUR FRIENDS ARE HELPING YOU MOVE, have everything in boxes before they get there. Your friends love you, but no one wants to watch you throw your underwear into bags.

—*APRIL SMITH*
BOSTON, MASSACHUSETTS

Consider

PACKING TAPE CAN BE EXTREMELY DIFFICULT to remove from picture frames, glass, and bubble wrap. Use tape as sparingly as possible, while maintaining the security of your objects.

—*ANONYMOUS*
BIRMINGHAM, ALABAMA

WHEN I MOVED TO DENVER FOR LAW SCHOOL, I had to downsize. I borrowed my dad's Volvo station wagon and decided that whatever fit in there, I could keep. I selected the one piece of furniture I couldn't live without, as well as basic luxury items, like my stereo and TV. I also included practical things, like dishes. It helped tremendously to have this simple goal because it forced me to consider what I truly needed, as opposed to what I was emotionally attached to.

—*LIBBY DEBLASIO*
DENVER, COLORADO

• • • • • • • •

NEVER MOVE UNIVERSITY BOOKS. If you really want to reference something from your social history class, you can always buy new textbooks on Amazon for peanuts (and you'll get the better, updated version!).

—*MICHAEL GARRITY*
TORONTO, ONTARIO, CANADA

• • • • • • • •

NOTHING MOTIVATES PEOPLE to help you move more than food. The underlying sentiment you should convey to friends who help you is gratitude. I like to move first thing in the morning. If you're going to ask someone to be at your home at 7 a.m., you should have breakfast waiting for them. And if you have a lot of things to move, give them pizza for lunch, too.

—*C.S.*
VIRGINIA BEACH, VIRGINIA

START FROM SQUARE ONE

WHAT TO UNPACK FIRST: toilet paper. It's a necessity.

—*ALYSSA AGEE*
SNOQUALMIE, WASHINGTON

BOXING TECHNIQUES

ATTENTION BOOK COLLECTORS: Don't fill up your boxes with books. Even a medium-sized box filled with books will be terribly heavy. Instead, line the bottom of your boxes with books, and then put lighter items on top of the books to fill the box up.

  —S.D.
   MANCHESTER, PENNSYLVANIA

* * * * * * * * *

TAPE BOTH SIDES OF THE BOX. Sure, it's funny when someone picks up a box and all the stuff falls out of the bottom, but not when it's your stuff.

  —DANNY GALLAGHER
   HENDERSON, TEXAS

* * * * * * * * *

TO FIND BOXES, I made trips to the liquor store, since their boxes are a size a normal person can carry, and many beer boxes have cut-out handles. Also, they have boxes divided into 24 slots (great for glasses) and four slots (great for cookie jars, canisters, small appliances). I called first to see which day and time was best to pick up boxes, since I did not want to be a pest.

  —JILL MARIE DAVIS
   WEEHAWKEN, NEW JERSEY

* * * * * * * * *

BIG BOXES SEEM LIKE A REALLY GREAT IDEA when you're packing, because they hold more and you need less of them. But then you're carrying a big computer monitor box of kitchen stuff up the stairs at your new place, and you remember that smaller ones weigh less.

  —MIKE EMERY
   UPPER ARLINGTON, OHIO

OH, BROTHER!

Never ask your 18-year-old brother and his exceptionally intelligent friends to help you move. My brother has a big truck and I thought, what better way to save money? So he and his friend went to pick up my couch and dining room table from my grandparents' house, where it had been in storage. They showed up at my new apartment that afternoon, minus my dining room table and two of the four cushions.

The best and worst part of the story is they weren't really sure where they lost everything along the 30-minute trip between my grandparents' house and mine. They just put everything in the bed of the truck, but didn't tie it down—or even put the tailgate up! I can laugh about this story now, but only because I am no longer sitting on the wooden boards of a couch with no cushions.

—L.N.
PHOENIX, ARIZONA

ALWAYS GET THE INSURANCE when you're driving something unfamiliar. I did it only because I was completely hung over at the time and wasn't thinking. But when, in my foggy haze, I parked in the alleyway of a one-way street, I crashed into the building, and the side mirror snapped off and shattered on the sidewalk. Fortunately, this incident only cost me $20—the price of the insurance. Without the policy, it would've been at least $200. Even if you're sober, something's bound to happen.

—LIBBY DEBLASIO
DENVER, COLORADO

IF YOU DON'T HIRE PROFESSIONAL MOVERS, then you have to understand that some of your stuff is going to get broken. There are no two ways about it. I'm not saying that you should use professionals —because it does cost lots of money—but if you don't you can say goodbye to some of your stuff because it's going to get dropped and break.

—*CHARLENE DEPASQUALE*
PITTSBURGH, PENNSYLVANIA

> **If you help me move, I'll supply a case of beer. A cheap pack, though. Not import. Bud Light. Plus pizza.**

—*JENNY DISALVO*
BOSTON, MASSACHUSETTS

I DIDN'T KNOW THIS UNTIL I STARTED ASKING questions, but U-Haul bases its prices on the number of available vehicles in a specific location. So, theoretically, if you rent a U-Haul in California and drive it to Colorado, it might cost you $100 to drop it off in Denver, but only $30 to drop it off in Colorado Springs. Definitely spend some time calling around to check out your different options. The savings are definitely worth it!

—*J.C.*
REDMOND, WASHINGTON

Pack an overnight bag. You won't remember what box you tossed your razor into.

—*APRIL SMITH*
BOSTON, MASSACHUSETTS

HELL ON WHEELS

MATTRESSES ARE NOT MEANT TO BE CARRIED ON THE ROOF of your car. It looks silly, it's an aerodynamic faux pas, and it's downright dangerous. My friend Eric and I discovered this when I helped him move many years ago. He didn't have much stuff, and it was a short move, so we figured why waste the $50 on renting a truck? We packed the car with all his stuff, then slapped the mattress on the roof with one little rope for luck, and drove off.

We forgot to consider that when a car is in motion, it must move a lot of air out of the way, and most of this air moves straight up, right underneath the mattress. We got about halfway there before the first string broke. Naturally we didn't have any extra string with us, so we did the obvious: We each rolled down our windows and grabbed onto the mattress handles. What a ride! Anything over about 15 mph and we were being lifted out of our seats. It was like riding a hang glider. Not to mention that it's hard enough to drive with only one hand without the added challenge of being pulled out of the car.

We made it safely, mostly due to luck, not common sense. Next time, however, I'm paying for the truck.

—*KEVIN SHOLANDER*
FORT COLLINS, COLORADO

. . . .

MAKE SURE YOU READ—and follow—the instructions on vehicle speed if you're doing any towing. I was towing a full-size Cadillac from Denver to Phoenix, and the warning on the tow package said DO NOT EXCEED 55 MPH. So there I was doing 80, and the vehicle started swaying back and forth in an uncontrolled manner. Those warnings are there for a reason!

—*J.C.*
REDMOND, WASHINGTON

BE PREPARED FOR A CHALLENGE if you have to ship your car. I met a lady who had shipped her car three times with the same company, and she recommended them. My car arrived on the west coast, safe and sound. The problem was, it arrived three weeks after I was hoping it would! I incurred $650 in car rental fees that I wasn't expecting.

—*ANONYMOUS*
SAN RAFAEL, CALIFORNIA

MAKE SURE YOU DRIVE ON WIDE ROADS. I once drove a moving truck down a pretty narrow road, with trees hanging near the edge. Sure enough, the side rearview nailed a branch and shattered. Also, if you must back up, particularly while at the gas station, have someone jump out and see if anything's behind you. I failed to do this and I backed into a tiny sports car, which had pulled up so close I couldn't see it in the (shattered) rearview.

—*JWAIII*
ATLANTA, GEORGIA

DRIVING THE MOVING TRUCK ISN'T AS HARD as it looks. You'll get the hang of it quicker than you think. What I learned is to 'live' in the mirrors. The mirrors on a big truck are much more important than on your passenger car. You really have to pay attention to what is happening on all sides of you at all times. And if you are not sure if you can make it, don't try.

—*BEN NOBLE*
YOUNGSTOWN, PENNSYLVANIA

GET ALL YOUR "ACCESSORIES"—like pictures, paintings and other decorations—put in place as quick as you can. You'll be surprised how quickly you'll feel at home when you have these familiar pieces of yours to look at.

—*DENISE LABATOS*
YOUNGSTOWN, PENNSYLVANIA

EXPLORING A NEW PLACE

THE BEST WAY TO FIND PLACES to hang out or eat are by tapping into local entertainment publications (like *Time Out New York* or *Washington City Paper*). Also, friends that have lived in a city longer than you have usually know a lot of different scenes or places to check out. Just keep your eyes peeled and pay attention to places around you as you go about your new city.

—*KATIE*
NEW YORK, NEW YORK

• • • • • • • • •

WHEN I ARRIVED IN THE CITY WHERE I NOW LIVE, I decided to explore. Going with instinct and whim, I frequented the coffee shops, restaurants, and pubs surrounding me until I decided upon my favorites. Even then, recommendations from friends revealed to me two of my now-favorite eateries that I would not have otherwise chosen to investigate. I have taken many opportunities to expand my social circle, conversing with strangers to whom I have been introduced, and socializing with the people on my M.A. program. I have found that an open mind and a willingness to experiment and to explore are fundamental to settling in to a new place. If you treat the process of familiarizing yourself with your environment as an adventure, a process of discovery, it is sure not to disappoint.

—*ERICA O'BRIEN*
BRISTOL, ENGLAND

IF YOU'RE GOING TO PAINT OR WALLPAPER, do it before you move all your stuff in. We unpacked everything and then had to move our stuff into the center of the room and back. It was so stupid.

—*T.F.*
MINNEAPOLIS, MINNESOTA

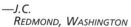

"Make sure you have a key from the landlord before moving in. Otherwise you may come back at 2 a.m. only to find he has locked all the doors, and you have no way to get in or contact him."

—*KEVIN K.*
CROWN POINT, INDIANA

PUT YOUR TV ON THE COUCH, and make sure its screen is facing toward the back. The padding will provide instant protection from vibration during the course of the move, and the screen is less likely to get scratched.

—*J.C.*
REDMOND, WASHINGTON

DOUBLE CHECK THAT YOU WILL HAVE A PLACE to park your truck and unload the contents. Some buildings have strict rules about parking. If you can get a reserved parking sign for that day, do it. Some cities will let you reserve a couple of spots for moving trucks. It is safer than double parking and clogging up traffic.

—*J.M.D.*
WEEHAWKEN, NEW JERSEY

• • • • • • • •

UNPACK YOUR LIQUOR FIRST. Get the booze out and set your stereo up. Make it fun

—*K.B.*
DIABLO, CALIFORNIA

LIST OF ESSENTIALS FOR MOVING DAY

When you're all packed up and ready to move, it helps to have a few items handy. Here's a short list to help make your move go smoothly.

- Bottled water
- Food for yourself and, if necessary, friends helping you move
- Lanyard to hold keys for old place, new place and transportation
- Dolly to move heavy objects
- Extra box tape
- Cash
- Clearly written directions to your new place

WITH A LITTLE HELP FROM YOUR (NEW) FRIENDS

THE KEY TO MAKING A NEW PLACE 'YOURS' is finding a bar, a small bookstore or coffee shop, and a job. Sooner or later, you'll have at least five friends who can make you feel like you belong.

—*REGINE*
LOS ANGELES, CALIFORNIA

• • • • • • • •

DON'T EXPECT TO FIT RIGHT IN INSTANTLY. When I moved, I found friends right away, but they weren't the ones who ended up being my best friends. Those people took many more months—and even years—to find. It was worth the wait.

—*JENNY W.*
NEW YORK, NEW YORK

• • • • • • • •

YOU NEVER KNOW WHEN YOU'RE GOING to make new friends. Once, my toilet clogged and I didn't have a plunger. So I went next door and knocked and this man with an English accent answered the door. I introduced myself and said, "I just moved in next door and I seem to be having some trouble with plumbing. Do you happen to have a plunger?" He didn't. I didn't know it at the time, but he was heading to the grocery store. I got a knock on my door about a half hour later and he had a plunger for me. He'd bought two— one for his apartment and one for mine.

—*ERIN*
FRANKLIN, MASSACHUSETTS

• • • • • • • •

YOU'VE GOT TO HAVE THE ABILITY to make new friends to make it through the transitional process. Usually, you can find lots of them through work. Other good ideas include joining groups for activities you enjoy, such as a book club or wine-tasting group.

—*FRAN WILLS*
LITTLETON, COLORADO

HELLO, DOLLY!

IF YOUR RENTAL TRUCK COMPANY OFFERS THE USE OF A DOLLY, take it! When I moved, my husband was deployed and I had to move everything to our apartment with just my sister's help. I didn't know how I was going to manage all the heavy furniture. With the dolly, we were able to move everything—from boxes to sofas—all in one day!

> —*ALLISON BENOIT*
> *HOUMA, LOUISIANA*

IF YOU'RE A GUY, YOU SHOULD SUCK UP your pride and hire a dolly. It'll save your back and be the best ten bucks you ever spent.

> —*B.N.*
> *MINNEAPOLIS, MINNESOTA*

AVOID GETTING DRUNK and making a fool of yourself in front of the new neighbors the first day. That can wait at least a week.

> —*PAM SASSER*
> *WHEELING, WEST VIRGINIA*

What Job? Where (and How) to Find One That's Right for You

Y*ou might have a degree. You might have a great résumé and cover letter. But you still might not have a job. The first step, of course, is deciding what you want to do. The second step is deciding whether this is realistic, or if you should do something else in the meantime. And the third step is getting out there and searching for a position. We asked others how they went about their first post-college job search, and what career-building advice they would give.*

IT'S ABOUT *WHO* YOU KNOW. Most of the really good jobs aren't even advertised. I got hired at my current job because one of my friends was the manager. That's the way the world works.

—D.S.
DENVER, COLORADO

NETWORKING IS A TERM YOU NEED TO BECOME FAMILIAR WITH. AND, NO, IT DOESN'T MEAN CLICKING FROM NBC TO CBS TO ABC.

—BOB MAGYARICS
CALLA, OHIO

HEAD LINES
Best Advice and Top Tips

- Do your research—find out as much as you can about the field you're interested in.

- Network, network, network—contact people in the industry to make important connections.

- Don't expect to start at the top—entry-level jobs allow you to really learn the business.

FIGURE OUT WHAT YOU DESIRE OUT OF LIFE. Take the time to figure out what motivates you and what makes you happy. That can take some trial and error. The people that I know who love their careers are the people who struggled a bit to get there. I didn't know where I wanted to go with my life until after college. I had been an anthropology major, and I was interested in documentary work, but I was still searching for the right path. After some traveling and soul searching for a few months, I solidified my desire to become a photographer. It took time and patience and working lots of part-time jobs while I took classes and developed my skills.

—*L.G.*
DURHAM, NORTH CAROLINA

NETWORK. FOUR OUT OF FIVE INTERVIEWS that I have been granted are because I had known someone at the company or had a friend who knew someone.

—*JERALYN*
AUSTIN, TEXAS

When I graduated from college, all I had was a degree in business and about five years of experience waiting tables. I had no idea what I wanted to do. I took a corporate job with high pay and a dental plan and all that, but I hated it. I actually enjoyed waiting tables and making crappy tips more than having a cubicle and a high salary. It dawned on me that I'd be happy managing restaurants, and that's what I do now. I remember thinking that once I graduated I would never have to work in a restaurant again, but it's hard to know what you want to do until you have actually done it.

—*Bill*
    Austin, Texas

> " Network at keg parties. Meet lots of people and hope one of them can line up a job for you. You never know where those keg party pals might end up working! "

—*Tony Hudoba*
    Blaine, Minnesota

Do what you love. Enjoy your work. This doesn't mean that you'll wake up every morning excited about going to work. I don't know anyone like that who isn't on prescription drugs. Life is life, no matter what you do.

—*Sara Walker*

FIGURING OUT WHAT YOU WANT TO DO

If you don't even know how to start, follow this well-defined process for finding your career direction.

1. **Identify your values.** The first step in finding a fulfilling career is to get clear on what is important to you—in other words, identifying your values. Remember that the set of values you hold dear today will change during your life. For example, when you first get out of college, you may identify adventure, intellectual stimulation, and friendship as strong values. At another time in your life, you may prioritize family, learning, and friendship. It's likely that no one job will honor all of your values, but it is important to understand what your values are so you know what trade-offs you are willing to make.

2. **Identify your interests.** You can identify your interests by paying attention to what you like to do. Spend some time reflecting on what you really enjoy. Notice what you enjoy talking about. What sorts of newspaper or magazine articles do you like to read? What television shows do you enjoy watching, and why? Do you have hobbies? What is it about these activities that you like? Keep lists of these things and notice the themes that arise. Some of these themes may translate into a career.

3. **Identify your skills and strengths.** Everyone has some. As you start to identify yours, make sure you recognize the things you like to do—and don't like to do—as well. For example, you may be good at math, but really don't want to use it in your job. It's not always easy to identify your unique skills and strengths on your own, so start asking your friends, family members, and coworkers to help you. Ask them questions such as, "What do you see as my greatest strength?" You may be pleasantly surprised at what you hear in response.

4. **Do your research.** Now is the time to research possible career paths. Look at your values, interests, skills, and strengths, and start to figure out which careers are compatible. Go to your school's or alma mater's career center, read their literature, and look through their resources. Check out the career section of your local library or bookstore. Get on the Internet. Start reading the paper. Research many different possibilities, paying attention to the career paths that intrigue you.

5. **Network, network, network.** This is the most important step: You have to talk to other people—a *lot* of other people. Talk to them about what they do, how they got there, and what it takes to be successful. As you listen to what they have to say, consider their words in light of your own values, interests, and skills. And pay attention to the most important indicator: your gut. If you are intrigued on a gut level, follow that lead.

6. **Repeat.** The job-seeking process is not linear; it's more like a squiggly line. Your networking may help you refine and clarify your interests, which in turn may lead you to do additional research. Just keep at it, and it will eventually lead you to where you want to be—in a good job.

—Ricki Frankel

AVOIDING THE DAILY GRIND

Not ready to commit to a 9-to-5 career? Here are a few productive distractions:

Peace Corps: www.peacecorps.gov

Freelance work: www.freelanceworkexchange.com

Work abroad: www.transitionsabroad.com/listings/work/index.shtml

AmeriCorps: www.americorps.org

FINDING A JOB YOU LIKE is the best possible scenario. But if you can't do that, find something related to what you want to do eventually. For example, if you want to become a magazine designer and eventually an art director, start as a publication assistant and work your way up. You can build connections, learn, and, most of all, keep your motivation and dreams alive.

—*M.K.*
HARTFORD, CONNECTICUT

· · · · · · · · ·

IF YOU HAVE TO TAKE a lower-paying job just to get some money, do it. But don't let that be the end of your job search. Keep on sending out résumés and networking; don't get complacent.

—*ALLEN BARKLEY*
DALLAS, GEORGIA

· · · · · · · · ·

Happiness is more important than success and always will be.

—*KAREN*
BOSTON,
MASSACHUSETTS

DON'T EXPECT THAT DREAM JOB RIGHT AWAY. If you are willing to do the grunt-work jobs, you will learn the business. And if you give it your all, most likely you will be rewarded for your efforts. My bachelor's degree was in art history, so I literally knocked on gallery doors in Cincinnati, where I was living, armed with my résumé and a don't-take-no-for-an-answer attitude. I started out helping out around a gallery and driving the owner's daughters to and from swim practice. I was running the entire business by the end of the summer.

—*DEIRDRE MORGENTHALER*
CASTLE ROCK, COLORADO

BELIEVE IN YOURSELF

A lot of people will tell you that when you're just getting out of school, you should get any first job you can get with your degree. But I think it's crucial that you try to get a job you love, particularly one that's in a field you're passionate about. During college, I worked as an intern at a National Public Radio station in Flagstaff, Arizona. I eventually turned that internship into a paying job. In my senior year of college, while my friends were out partying every night of the week, I was getting wonderful experience covering city council meetings, news events, and writing and filing stories for the morning news. It prepared me for what was to come.

After college, I worked at Dillard's department store for a year and lived at home, saving money for my dream to move to New York. My parents, friends, and relatives told me I was crazy not to just take any job. I followed my heart, moved to New York City, and took an unpaid internship at WNBC-TV because I knew it would lead me to great things: contacts, experience, news stories, and more. I learned how to produce shows, field produce, cover news events, answer calls on the news desk, and write news copy. Nine months later, I landed my first real job as a video journalist at CNN. After six years, I had received six promotions and had worked my way up to a futures planning editor on the national desk. While my friends worked boring nine-to-five jobs they dreaded every day, I did something I totally loved every minute of the day.

—MELANIE
MARICOPA, ARIZONA

ASK THE EXPERT

Informational interviewing: *What is it, and why do I have to do it?*

Although it has an imposing name, informational interviewing is nothing more than talking to people to gather more information about a particular job. It is a critical part of your research and job-search process, and it's the best way to find out if a job is actually of interest to you. Talking to people will give you information that you cannot learn from reading. You might ask people about what they do, their career path, their industry, or their company. Most people want to be helpful, and enjoy speaking to others about what they know. If you are interested in learning more about a certain career path or what it is like to work for a particular company, you need to find people who know something about those things. Ask everyone you know – and everyone you speak with – for introductions to people who can give you the kind of information you are looking for. The process of talking to as many people as possible can help you narrow down what you want to do.

People often ask me how to contact someone for an informational interview. For most people, sending them an email, if you have their address, is fine. If not, a telephone message will work just as well. If you got their name and contact information from someone else, say, "So-and-so suggested I call you. I am looking for information about [job or company], and I was wondering if we could find some time to have a conversation." If someone doesn't respond to your request, don't take it personally. Just contact the next person. Through the process, you will learn quite a bit that will help you decide what you want to do, and you will begin to build your own career network.

—Ricki Frankel

YOU HAVE TO WORK, so you might as well make as much money as possible. Why work if you're going to struggle to get by? Find something that pays the most money you can earn with your experience and talents. Screw that "do what you love" stuff: Do something that makes money, then do what you love at home.

> —*D.S.*
> *BOSTON, MASSACHUSETTS*

• • • • • • • •

SOMETIMES IT'S BETTER TO FIND out what you *don't* want to do. Every job is a learning experience. You have no idea what you're going to be good at. You have to give everything a shot.

> —*RAY*
> *ROCKY MOUNT, NORTH CAROLINA*

• • • • • • • •

CLASSIFIED ADS SUCK. Most quality jobs aren't advertised in newspapers. I've found 80 percent of my positions via networking and going through recruiters who found my résumé on monster.com.

> —*ROB SALTER*
> *MUNCHENGLADBACH, GERMANY*

• • • • • • • •

WAITING TABLES IS A GREAT THING to know how to do. You can get a job almost anywhere in the world, make ends meet at times in your life when things aren't going well, and always have something to fall back on. But it can also be a trap. It's likely that you can make more money waiting tables than at most entry-level jobs in the professional world. It's not a skill I would ever trade in, but I think it's important to keep your goals in mind and make sure you are always working toward them.

> —*J.*
> *BINGHAMTON, NEW YORK*

Consider

Don't let business cards get lost in the vacuum in your pockets or bottom drawer. Develop a system, enter everyone you meet into a database, or send them a LinkedIn request.

—*NADIA*

PRIVATE SECTOR'S LOSS

Twenty-seven percent of 2009 college grads planned to get a job in public service – up from 23 percent in 2008.

MEET AS MANY PEOPLE AS YOU can who work in the industry you want to break into. I wrote a number of emails to contacts and asked if I could take them out for a quick coffee and discussion. I always mentioned the fact that I would love their good insight, and I think most were flattered. It's true that "important" people are busy, but many people like to feel like they have influence and are admired; many will take time out of their day to share their story with you. It's more important in these meetings to ask questions than to sell yourself. Remember, it's not a job interview; it's a chance to show how committed you are to pursuing your goals and learning about the industry. You'd be surprised: Many of these meetings lead to a job later on, or to a good referral to another person in the field who may have work for you.

—ANDREA
TORONTO, ONTARIO, CANADA

• • • • • • • •

DO RESEARCH ON DIFFERENT JOBS. Find out how much jobs pay, what skills are required, and what a typical day would look like. A job might seem attractive, but when you learn the day-to-day workings of it, you might change your mind.

—CHRISTOPHER
HAVERTOWN, PENNSYLVANIA

• • • • • • • •

FIND A JOB YOU TRULY LOVE. If it's a job that you believe in and you enjoy doing, you'll work harder and want to stay longer. The temptation to call in sick or the habit of being continuously late will be obsolete if you wake up each morning thinking, "I can't wait to go to work!"

—LACEY CONNELLY
CHICAGO, ILLINOIS

YOU ARE A FUNGIBLE WORKER BEE. Get over your pride and use your connections. "Referred by so-and-so's tennis partner" scrawled by the HR person at the top of your résumé may be the only thing separating you from the other fungible worker bees.

> —*D.M.*
> *NEW YORK, NEW YORK*

• • • • • • • •

EVERY JOB I HAVE HAD since graduating has been through connections. When you are looking for jobs, contact anyone you know in the field. They may be able to inform you of open positions, be your reference, or write a recommendation.

> —*RACHEL WIECK CUPIT*
> *NEW ORLEANS, LOUISIANA*

• • • • • • • •

ALL OF MY REALLY GREAT TEACHING JOBS have come from education fairs. I've found that when you meet the recruiter in person and have that personal contact, it makes a huge difference.

> —*ELIZABETH*
> *FORT WAYNE, INDIANA*

• • • • • • • •

KNOW PEOPLE IN THE RIGHT PLACES or get your foot in the door somehow. This is a better way to introduce yourself to a company than by storming the HR office with a baseball bat.

> —*JESSE AMMERMAN*
> *CHICAGO, ILLINOIS*

Do what you enjoy or you won't *have* a life after college.

—*J. KYLE KISER*
SCOTTSDALE, ARIZONA

THE VERY LEAST YOU CAN DO in your life is to figure out what you hope for. The most you can do is live inside that hope, running down its hallways, touching the walls on both sides.

> —*BARBARA KINGSOLVER*
> *2008 COMMENCEMENT SPEECH AT DUKE UNIVERSITY*

Even when you're starting out, I think it's really important to work to live, and not live to work.

—*Anonymous*
Atlanta, Georgia

Since it is difficult to find a job now, I would focus on just getting SOMETHING that can pay the bills. Remember that your first job isn't going to be the job you have forever. I have been out of college for five years, and have had four jobs. I know people the same age as me who have had six or seven jobs. It's OK to jump around, and it's totally normal to feel unsatisfied with what you're doing. At some point I was working a job that I thought would be perfect for me, and I was very unhappy. I realized that it wasn't what it seemed to be. It was "back to the drawing board". I really like what I'm doing now, and it was almost a happy accident that I landed in this position.

—*Shira Pinsker*
Washington, D.C.

• • • • • • • • •

People say you shouldn't sit behind a computer screen when job hunting, but there are a lot of great jobs on the Internet. Go to university websites, and don't forget about Craigslist. But no matter where you search for your job, remember that you must keep interviewing. Even if you know that the job isn't exactly what you would like, interviewing for it is great practice and helps you build interviewing skills for the job that you really want.

—*Kristin Anne Bradley*
Aventura, Florida

• • • • • • • • •

If you're looking for what you want to do, you should intern with companies to try out different jobs and make sure you like them. It's a good way to see what's out there, and it looks good on a résumé. It looks like real experience, as opposed to working at a bar.

—*Vanessa*
New Jersey

TIPS: FROM JOB SEARCH TO JOB *FOUND*

- Get out there! Go to every free and low-cost networking, industry, and alumni event you can find. You never know where you'll hear about a new opportunity, or meet someone who is looking to hire, or who knows someone who is looking to hire.

- Allot a certain amount of time each day for online search and emailing résumés. But don't permanently station yourself in front of your computer; spend a substantial amount of time each week meeting with people you know and networking.

- Seek out trusted, positive mentors who can both circulate your résumé and suggest new directions for your job search.

- Be open to many different kinds of opportunities. You have to start somewhere. You don't need to find a job for life; focus on the coming year.

- Be creative and forward-looking. Take time to research and think about what the jobs of the future will be. Consider how you could apply your skill sets to these new opportunities.

- Consider entrepreneurial jobs. New companies will likely not have a high starting salary, but payoffs can be large if the company is successful. Most importantly, you can learn a tremendous amount in the less structured entrepreneurial environment.

- Check to see if any of the companies you're interested in might have a project that you can work on. They may not be able to compensate you for your work, but if you have the time it could be a great way to showcase your talents and abilities while gaining valuable experience.

—Shannon Duff

A LEAP TO LAW

Don't limit yourself with a preset career path. I never thought I would be considered for a high-paying corporate law job. I was an art history major at a liberal arts college, and I didn't know the first thing about finance or corporate law. I did manage to get into law school, though, and my parents were telling me to think about representing children.

After I got to law school, I found out that if you get a certain GPA your first year, the law firms track you down and throw jobs at you. Who knew? So I took a summer position because the money was good, and then I found out finance is actually pretty interesting, especially when combined with all the recent corporate scandals. Who knew again?

So I took a permanent offer after graduation. The law firm probably won't be my final destination because the hours are hellacious, but I am confident that working there will present some other opportunity I hadn't thought of before, just like law school did. It's like going from one handle to the next on the monkey bars.

—D.M.
New York, New York

Ever since I was young, I've wanted to work with NASA and the space shuttle program. Currently, I am a crew systems engineer for the government. Achieving your goals means taking one step at a time; it means figuring out where you want to be and taking the steps to get there. I may never get there, but I'm having a heck of a time doing it.

—Michelle
Dayton, Ohio

When I graduated college, I wanted to be a writer. I enjoyed it, I was pretty good at it, and I hated math. But that didn't stop me from applying to be a stockbroker at one point. They gave me a test during my first interview; I remember a lot of numbers on it. I did so poorly that the guy who gave me the test thought there must have been some sort of mistake, so he offered to let me take it again. My first job out of college was in sales. After I failed at that, I waited tables, telemarketed, and worked as a greenskeeper for a country club. It was around that time that I took a tour through a CNN newsroom. I looked around and saw people my age writing and producing the news. They weren't wearing suits, and they weren't dealing with numbers. I knew it was what I wanted to do, so I got an internship at a local station and worked my way up from there.

—*J.A.*
Atlanta, Georgia

• • • • • • • •

You should never disqualify any experience you have. You never know where something is going to lead. I went to school for religion and philosophy, but I put myself through school by cooking. After I graduated, I kept cooking because I enjoyed it and because it's what I was most qualified to do. Now, I have a pretty good career as a chef.

—*Ryan*
Chapel Hill, North Carolina

• • • • • • • •

Do something, anything. If you start moving forward, doors will open. More than anything, creativity is what drives the American economy. If you demonstrate practical creative thinking, people will track you down.

—*Daren*
Decatur, Georgia

Remember, it's called *networking*, not *partying*.

—*ANONYMOUS*
SHARON, NORTH
DAKOTA

FOR THOSE THINKING OF MOVING to New York, my advice is just to bite the bullet and move—no job will consider you or take you seriously unless you have that New York address on your résumé. I thought I could go on interviews while I was still in college spring semester and secure a job for the fall (like all my banking/business school friends had done) but I was completely wrong. Interview after interview that I went on in the spring of my senior year ended with, "Well, call us when you get up here. We won't know anything until then." So I moved in August, sublet an apartment I found on Craigslist and basically spent my days running around the 100 degree city in my "Bat Mitzvah" suit (as my new boss likes to call it), going on interviews and meeting brokers to look at apartments in between.

—*ROBIN*
NEW YORK, NEW YORK

WORKING ABROAD

A list of the top 10 countries where American students want to start a new career:

1. United Kingdom
2. China
3. United States
4. France
5. Australia
6. Japan
7. Germany
8. Hong Kong
9. Spain
10. Italy

THE COLLEGE NETWORK

USE YOUR PROFESSORS AS RESOURCES. After college, I went to Europe for four months, and when I came back, I scheduled a meeting with my favorite professor. I asked him if he had any suggestions on how I should move forward after graduation. This professor helped me. He knew somebody at a PR firm and called his contact for me. This led to my first job after college!

—MARIANA
SAN FRANCISCO, CALIFORNIA

● ● ● ● ● ● ● ● ●

USE ALUMNI ASSOCIATIONS. My college found my first job for me. The school had an outplacement program that didn't cost me a dime. All I had to do was meet with a counselor to tell what sort of work I was looking for, what field my degree was in, and what kind of money I was looking for. That was it. They would periodically mail job openings to me that they felt were a good fit. Those people are usually well connected with the business community in their area, so this can be a big help.

—MATT TIMMONS
CALLA, OHIO

AS SOON AS YOU KNOW what you want to do with your life, start getting experience. I work in radio, and it is really hard to get a paying job without first having some experience through an internship, volunteer work, or both. I worked at my college radio station and I also volunteered for a nonprofit organization. There are so many nonprofits that need help, and you can always find at least one that will give you the experience you seek.

—LIZ POPE
AUBURN, CALIFORNIA

Consider

USING INTERNSHIPS

After I graduated, many fields of work were tight and had few jobs available, so I used the time to work in internships. The internships were helpful because I was able to be employed while looking for a permanent position or another internship. I did four or five internships (each about four to six months long). I sought out internships at places well-known in my field and places that had the reputation for hosting the best internship programs.

Also, network with friends in the field. Find out where your friends or people you meet have interned, and apply to that internship. I know that a lot of students I worked with at the paper in college were interning each year with companies that previously hired students from our school. Many employers are impressed by students who previously worked for them, and they will go back to that school to find more employees.

—*BRETT*
CHICAGO, ILLINOIS

· · · · · · · ·

FIND WHAT INTERESTS YOU and be willing to work for free in an internship or something. I was a photojournalist and went to a paper out of college and told them I'd work for free. It took a few months for them to realize they should hire me, but I ended up getting a great job shooting for United Press International.

—*PAUL DIAMOND*
SEATTLE, WASHINGTON

· · · · · · · ·

GET YOUR FOOT IN THE DOOR. I ended up getting my first job at the place where I had interned. The company was being uprooted to a new location, and they were really hurting for people. They brought me in as a temp.

—*ANONYMOUS*
BROOKLYN, NEW YORK

GET IN ON THE GROUND FLOOR. I was going to graduate school for education, and I knew I wanted to find something related to kids. I found an ad for a company, and I originally went to work as a tutor for them. Then things happened! I became a teacher at the new school they were starting, working 25 hours a week in the beginning. Eventually I moved into the administrative offices. Three years later I was the dean of students at the school, which had grown from a handful of students to something like 85.

> —REBECCA SHENN
> NEW YORK, NEW YORK

> There's a reason everyone tells you to follow your passion – because you should! The money will follow.
>
> —NADIA

· · · · · · · ·

❝ Find a career that has the potential of earning you money, but do something you're interested in. At the end of the day, what people strive for is happiness. ❞

> —JANNA
> TORONTO, ONTARIO, CANADA

· · · · · · · ·

FIND FRIENDS WHO LIKE THEIR JOBS. I got the best job I ever had through a friend, and it's a job I never would have gotten otherwise. People think of networking as trying to chat up people you don't know, but it's as simple as contacting the people you already know and letting them know you need a job.

> —CHRISTINA
> CHAPEL HILL, NORTH CAROLINA

BEYOND 'YOU NEED TO NETWORK'

By the time you have graduated, you will have heard the mantra "it's all about networking and connections" so often that it is probably embedded in your consciousness. But that doesn't mean you know how to network effectively. So, how do you go about networking? Here are some starter tips:

"The Love You Take …"
First, change your point of view. Keep in mind that social networks are defined as "mutually reciprocal relationships." The Beatles once sang, "The love you take is equal to the love you make." That general theory can be applied here. You are much more likely to develop important contacts and career connections if you can show people that you are not always "on the take." Indeed, you will be pleasantly surprised by the results when you make it clear to people that you do not expect favors from them – rather, what you are seeking is to give and receive time, advice and guidance.

You may wonder: What exactly you are in a position to give at this stage of your career? The answer is, when you recognize someone's achievements and then ask for their advice, you are giving respect and acknowledgement. Indeed, this is valuable and worthy.

Make the Connections
It is important to expose yourself to as many different environments as possible where opportunities exist to connect. This applies as much to online social networking as it does to doing so in person.

One common approach is to choose a group or association that is relevant to your area of interest. For example, if you are a marketing graduate, join the American Marketing Association. Chances are there will be an active group close to where you live as well as one online. Volunteer for these organizations at every opportunity, because it will get you visibility very quickly, often more so than in your work environment.

Joining a social group for sports or church can prove equally useful.

Start a Conversation

While the ability to connect is critical to the networking process, it is your skill at meaningful conversation that often solidifies the relationship. Although the prospect may be terrifying, you should realize that starting a conversation anywhere, at anytime, is much easier than you think.

You can start a conversation with a comment on anything from the decor of the room, to the accident you witnessed on your way in, to a compliment on the pin someone is wearing. In most cases, the other party will respond, and thus a conversation begins.

How do you keep that conversation going? Follow the advice of Dale Carnegie who characterized people who talk about themselves as "bores," people who talk about others as "gossips," and people who talk about you as "brilliant conversationalists"! Indeed, if you are at a loss for something to talk about, always remember that most people are happy to talk about themselves.

You can start the ball rolling by asking them about the various phases of their lives: their past, present and future. You can always ask someone where he or she went to school, or when they first knew they were interested in a particular career. You can ask what their greatest challenges are, and what they like most/least about their job. When asking about a person's future, good questions can be anything from their plans for their next vacation to their career aspiration.

Become a Collaborator

The essence of *sustained networking* lies in collaboration and an ongoing attitude of mutual reciprocity. Maintaining relationships requires specific, sustained effort, and the more thoughtful you can be, the more memorable you will be.

If during your conversation you picked up a person's particular area of interest, think about sending him or her an article or book suggestion that is pertinent. And the next time you hear of a spectacular career move by an executive you want to impress, send him or her a congratulatory note on reaching the next phase of an extraordinary career.

—Nadia Bilchik

DO NOT BE CONSTRAINED by your own expectations or anyone else's. You can always go back to a 9-to-5 job, but you might get to an age when you will feel too old to take risks and explore the world. Better to do the latter when you're young.

—*KAREN*
BOSTON, MASSACHUSETTS

• • • • • • • •

YOU HAVE TO FOLLOW YOUR HEART. This is the most important decision you will make. Don't choose a career because you think you can make bundles of money at it or because it's the career that your dad chose or because your friends think you'd be good at it. Choose the one thing you love to do and do it to the best of your ability. For me, it was teaching kindergarten. I knew that's what I wanted to do, and I have never regretted it. I know I could have made more money in other fields, but I love working with kids at that age.

—*MIA O'MALLEY*
BOARDMAN, OHIO

• • • • • • • •

BEFORE I FIGURED OUT what I wanted to do with my life, I worked in retail for five years. Retail is a good place to find yourself. It's a nonstressful job, it will build your wardrobe and make you look sharp, and you might earn enough money to get a little independence. You can also learn practical skills; you get comfortable talking to lots of people. I also found it easy to ask customers for advice. In this role, you're always in the position of subordinate, and it's a good opportunity to ask regular customers about their lives and how they got to where they are (people love talking about themselves). You can't find this in a textbook.

—*MATTHEW WISE*
TORONTO, ONTARIO, CANADA

'NET'-WORKING

In today's world, you should absolutely use the Internet to get leads for your job search—just be sure not to rely on it as your only source of job leads. Company websites, job search sites like Monster.com, your alumni network, and others are all sources of leads—and, of course, great sources of research about what kinds of jobs are available and who is hiring. Just remember, when you respond to a lead from the Internet, yours may be one of several hundred faceless résumés someone is reviewing. It can be discouraging to send résumés out and receive only silence in response, but if you're not called, don't take it personally.

Keep in mind, however, that personal connections are still the best way to get a job. In fact, 80 percent of job seekers find their jobs through personal connections. People you know will introduce you to hiring managers, and then your résumé will no longer be faceless. That's why you cannot rely on the Internet as your sole source of job leads—but don't ignore it as a possibility.

—Ricki Frankel

"NETWORKING, NETWORKING, NETWORKING" has always been my motto. When I meet someone, even in a casual environment like a bar, I always ask about his or her work because there's a chance we could be helpful to each other professionally. One of my college professors brought in a guest speaker who was a partner in an advertising agency. After his speech, I approached him and asked if I could come down to his office and learn more about what he does. He was happy to have me, and during my tour of his office, he told me that he could see me working as an account manager, which is now my position in a Chicago advertising agency.

—MUHAMMAD SHABAZZ
CHICAGO, ILLINOIS

NETWORKING DOS AND DON'TS

Do: Let everyone know you are searching for employment. Tell your family, tell your friends, tell any of your close professors or mentors. Let them know what you are generally looking for in a job, or if there is a new field you want to break into. Use a career networking site, such as Linkedin.com. It's similar to Facebook, but you connect to others on a professional rather than a social level. Your close contacts may already know of something, or they will keep you in mind if something new comes up.

Do: Find out if your alma mater has a networking site especially for alumni. If so, contact your fellow alumni who work in the field you are interested in. Ask them for tips about educational paths, résumé builders, or good interview practices, or if they know of any companies who are hiring.

Don't: Ask for a job. Leave it up to your alumni correspondent to offer you an interview, or to put you in touch with his or her employer. You do not want to put someone else in the awkward position of saying, "No."

Do: Ask a friend or mentor, who's an "insider" at a particular company, to put in a good word for you. Please use this method with caution, however. You should only ask those whom you know are genuinely impressed with your work.

Don't: Ask a parent or close relative who's an "insider" at a particular company to put in a good word for you. Praise from a parent or close relative may not appear sincere. Of course you're amazing to them—they love you!

—*Sarah Franco*

USE YOUR FRIENDS TO GET A JOB, but make sure they know your experience. My friend had long known about a job opening at his workplace, but he didn't know my experience or background. "Send me your résumé," he said when I asked if there were any openings there. Within a week, I had a phone interview. In two weeks, I had the job.

> —*NICK*
> *NEW CITY, NEW YORK*

• • • • • • • • •

FREELANCING IS A GREAT WAY TO WORK. I started taking freelance assignments and loved it. I also learned more about what kind of work I like to do. And every job is new and refreshing.

> —*L.C.*
> *PITTSBURGH, PENNSYLVANIA*

DEAD ENDS

If your career goals include one of the following jobs, watch out. Forbes.com says they will disappear in 20 years.

- Grocery Store Cashier
- Film Processer
- CD Store Manager
- Union Organizer
- Encyclopedia Writer
- Miner
- Construction Worker
- Fighter Pilot
- Call Center Rep
- Oil Wildcatter

WATCH OUT!

IF YOU EVER SEE A JOB IN THE CLASSIFIED ADS promising that you will make $600 a week while training for a management position, skip over it! All you will be doing is selling perfume for a tyrant who will promise you your own office if you keep up the hard work. Eventually you will get tired of working for free, and they'll find another sucker. It happened to me.

    —ANDREA PARKER
     CHICAGO, ILLINOIS

WHEN LOOKING FOR A JOB ONLINE, make sure you do your homework. I found a job on Craigslist that sounded great, but I ended up working for a lunatic. The job had all of the warning signs—like "Work out of your house"—but I was desperate. Do a lot of research before you take a job and ask a lot of questions during the interview.

    —KATIE
     SAN JOSE, CALIFORNIA

I TRIED MAKING A CAREER out of my hobby, which was cycling, and I spent four years working full time in bike sales. But as fun as it was at first, I got so burnt out that I quit and didn't even look at a bike for a year. It became all-encompassing: It was my work, it was my fun. There wasn't anything else in my life. Unless you can really separate the job from the hobby, don't try it.

    —TIM MURPHINE
     VALDOSTA, GEORGIA

BE RELENTLESS. When I decided to pursue a career, I went at it full speed. I got a list of the top 20 PR firms in San Diego and researched all of them, found the contact person and systematically called and asked for a job. From there, I just went after it and got the interviews. Persistence is key.

    —STASIA RAINES
     SAN DIEGO, CALIFORNIA

FIND SOMETHING YOU ARE PASSIONATE ABOUT, and speak to as many people as you can who work in that industry. Especially in a recession, when there is intense competition among recent college graduates for work, your chances of finding a job that a) interests you and b) pays your bills are much higher if you can build a professional network of folks who also work in your preferred industry. In addition to telling you what you need to know about the experiences and skills that specific employers value most in job candidates, your contacts may know other people who are hiring. A personal recommendation on their behalf often makes a big difference in whether you are invited to interview for an open position, and whether you are extended a job offer. Perhaps most importantly, a professional network is a great resource for making an informed decision about whether a specific employer—or more broadly speaking—a specific career path is a "good fit" for you.

—*ANONYMOUS*
DECATUR, GEORGIA

• • • • • • • •

WHEN I GRADUATED, I thought that I was supposed to be in sales or something corporate, because that's what my dad did. And when you're graduating, all the companies that come on campus for interviews are offering big corporate jobs. I thought I had to take one of these jobs, but I had no interest in it. Now I know that it's OK not to want a corporate job.

—*JENNIFER*
PLEASANTON, CALIFORNIA

• • • • • • • •

DON'T SETTLE FOR JUST ANYTHING. Upon graduating college, I took a job at a recruiting firm in Washington, D.C. It was your ̶ ̶ ̶ ̶ ̶ ̶ ̶ ̶ ̶ ̶ 5̶ ̶ hour-a-week, coat-and-tie-wearing nightmare. I hated i̶ Consider quit, I've worked at summer camps and ski slopes, back ̶ ̶ Europe, toured the United States, hiked parts of the Ap ̶ ̶ Trail, and have now combined my passions for the outo ̶ cation by teaching outdoor education classes at a unive ̶

—*WHIT ALTIZER*
OXFORD, MISSISSIPPI

WHEN YOU FIRST GET OUT OF COLLEGE, it's best to think "job" instead of "career." You need to pay off those student loans, put down a deposit on your new apartment, buy career clothes, and get set up in your adult life. You also need to learn the ropes and build the experience that will take you to the job you're going to love. It does not happen overnight.

—*ANONYMOUS*
SAN FRANCISCO, CALIFORNIA

" There is something to be said for chasing your dream until it dies. However, it is also important to do what you are good at, what comes naturally. Everyone has their own individual strengths, and when you play to those, you will be successful no matter what you do. "

—*BILL WALKER*
SEATTLE, WASHINGTON

FOLLOW STEPS, GET JOB

1. **Clarify your interests, skills, and goals.**
   As a starting point in the job search, it is best to spend time identifying your interests (what you like to do), your skills (what you are good at doing), your values (what's important to you), and your personality (what qualities you possess that complement your other skills).

2. **Research and explore your options.**
   Talking to alumni and others about what they actually do on a day-to-day basis can help you further identify your options and decide whether or not they are a good fit for you.

3. **Identify and research specific prospective employers.**
   Go to career fairs, meet people through your alumni associations at school, look online at job sites like Monster.com, and realize the importance of networking.

4. **Initiate contact, submit applications, and generate interviews.**
   Polish your résumé and cover letters. Contact the companies you are interested in. Request an opportunity to interview for information or to discuss job opportunities.

5. **Create a notebook, keep records, and follow up.**
   Keep copies of cover letters and résumés you submit. Maintain a contact list of all prospective employers. If someone tells you to follow up on a certain date, make note of that date and be sure to follow up.

WHEN I STARTED MY SEARCH, I blindly sent résumés to several human resource departments and answered ads at large firms. After they blew me off, I called my old professors and acquaintances and asked them if they knew anyone looking for help. I found that there were a lot of jobs out there that were not posted anywhere. I think most people, when hiring, go to someone they know and respect before they place an ad.

—ANONYMOUS
LOS ANGELES, CALIFORNIA

• • • • • • • •

KNOW THAT YOU MIGHT need a second job. When you start your career, you usually have to start at the bottom: not only at the bottom of the job pool, but also at the bottom of the pay scale. I work in radio, which doesn't pay much in the beginning. Knowing that, I always have some kind of second job that helps me pay the bills.

—LIZ POPE
AUBURN, CALIFORNIA

• • • • • • • •

I HAD WANTED TO BE A SINGER for as long as I can remember. But my school had a job fair where a brokerage house offered me very good money to work as a stockbroker. I did this for almost a decade, but I was miserable. Finally, I quit and started pursuing my dream of becoming a singer. Once I took that step, all kinds of opportunities appeared. My singing career is going very well. Although I still have a long way to go, I've never been so happy in my life.

—CARMEN C.
OAKLAND, CALIFORNIA

FINDING OUT WHAT MATTERS TO YOU

If you're not sure what career direction to take, try the exercise below, which will help you realize what personal values are important to you. Understanding your own values can help you figure out what you want from your career as well as your life. Revisit your list throughout your career; the items will shift in importance at different times in your life.

Rate the following values on how important they are to you on a scale of 1 to 5, with 1 being extremely important to you and 5 being not at all important. Go through the list again and choose your top 10 values. Then narrow it down to your top 5 values.

- ☐ Achievement
- ☐ Adventure
- ☐ Affection
- ☐ Aesthetics
- ☐ Autonomy
- ☐ Caring
- ☐ Challenge
- ☐ Change and variety
- ☐ Competition
- ☐ Cooperation
- ☐ Creativity
- ☐ Direct people contact
- ☐ Economic security
- ☐ Excitement
- ☐ Expertise
- ☐ Family
- ☐ Freedom
- ☐ Friendship
- ☐ Health
- ☐ Independence
- ☐ Influence
- ☐ Integrity
- ☐ Intellectual stimulation
- ☐ Knowledge
- ☐ Leadership
- ☐ Leisure
- ☐ Location
- ☐ Loyalty
- ☐ Moral value
- ☐ Opportunity for advancement
- ☐ Parenthood
- ☐ Pleasure
- ☐ Power
- ☐ Responsibility

☐ Recognition   ☐ Spirituality

☐ Security   ☐ Wealth

☐ Service   ☐ Wisdom

☐ Social Service   ☐ _____

                             Other

☐ Stability

TOP 10 VALUES

_____

_____

_____

_____

_____

_____

_____

_____

_____

_____

—Nadia Bilchik

The Hunt: Résumés and Cover Letters

*I*t's true: 16+ years of school comes down to a couple of sheets of *paper. Or rather, you now need to smash your life, your experience and what you can offer a company neatly, succinctly, and impressively into a résumé and cover letter. And don't make any typos! That is, if you want to get a job. While there are plenty of websites and books out there that offer guidance, we asked the masses what didn't work for them, what did, and what they would advise as you try to lift your résumé to the top of the pile.*

BUY SOME PLAIN BUT TASTEFUL NOTE CARDS with matching envelopes. You'll be writing a lot of bread-and-butter notes during your job hunt. And follow up. Follow up. Follow up. Your mother is not around, so you'll just have to nag yourself.

—*N.*
BROOKLYN, NEW YORK

PLEASE USE SPELL-CHECKER ON YOUR RÉSUMÉ. MISSPELLING A WORD MAKES YOU LOOK LIKE AN IDIOT.

—*ANONYMOUS*
ATLANTA, GEORGIA

HEADLINES
Best Advice and Top Tips

- When it comes to résumés, stick with basic fonts and paper colors.

- There are plenty of résumé guides out there. It's most important to create a résumé you feel comfortable with.

- Cover letters or emails should be individually written to each company and, if at all possible, addressed to a specific person.

Don't send everyone the same standard cover letter. Change it for different jobs.

—*SEMA*
VAN NUYS,
CALIFORNIA

THE DAMN GOOD RÉSUMÉ GUIDE is the only book anybody should ever use to help them write a résumé. It took me through both the chronological and functional formats and taught me how to do a skills inventory and write out my exact qualifications in a marketable fashion. I've actually had several people compliment my résumé.

—*R.W.*
FORT COLLINS, COLORADO

• • • • • • • • •

DON'T SCRIMP ON THE QUALITY OF PAPER you use for your résumé. Trust me, I have an aunt who works in HR; it matters. I know it seems crazy to spend that kind of money for a thicker, better-looking piece of paper. But if you ultimately get the job, it's worth it. And buy cream-colored. Never white. It will make it stand out from the others.

—*ANONYMOUS*
SOUTH BEND, INDIANA

POTENTIAL EMPLOYEES CAN SEE right through generic form letters. Every résumé and cover letter should be tailored to each specific position. If the company says it's looking for someone with experience with X, Y, and Z, then you'd better list your experience with or knowledge of X, Y, and Z in the résumé. Your résumé and cover letter should basically be a rewrite of the job description. Show you aren't just looking for *a* job; you're looking for *this* job.

—*KELLY WILKES*
ATLANTA, GEORGIA

• • • • • • • •

" Using action words is good; writing big words for the sake of sounding important is bad. If you find yourself writing *amalgamate*, you're way off track. Try *merge*. "

—*J.A.*
ATLANTA, GEORGIA

• • • • • • • •

LESS IS MORE WITH RÉSUMÉS and cover letters. Don't tell me everything about yourself. And don't use big words to impress me. I look for honesty and enthusiasm; they're hard to fake. Say things like, "I'm really good at this. I'm not good at this yet, but I'm dying to learn. I'm a quick learner and a hard worker, and what I don't know I can make up for in my desire to learn."

—*ANONYMOUS*
ATLANTA, GEORGIA

BASIC RÉSUMÉ TIPS

- Use a clean, readable font. Font size should never be smaller than 11pt.

- Bold and enlarge your name at the top of the résumé. Include your contact information, including your phone number and a professional email address. If you have a personal website that illustrates your talents and matches your career goals, include the URL.

- Objective: Include a one- or two-sentence summary of what you're looking for that stresses what you'll add to the company, *not* what you're looking to get from a job.

- List your experience chronologically, with your most recent job first. List accomplishments with each position, including any promotions, awards, or increases in responsibility. If you can quantify your achievements with hard numbers or cause-effect examples, do so.

- If your résumé is two pages long, make sure to fill the second page at least halfway down the page – or condense it to one page. Two-page résumés should have "Continued" at the bottom of the first page, and your last name and "Page 2" at the top of the second page.

- Not in a creative field? Don't use fancy graphics. In a creative field? Don't use fancy graphics. Save it for your portfolio.

- Be consistent: If you spell out the state in your address, such as New York, spell out the states for your jobs.

- The Internet contains a number of sites listing dozens of strong résumé verbs. Look them up, and use them.

- Don't forget to mention your relevant technical and computer skills – even if editing on iMovie is just one of your hobbies. Always include memberships in professional organizations. Listing your personal interests is optional.

- Education: Include your degree, major, minor, date of graduation and the school's name and location. GPA is recommended only if you received higher than a 3.0.

- Read, edit and re-read your résumé to make sure it's clear and typo-free. Do it again. Ask your friends and family to read it. Be open to their advice.

- Consider creating several versions of your résumé, each tailored to the type of position you're applying for.

—The Editors

THE FORWARD-LOOKING RÉSUMÉ

Your résumé should reflect your next job, not your current job. It should tell the reader that you can do the job you're after. If you need to translate your experience into new words that better describe the new job, figure out the jargon and do the translation.

—Ricki Frankel

WHEN WRITING YOUR RÉSUMÉ, see if your school/university has a career center. Even an old English teacher or professor might be able to help you. Texas Tech has a career center, and I went there and got mine checked and rechecked. I also had classes where my résumé was a project, so I would update it and check it through their center again.

—*MICAH KARBER*
SILVERTON, TEXAS

• • • • • • • •

66 Spell-check your cover letters. I received one cover letter back and the woman had taken a red pen to it. I was like, 'Oh, let me eat my piece of humble pie.' Apparently seven years of college hasn't taught me much. 99

—*LEANNE*
ATLANTA, GEORGIA

• • • • • • • •

IT IS IMPORTANT TO LIST EXPERIENCE, and it doesn't necessarily have to be in the field you are trying to get into. I am in public relations; however, leading river-rafting expeditions through Class IV rapids shows that I am a "take charge" kind of guy.

—*ANONYMOUS*
SANTA CRUZ, CALIFORNIA

COVER LETTER DOS & DON'TS

Stop wondering whether or not to include a cover letter when sending a résumé: always *write a cover letter, every single time. Your cover letter is a major opportunity to focus the reader on your skills and abilities, and to highlight your assets. In today's world, it is perfectly acceptable to send a cover letter with your résumé via email. Here are some things to do—and some things to avoid—in cover letters.*

DO

- State your reason for writing.
- Be brief and specific.
- Be positive.
- Use your own words.
- Summarize your qualifications.
- Tell them how you will follow up.
- Write to an individual by name, if possible.
- Use good paper, if you are sending a physical letter.
- Attach your résumé.
- Include your contact information (phone number and email).
- Check your spelling and grammar (and just running spell-check is not enough).

DON'T

- Ramble.
- Include unnecessary words.
- Use big words to impress.
- Leave the reader unsure of the action.
- Begin with "Dear Sir/Madam".
- Hand write your letter.

—The Editors

LYING DOESN'T PAY

WHEN APPLYING FOR A JOB, many people take the risk of exaggerating their education, skills, knowledge, ability, and experience. Perhaps they think they'll never get caught in a lie, but they're wrong. Lying, or even overstatements, can cost you the job.

Today, most employers conduct a background check on all applicants. Depending on the employer and the nature of the job, the background check may include verification of the applicant's prior employment, education, credit history, criminal conviction history and other sensitive information. Even if an employer finds out negative information about an applicant through a background check, he still may consider the applicant for employment. But if the employer learns that an applicant has not been honest in the application process, he probably won't hire the applicant at all. Despite the temptation to misstate or enhance information, the applicant will benefit more from being honest and straightforward.

Try to turn negative history into a positive statement: "I have a lot of experience and am proud of my ability to manage corporate budgets. If I had put half of this corporate diligence into the management of my personal affairs my credit rating would not be anywhere near as bad as it is."

—*Angela J. Reddock*

• • • • • • • •

IT'S A BAD MOVE TO LIE ON YOUR RÉSUMÉ. Someday you will get to be good and comfortable with your future coworkers. After a few cocktails, you will inevitably begin to talk about how the beverage company that you once owned was no more than a lemonade stand on the corner of 53rd and Garfield.

—*DAVE HUDSON*
ST. CLOUD, MINNESOTA

IF YOU LIE ON YOUR RÉSUMÉ, you're preparing yourself to be incompetent in your job. Why not just seek out the opportunities that will get you the experience to truly prepare you for the job so you don't have to lie?

—*PATRICIA DREY*
SAINT PAUL, MINNESOTA

* * * * * * * * *

AN EXPERIENCED INTERVIEWER will know right away that a young thing only a year out of college didn't "manage" a million-dollar project for any sane company. Saying so on your résumé only makes you look immature.

—*K.A.*
BROOKLYN, OHIO

* * * * * * * *

REASONS YOU SHOULDN'T LIE ON YOUR RÉSUMÉ:

1. Because lying is wrong and stupid.
2. Because you may get caught.
3. Because you may get fired.
4. Because you may get sued for various reasons. You could end up with a job you legally cannot do. You may end up screwing something up for your employer, and they may sue you. You may screw something up for a client, and they may sue you. Even if you don't screw something up and you worked on something you weren't supposed to, it creates an excuse for you and your employer to get sued. We live in a very litigious society.
5. What would your mom think?

—*T.C.*
MINNEAPOLIS, MINNESOTA

I KNEW WHEN I WAS IN COLLEGE that I wanted to be in television production. I also knew that my competition was tens of thousands of other recent graduates with the same skill set, a similar educational background, and probably the same internship experience. Knowing this, I had to think of a way to make my résumé stand out, so I spoke to a friend of a friend who had worked in television for 10 years. She told me the best thing to do was to have a perfectly formatted résumé. If your first internship on your résumé is in all caps, make sure the rest conform. If you use bullet points to list your experience for your first internship on your résumé, do the same for every internship you list. It's important that your résumé looks perfect and has no mistakes.

—*SEMA*
VAN NUYS, CALIFORNIA

● ● ● ● ● ● ● ●

WHEN YOU'RE FRESH OUT of college, it's important to set yourself apart from all of the other recent grads. It goes without saying that grades and internships are important, but equally important (or more so) is demonstrating that you can put your education to work in the real world. For example, when I was seeking my first job in PR, I submitted a news release about why I was perfect for the job instead of a typical résumé. No matter what field you are in, you can come up with a clever and memorable way to present yourself and your capabilities.

—*D.B.*
COPPELL, TEXAS

MY INTERVIEWER LOOKED at my résumé and said, "Nice objective. Wouldn't you say your objective is to get this job?" My cheeks burned as I said, "Yes." Never, ever put your objective on your résumé. Why? Your interviewers know your objective. They don't need any grand pronouncements such as, "My objective is to find a job with a global multimedia conglomerate that will maximize my people skills and problem-solving talents." It's useless information and wasted space at the top of your résumé.

—ADAM DREYFUS
NEW CANAAN, CONNECTICUT

● ● ● ● ● ● ● ●

" Change your email address to something professional. Don't have the one you had from high school, such as soccerchick1. Make it generic. "

——ERIN BLACK
PITTSBURGH, PENNSYLVANIA

● ● ● ● ● ● ● ●

BE CREATIVE WHEN SENDING OUT YOUR RÉSUMÉ.
I got a little desperate on the job hunt so I blew up my cover letter and résumé to about 18 inches by 33 inches each. I made a sandwich board out of it and, at the beginning of the workday, walked outside of a building that housed several shops I would have liked to work for.

—BRANDON
DALLAS, TEXAS

TOP RÉSUMÉ DON'TS

Your résumé is a paper representation of you. Or rather, it's the person you want to be in the eyes of your employer. That means there are some basic rules to follow when creating your résumé. Specifically, there are several things you don't want to do—assuming you want to find gainful employment.

❏ **DON'T SEND OUT YOUR RÉSUMÉ WITHOUT HAVING SOMEONE PROOFREAD IT.** Or three someones. Typos are inexcusable on a résumé and generally mean you won't even make it to the interview stage.

❏ **DON'T FORGET YOUR CONTACT INFORMATION:** home address, phone and email are all imperative. You never know by what means your future boss will want to contact you. And be sure to update your email address to reflect your newfound maturity—addresses like "hot4ubaby" or "pinkieprettyone" belong to someone who is looking for something other than a job.

❏ **DON'T FORGET TO INCLUDE THE LOCATIONS OF YOUR VARIOUS JOBS.** Employers want to know where you've lived and worked.

❏ **DON'T USE CUTE FONTS.** They don't reflect creativity; they are a sign of immaturity.

❏ **DON'T USE WACKY PAPER.** Sure, it's OK to stand out from the pack by picking a slightly different hue for your résumé. But that one with the paisley? No.

❏ **DON'T INCLUDE PERSONAL INFORMATION.** Your marital status, age, race, family, and hobbies are things you can discuss at the appropriate time; after you discuss your salary.

❏ **DON'T LIE.** You need to back up everything on your résumé. If you claim to have visited Paris in college, you need to be prepared to show pictures of your visit. And don't fudge dates to make it look like you've been employed all your life—it will only confuse you during the interview.

❏ **DON'T EXAGGERATE YOUR TALENTS.** If you can speak a little Spanish, don't be tempted to say you are fluent. If you once used InDesign and were confused by it, don't claim it as one of the many computer applications you've mastered.

❏ **DON'T MAKE A JOB SOUND MORE IMPORTANT THAN IT WAS.** Some grads try to jazz up their résumé by making a stint at an ice cream shop sound like three months at the United Nations. Employers once had odd jobs, too. Skip the ice cream shop listing, or simply state what it was, without exaggeration.

❏ **DON'T BE MODEST.** If you won an award in college, mention it (assuming it's not something like Most Likely to Get Drunk). If you excelled in sports, mention it. If you traveled for a year abroad, mention it.

—Andrea Syrtash

DURING AN INTERNSHIP, keep a journal of what you did or learned. Find a way to describe each experience as you might talk about it on your résumé or in an interview. Practice using descriptive words and phrases to explain what you did and learned. If you screwed something up, tell what went wrong and what you learned from it. A common interview question involves something you did wrong. You can be prepared with an example of what went wrong, followed with what you learned and what steps you took to make sure you will not repeat the error.

—*B.G.*
MANKATO, MINNESOTA

• • • • • • • •

IF YOU ARE ANSWERING AN AD, make sure you read it in its entirety. You may see that something they are looking for taps directly into your skill set, and you can use it to your advantage when writing your cover letter. I read an ad from a shopping network looking for production assistants. In addition to the usual requirements, I noticed they were looking for someone with nice hands for possible hand modeling. In my first paragraph, after mentioning my education and experience, I wrote, "And did I mention my beautiful, olive-skinned, silky-smooth hands?" I got a call to come in for an interview and was hired on the spot.

—*SEMA*
VAN NUYS, CALIFORNIA

• • • • • • • •

FOCUS ON YOUR ABILITY TO communicate and work with others, that you're a "team player," that you "network," and so on. Your outgoing personality can come out of that without the direct reference to your status as "Frank the Tank."

—*B.G.*
MANKATO, MINNESOTA

BE BOLD. Write a letter to the top person of an organization (CEO, President, Managing Partner, etc.) and include your résumé. What is the worst that can happen? That person doesn't get back in touch with you? If that's the case, write them a follow-up letter. If they don't respond, move on. There are too many good jobs out there to let the fear of not getting a letter or call back get in your way.

—*ZACH*
DALLAS, TEXAS

• • • • • • • •

IT'S IMPORTANT TO MENTION education, but nowadays that isn't what sets you apart. If you have any work experience at all, even an internship, focus on that in your cover letter rather than your education. In my first cover letter, my entire first paragraph was devoted to my education even though I had some very solid internship experience. I didn't get any responses from prospective employers when I sent that one. Then someone I trusted who had experience in my field looked it over and had me change it to something like this: "I am a recent graduate of the Cinema and Television Arts program at California State University, Northridge. I have more television work experience than most alumni two years out of university." Then I went on to concisely mention my internship experience. This letter received an immediate response.

—*SEMA*
VAN NUYS, CALIFORNIA

• • • • • • • •

FIND OUT WHAT KIND OF SOCIAL ACTIVITIES the staff takes part in as a group. I was applying to an office that had a lot of potlucks, so I sent one of my favorite recipes in with my résumé. They liked the idea (or they liked the broccoli and cheese casserole!) and I got the job.

—*KARI RIDDELL*
HALIFAX, NOVA SCOTIA, CANADA

YOUR *OTHER* REFERENCE: GOOGLE

I HAVE A MYSPACE ACCOUNT. The interviewer for my current job asked me if I did, and I instantly thought, "Oh my gosh ... what do I have on there, and is it really bad? What do my friends have on their pages? Or my boyfriend?" The worries went on and on. Steven, my interviewer (now my coworker), told me a story of a woman he interviewed whose MySpace account was so bad he didn't hire her. Thankfully, my profile was very general and not incriminating. When you create your MySpace account, think of future employers looking at your profile.

—*KRISTIN ANNE BRADLEY*
AVENTURA, FLORIDA

• • • • • • • • •

I RECENTLY HEARD ABOUT A STUDENT who lost out on a job because the company Googled her and found photos of her engaging in risky behavior. I have Googled my own student employees in the office and found some pretty surprising things. I had to tell one guy to clean up his act because what I found was not good. To get students thinking about this earlier in their academic careers, I have Googled all of my students. You may not even realize what is out there; someone else may post pictures or personal information about you without your knowledge. This can, unfortunately, associate you with someone who is engaging in risky behavior or expose risky behavior of your own that you would not have posted on the Internet. If a prospective employer finds something negative, it's too late. Someone else's values and experiences come into play, and whatever he or she has found can influence hiring decisions.

—*JULIA BARLOW SHERLOCK*
MOUNT PLEASANT, MICHIGAN

GOOGLE YOUR NAME, YOUR PHONE NUMBER, your domain name, and your email address, and clean up your digital trail. It will save you in the long run. I've been Googled, but employers haven't found anything incriminating because I'm not dumb. When they searched me under my own name, they found a bunch of food photos I posted in various food blogs. And they were impressed.

—*ANONYMOUS*
SAN FRANCISCO, CALIFORNIA

IT'S VERY IMPORTANT to know how much employers look at things like Facebook, MySpace, LinkedIn, and other networking sites. They use your profile as an introduction to you, and if you have sloppy pictures of yourself, or if you express any questionable opinions, you should change them to a more…edited nature. Otherwise, when you apply to jobs, you could be penalized without even realizing it.

—*JULIA*
NEW YORK, NEW YORK

EMPLOYERS DO RESEARCH ON FACEBOOK. If you're posting pictures of you and your boyfriend making out or your friends smoking pot on the weekends, I will know about it if you let me. Please, don't let me know about that.

—*ANONYMOUS*
ATLANTA, GEORGIA

DON'T TRY TO DESCRIBE A JOB as something it isn't. For example, I was once an Elevated Tri-Granular Digestible Substance Coordinator; I poured cereal fixings into a hopper for five bucks an hour. Anyone who is worth his merit as an interviewer is going to see right through this, and your résumé will become humorous fodder for the breakroom wall.

—*DAVE HUDSON*
ST. CLOUD, MINNESOTA

• • • • • • • •

I WANTED TO BREAK INTO the publishing field in New York, so I went to the newsstand, picked up every magazine for which I wanted to work, and wrote down the names and addresses of their editors in chief. I spent about $200 to send 40 or 50 Priority Mail letters to those editors. I introduced myself and told them about my goal to work in publishing. I received 10 responses in all, including personal letters from the editors of *CosmoGIRL!* and *Esquire*, in which they told me to stop by to see them when I got to New York. I met both of those editors; the editor of *CosmoGIRL!* even gave me invaluable career advice.

—*CHRISTINA*
NEW YORK, NEW YORK

A Book by Its Cover: Interviewing For the Position

Y ou made it over the first hurdles: You wrote your résumé and got it in front of a prospective employer who wants to talk to you. Now you have an interview—congratulations! Interviewing can be alternately fun and nerve-wracking, depending on the job and the interviewer. The most important thing you can do is prepare, and we've put together some tips for doing this. Research, prepare, and practice, and you should do fine.

HERE'S A DIRTY LITTLE SECRET: Chances are, the person sitting in front of you has never read your résumé, especially if you're fresh out of college. So bring a copy with you.

—*ADAM DREYFUS*
NEW CANAAN, CONNECTICUT

"INTERVIEW" WITH YOUR PARENTS OR FRIENDS. IT WILL REALLY HELP YOU IN THE REAL INTERVIEW.

—*SANDY PRESCOTT*
MEDFORD, NEW JERSEY

HEADLINES
Best Advice and Top Tips

- Research the company before your interview.

- Practice answering typical interview questions.

- It's OK to be nervous.

- Tell the truth; it's better to admit to something negative than to be caught in a lie.

- Present yourself in the best way, from what you wear to the language you use.

- Buy a stack of thank-you cards – and use them after each interview.

I once heard that for every 50 people interviewed, one person is hired. So make sure you go to 50 interviews before you get frustrated.

—DAVID ARENSON
JERUSALEM, ISRAEL

THE WORST THING YOU CAN DO is come to a job interview with an attitude. It doesn't matter how great you were in college, how many internships you had, how fabulous your GPA was, or how many extracurricular activities you participated in. When you get into the real world, all that matters is what you can do for your employer. I remember coming to my first job interview thinking that with my full academic scholarship, great GPA, and impressive alma mater, these people would be lucky to have me. I was wrong. In the economy at the time, I was lucky to get any job at all.

—ASHLEY
IRVING, TEXAS

NEVER FLIRT DURING AN INTERVIEW, even after the questions are over: the interview is *not* over until you leave the building. The guy who interviewed me for a customer service position was so extremely attractive that he had me smiling throughout the whole interview. When he was done asking professional questions, he asked why I had been smiling. I knew he knew why. I told him that he was cute. Later that night he called me and, in so many words, asked for a one-night stand. I told him no, and I didn't get a callback for the job, either.

—*A.P.*
CHICAGO, ILLINOIS

• • • • • • • •

DON'T LIE ON A JOB INTERVIEW, especially if you want to work for a bank. I applied for a bank teller position, and after the question portion of the interview, they had me do a surprise poly-graph test. They asked me if I had ever stolen anything, and I said no, even though I stole candy bars when I was little. I failed that question and didn't get the job. I should have been honest. They know that everybody has stolen something.

—*RUBEN REEVES*
CHICAGO, ILLINOIS

• • • • • • • •

WHEN YOU'RE INTERVIEWING, make sure you have a bottle of water. If you're shaky, sweaty, dry-mouthed, or simply grasping for an object to hold on to for dear life, a bottle of water is always a good option. Nothing huge, not a 50-gallon bottle. Just something that can fit in your bag or that you can hold in your hand until you're ready to go in for the interview.

—*MEGAN*
SYRACUSE, NEW YORK

When asked what your weaknesses are, always say that you are a workaholic. Works every time.

—ANDREA PARKER
CHICAGO, ILLINOIS

EVERYONE HATES THE STANDARD questions (like "What can you bring to the company?"), but if you have a generic résumé, you get asked generic questions. Interviews are as much about the actual interactions as they are about the things being discussed during the 10 to 15 minutes you're there. So, avoid the on-the-spot beauty pageant questions and the danger of rehearsed-sounding answers by making your résumé speak for you and giving the interviewer something different and more natural to discuss. My résumé worked because it included things that demonstrated my value to an employer while providing something to talk about at the interview.

—T.C.
MINNEAPOLIS, MINNESOTA

• • • • • • • •

SHOW CONFIDENCE. I really think that if you go into an interview knowing you're qualified for the position, you will inevitably exude that confidence, which will increase your chances.

—JIM
HOBOKEN, NEW JERSEY

INTERVIEW QUESTIONS on any of the following topics are considered discriminatory. You have the right to not answer them.

- Race
- Age
- Sex
- Religion
- National origin
- Birthplace
- Disability
- Marital/family status

ALWAYS BE PREPARED for weird questions in an interview. I was applying for a teacher's assistant position at a day care center, and I was asked to quickly think of a nursery rhyme and sing it. I was caught off guard because I had never been asked to sing anything in an interview. It took me about five seconds, but I sang "Itsy-Bitsy Spider" with no rhythm. I didn't get the job; I guess I wasn't enthusiastic enough.

—*ZAKIA SIPP*
CHICAGO, ILLINOIS

• • • • • • • •

"If you're a small person, learn how to have a powerful hand-shake. People won't expect it from you and will be surprised when they realize you're much stronger than you look. "

—*MELANIE*
MARICOPA, ARIZONA

• • • • • • • •

WHEN I WAS INTERVIEWING, I was really sweet and really upbeat. I'm extremely outgoing, so I just took the qualities I have and used them to my advantage. It really worked! Have enthusiasm for what you're interviewing for. Your potential employer will recognize it.

—*KRISTIN ANNE BRADLEY*
AVENTURA, FLORIDA

I WAS INTERVIEWING FOR A JOB ONCE, and my competition for the job had a connection at the company. In other words, I knew going in that I wasn't getting the job, so I did something that I regret. I was so annoyed during the interview I just blurted out, "This interview has gone far enough. You know you are asking me these questions to be polite. You know you've already decided to hire the other person." After that I excused myself and left. If I had to do it again, I would have answered the questions, tried to see it as a positive experience, and walked out with my head high.

—*ANONYMOUS*
PASADENA, CALIFORNIA

• • • • • • • •

IN ANY INTERVIEW, when they ask what your "worst" qualities are, tell them something that can be good, like, "Sometimes I'm a little too detailed."

—*LISA OLKON VANDESTEEG*
ST. PAUL, MINNESOTA

THE DAY BEFORE THE INTERVIEW ...

- Call the person who scheduled your appointment and ask for a detailed job description; the name and rank of the person you will be talking to; what the interviewer's expectations are; and what the dress code is.
- Search the Web for information about the company; it will give you something to talk about. Look for news on products, quarterly earnings, or company officers.
- Write down and memorize three stories that highlight your personal achievements or work you are proud of.
- Lay out your interview outfit that night. Go to bed early and get a good night's rest.

HEADS UP:
PREPARING FOR INTERVIEWS

- **Practice, practice, practice.** Look at lists of potential questions and write out your answers. Know what case you want to make for yourself; be specific about what strengths, skills, and experience you have; and be prepared with examples of how you used them and how that relates to the position you are interviewing for.

- **Study.** Read the job description and know your résumé. Find out about the company and about the field you are interested in entering. If you can, read up about the people you are going to interview with.

- **Prepare stories.** Go through your résumé and prepare at least three or four stories that you can tell about your experience. These stories should illustrate how your background qualifies you for the job you are interviewing for.

- **Prepare to turn the negative into a positive.** Everyone has something in their background they don't want to address. Prepare to counter the negatives you may have to address, with a positive outcome or interpretation.

—Ricki Frankel

REMAIN CALM. If you're nervous, get that emotion under control. I always use the technique Mr. Brady taught Marcia on *The Brady Bunch:* Picture the interviewer in his underwear.

—J.B.
DEERFIELD, OHIO

YOU MUST SEEM INTERESTED IN OTHER PEOPLE, and you must learn to listen. The young people I meet so often just want to talk about themselves and are likely to bring the conversation back to themselves no matter what the topic is. When I interview a recent graduate for a job, I look for people with emotional intelligence—someone who asks questions and retains information, not some-one who wants to tell me their whole history and how their personal experiences are like my own.

—*MEL MILLER*
BRISBANE, AUSTRALIA

" Patience, patience, patience. Potential employers can sense when you're desperate, and they don't hire you. It's when you're relaxed and rolling along that the best job prospects seem to come. "

—*KAREN CULP*
SPRINGFIELD, MISSOURI

NEVER TALK ABOUT YOUR COLLEGE party days. If people ask me about college, I tell them about the organizations I was involved in and how they influenced my decision to go into my pro-fession. If they push me about it, I just change the subject.

—*JOHN FOCKE*
MARQUETTE, MICHIGAN

I WANT A RAISE! BEFORE I START!

For your first professional job out of college, I don't think negotiating salary is much of an option. You really have no power in this negotiation. You need to get busy building your résumé more than they need you. I made the mistake of asking for a few thousand dollars more with a job, and then I didn't get it. A friend of mine later told me to keep in mind that the person making the offer is not the person who set the salary or who has the power to give you more money. This is especially true in big companies. By asking for more money, you are putting that person in a bad position because they have to go back to their boss with your counterproposal. It's not a good situation. Later in your career you will be able to wheel and deal. But not with the first job.

—*TRAVIS LINDEN*
HARRISONBURG, VIRGINIA

WHILE I WAS WAITING for a job interview in a company's reception area, an employee ran past in tears and said to me, "Don't take a job here, no matter what they offer you. This place sucks!" The interviewer was, in fact, a strange person. I did an extra-thorough job of checking the company out with past employees and, sure enough, they confirmed the crying woman's opinion. I turned down the job offer. Lesson learned: No matter how great a job sounds on the surface, always go with your gut and do some behind-the-scenes research.

—*NANCY SHENKER*
THORNWOOD, NEW YORK

Arrive at the interview with a box of doughnuts for the office.

—*SHARON HAROWITZ*
VANCOUVER, BRITISH COLUMBIA, CANADA

FACEBOOK-PROOF YOUR JOB SEARCH

I once inquired about a job at a community service organization. The following day, that organization added me as a friend on Facebook. "Wow," I thought. "Did my question impress them that much?" The answer, of course, is no. In reality, they were attempting to gain access to my Facebook profile to make sure that I was a fine, upstanding college student.

There is no hard data on how many employers snoop job candidates' online profiles, or how many otherwise stellar applicants have been denied employment as a result. Nevertheless, anecdotal evidence suggests that it does happen. So, do not let a little Facebook indiscretion get between you and your dream job. Follow these tips to Facebook-proof your job search.

1. **A Little Privacy, Please.** I like to think of my Facebook profile as a gated community. I let some people in (specifically, my friends, family, and close coworkers), and keep others out (specifically, ex-boyfriends, strangers, and other unsavory individuals). Facebook's settings are completely customizable. At the very least, you should allow only your Facebook Friends to have access to your profile. This way, a prospective employer will be clueless to its contents.

But if you still insist on keeping your profile open to your network, or to all of Facebook . . .

2. **A Picture is Worth a Thousand Words.** It's an old cliché, but it's true. Consider what a prospective employer may think of your scandalous Spring Break vacation photos from Cancun. Irresponsible? Incompetent? Unreliable? This is not the message you want to send. Snapshots of your cats, your grandmother's 80th birthday party, or a quiet evening with friends are a much better option. A good job is more important than the whole world seeing you drunk as a skunk in a string bikini, no matter how fabulous your abs are.

3. **Just Say No to Sex, Drugs, and Rock 'n' Roll.** Remove all references to illicit drug activity, alcohol-fueled shenanigans (even if you're of-age), and, ahem, your activities in the boudoir. Rock 'n roll is actually probably OK. Probably.

4. **Mama Always Said: Don't Talk About Politics or Religion in Polite Conversation.** And don't put it in your Facebook profile, either. Look: Your prospective employer will have a serious problem if he or she refuses to hire you on the basis of your political or religious views. But why make yourself vulnerable to this sort of discrimination? Leave those spaces blank, even if your political or religious views happen to be in the majority.

5. **Both Accent and Inflection Show Polish to Perfection.** You do not have to go quite this far, but your Facebook profile should demonstrate that you have a basic understanding of the spelling and grammatical rules of your native or target language. Good: My name is Sarah. I graduated from Middlebury College in 2008. I really enjoy yoga, making jewelry, reading, photography, and cats. Bad: my nam is Sarah. I graddated from Middleberry Collage in. 2008. I really enjoy yoga and jewelry (making it), and redding, phtography, and catz. lolz!!1! With material like this, how will a prospective employer ever believe that you can write a report, communicate clearly and professionally with clients, or that you typed your own résumé?

—*Sarah Franco*

• • • • • • • •

MAKE ALL SOCIAL NETWORKING PROFILES PRIVATE. You never know who's looking you up before you come to interview!

—*KELLI*
ATLANTA, GEORGIA

Consider

IT HELPS TO BRING ALONG A FRIEND for moral support during your first job interviews out of college. My friend went with me to one of my interviews at a placement agency in New York City and waited out on the street. It turned out to be one of my worst interviews: The interviewer kept telling me, "I don't think you're ready to go out and work." I didn't have much confidence in myself at that point, and I could only whisper back, "No, I am ready." I walked out of the interview in tears, but my friend calmed me down and helped me recover my ego.

—*MICHELE*
ROCKAWAY TOWNSHIP, NEW JERSEY

• • • • • • • •

INFORMATIONAL INTERVIEWS are always a good thing to do. You never know when people will follow up and make you an offer or ask to see you again. I didn't know if I was going to move to San Francisco, but I decided to have an informational meeting with a company just in case. Months later, I got a call from the director who told me that there was an opening. I had just figured out that I was San Francisco–bound shortly before she got in touch. It seemed so easy, and the timing was great!

—*MARIANA*
SAN FRANCISCO, CALIFORNIA

• • • • • • • •

IF YOU'RE GOING TO WEAR HEELS, be sure you can walk in them. Nothing screams amateur like tripping in your stilettos.

—*MEGAN*
SYRACUSE, NEW YORK

TELL ME ABOUT YOURSELF – BUT NOT *EVERYTHING*

I'll never forget my first on-campus interview when I was graduating from college. When the interviewer said, "Tell me about yourself," I started with where I grew up and told my life story from there. I didn't get the job.

When interviewers say, "Tell me about yourself," they aren't giving you carte blanche to tell them every little thing. You should prepare for this question and its sibling: "Walk me through your résumé." Essentially, you want to build a story that explains how your background has given you a unique set of experiences that qualifies you for this job. You don't want to go into too much detail; they can ask for more detail in the interview. Start with something like, "I've always wanted to do … " or "The reason I am here is … " Then, begin walking them through your relevant experience (*relevant* being a key word). Make specific points about how your experience qualifies you for the job. And be succinct, but ask if they want more detail about any particular point.

—*Ricki Frankel*

NEVER ANSWER A QUESTION that you really don't know the answer to. Don't make stuff up. You've got to earn respect and loyalty through honesty. In order to do that, you have to be straightforward.

—*S.F.*
TAMPA, FLORIDA

● ● ● ● ● ● ● ●

I ALWAYS CHEW A PIECE of mint gum on my way to interviews while listening to calm music in the car. It always helps me relax before all the questions. I just make sure I spit out the gum before I walk in the door to the interview.

—*MELANIE*
MARICOPA, ARIZONA

Consider

INTERVIEW PREP 101

Any job interview will go more smoothly if you are prepared for it. Interview questions, especially for entry-level jobs, tend to be the same or very similar from one company to another. If you know what you would answer to some or all of the questions below, you'll feel more relaxed and exude confidence and compe- tence. Careful, though; this list doesn't cover everything. You'll probably have to field a few surprise questions as well.

- Tell me about yourself.

- Walk me through your résumé.

- Why are you interested in this job?

- Why are you interested in this company?

- What would your former boss (or peers) say are your strengths and weaknesses?

- Tell me about a time when you had to juggle several different projects at the same time.

- Tell me about a time when you failed at something, and what you learned from the experience.

- Tell me about a time when you took a risk.

- What was the most frustrating experience in your last job, and how did you handle it?

- What motivates you?

- Where do you see yourself in five years? In 10 years?

- How much training will you need to do this job?

- What is your most effective work style?

—The Editors

IF A JOB LOOKS LIKE IT'S NOT PERFECT, don't shoot yourself in the foot during the interview by acting like you don't care. I recently got a job for which more than 50 people were competing. The other applicants were all more qualified, with experience in the field and relevant postgraduate degrees, neither of which I have. After I was hired, my boss told me this and said the reason I was hired over everyone else was simply because they liked me and thought I had "good energy." My boss told me it seemed like the other applicants saw it as just another job, something to tide them over. The funny thing is, that's true for me, too. But I acted like I was really excited to have the chance to do the job.

    —FRED
      WASHINGTON, D.C.

AN INTERVIEW WORKS BOTH WAYS. Do not let the interviewer disrespect you or bully you, because you are interviewing him or her as much as he or she is interviewing you. Bullies count on the fact that you are going to cower. Don't.

    —ANONYMOUS
      ATLANTA, GEORGIA

THE MOST IMPORTANT THING IN AN INTERVIEW is having fresh breath. Everything after that is gravy.

    —A.G.
      HUBBARD, OHIO

ASK THE EXPERT

Do they really want to know my weaknesses?

At some point in an interview you will be asked, "What are your greatest strengths and weaknesses?" My college's career center recommended that you state a weakness that could also be seen as something positive for the company, like, "I'm a perfectionist. I work too hard to make sure my projects are 100 percent." When I interview people, I'm actually looking for evidence of self-reflection and an ability to learn—although I am not looking for what you are working on in therapy. My recommendation? Choose one of your strengths, talk about how you rely too much on it, and then explain what you are doing to address it. For example, if you are a perfectionist, talk about how perfectionism both serves you and sometimes gets in your way, and what steps you are taking to recognize the difference.

—*Ricki Frankel*

SINCE I'M A GUY and the interviewer was a woman, I did the only thing I knew how to do as a naive young student: I smiled in a flirtatious sort of way. I wouldn't advise others to do the same; however, I did get the job.

—*ANONYMOUS*
LOS ANGELES, CALIFORNIA

• • • • • • • •

IF YOU HAVE THE TIME, take a practice run to the interview location. If you get lost, it's better to get lost on a day when you don't have an interview. Also, it's always a good idea to scope out the parking, so you're not walking miles or paying $20 for an hour.

—*J.W.A.III*
ATLANTA, GEORGIA

SO MANY PEOPLE DON'T REALIZE that looking for a job is exhausting and a long, drawn-out process; I didn't when I was looking for mine. Patience really is a virtue; your time will come if you allow it to. I wanted to give up after every unsuccessful interview, but I kept pushing forward. If you think professionally and do everything to the best of your ability, you'll know you did all you could have done to land that job.

—*KRISTIN ANNE BRADLEY*
AVENTURA, FLORIDA

MY BEST INTERVIEW

THE BEST INTERVIEW I had was for my current job. I felt confident, prepared, relaxed, and excited at the great opportunity I might have. It went well because I did my homework. I researched the agency and knew who its clients were and what the agency's outlook was. It was also my second interview with them, and I felt confident that they liked what they had previously seen of me. I took my time, didn't rush my answers to questions, and took a breath and paused if I was trying to come up with an answer. Overall, I felt like I would be a good fit with the agency, and I did my best to convey that to my interviewers.

—*MEGAN*
SYRACUSE, NEW YORK

DO YOUR RESEARCH

WHEN YOU GO IN FOR AN INTERVIEW, understand why you want to work for this company; not just the job, but the company. That's critical. Read everything about that company. Spend hours researching it. Go online and find out all the information you can. People who sit across from me and flatter me with what they know about the company are the people who impress me. And don't ask stupid questions like "What does your company do?" "What does your department do?" "Who's your customer?" I can't tell you how many people have done that with me.

—*ANONYMOUS*
NEW YORK, NEW YORK

. . . .

IN ONE FAILED INTERVIEW, THE INTERVIEWER was asking me questions about doing general things like answering phones and greeting people. He was summing up, saying, "So you can do this, and you can do that, and you might even be able to participate in various presentations to clients." I was feeling all jolly and happy, thinking I could definitely show up at this company, answer some phones, and give some killer speeches. And then the interviewer said, "Can you tell us your idea of what we do here?" I had no clue! After 15 minutes of a purely brilliant interview, there was this deadly awkward pause. My eyes desperately searched the room, and I noticed a sign over the door that said something about party planning, so I babbled something about that. The interviewer said curtly, "That's not our company. We have nothing to do with that." I wasn't too jolly or happy after that. I had made one of the gravest interview mistakes.

—*JESSIE*
PHILADELPHIA, PENNSYLVANIA

DON'T GO INTO A JOB INTERVIEW knowing more than your potential boss. I once did a lot of research before an interview, and I clearly made a potential employer uncomfortable when I brought things up that he wasn't prepared to discuss. Keep in mind that while you want to impress the staff at the office, many people are insecure about losing their jobs and may be scared of competition. So, in a job interview, show that you're willing to learn. Show ambition but don't ever say something like, "I want to learn to run my own business one day."

—*MATTHEW WISE*
TORONTO, ONTARIO, CANADA

• • • • • • • • •

DO NOT GO INTO AN INTERVIEW WITHOUT LEARNING about the company or person you will be meeting. I studied for a week for my interview. I wanted to know that I could answer anything I was asked. First, I educated myself on the company. Then I found out who their clients were and the products they sold. During the interview, I was asked how I could make improvements for some of their clients, and I was very prepared. It paid off.

—*ANONYMOUS*
SANTA CRUZ, CALIFORNIA

• • • • • • • • •

THE NIGHT BEFORE AN INTERVIEW, I look up the person I'm supposed to talk to and find something I have in common with him or her, like sports. My thinking is that all of the competition has the same qualifications as I do, so my biggest goal is trying to make some sort of personal connection. I want the interviewer to leave the interview saying, "Oh, I remember that guy; he talked to me about gardening."

—*ANONYMOUS*
LOS ANGELES, CALIFORNIA

WHAT ARE THEY LOOKING FOR?

WHEN I'M HIRING, IN ADDITION to educational background, I always look for sincerity. I never want to sit down with someone and feel as if that person were pushing a tape recorder button and giving a set speech. I want to feel that they are present, honest, and not just telling me what they think I want to hear. Over the course of my career, I have interviewed hundreds of people, and the best have been concise, straightforward, confident (with some humility), and honest about what they have and have not done.

—*JANE*
MONTCLAIR, NEW JERSEY

• • • • • • • •

WHEN I THINK ABOUT PEOPLE WE INTERVIEW, the single most important attribute is what I would call personal responsibility. It goes to the whole issue of how people see the world. Do they view their success and failure as their responsibility, or are they victims, claiming a previous boss as stupid or blaming a bad teacher in their past? I always prefer to work with people who, from the start of the interview, show evidence of taking responsibility and show initiative. I would rather hire a person like this with less experience than someone with more experience who doesn't have the right frame of mind.

—*DAVID FRIEDMAN*
MT. LAUREL, NEW JERSEY

MY NO.1 PIECE OF JOB-SEARCH ADVICE: Show that this firm and that specific position is what you want most in this world. Show passion! Employers want to know that they are getting someone who will be passionate about what he is doing.

—*BARAK*
TEL AVIV, ISRAEL

AN INTERVIEW IS A TWO-WAY STREET

Interviews are not only for employers to decide whether they want to hire you. You get to use the interview process to figure out if you want to work for *them*, too. You will know, if you are meeting with several people, whether you like the people who will be your future coworkers and bosses. They don't have to become your best friends, but you do want to feel that you can be comfortable in the work environment. When the interviewer asks you if you have any questions—in addition to specific questions about the job and company, ask questions about the corporate culture. Ask about hours. Ask how long people usually stay at the company, and where they go when they leave. Ask questions that will help you figure out whether this company is the type of place you want to work and whether you would be comfortable there. Ask about the person you would be working for and his or her management style. While you may not like the answers you receive, you will probably get a sense of whether someone would be a good boss for you. Some possible questions are:

- What would your expectations be of me if I were working for you?
- What is your management style?
- How would you measure success?
- What are the other people I would work with like?

When interviewing with prospective coworkers, ask similar questions. Specifically, ask, "What is it like to work for this person?"

You'll learn a lot from the answer.

—*Ricki Frankel*

DRESS FOR SUCCESS

LOOK YOUR BEST IN AN INTERVIEW. Make sure that your clothing fits correctly, is neat (no wrinkles or stains), not too flashy (no huge floral prints or outrageous colors), and is a suitable style for the business environment. This is as important as saying the right things in the interview, because an employer who hires you is also hiring you to be a representative of their company. In representing their company, they want you to look your best.

> —*JULIA*
> *NEW YORK, NEW YORK*

• • • • • • • • •

IT'S SAD THAT WE JUDGE BOOKS BY THEIR COVERS, but it's true. We just hired for an entry-level position at my company. We knew that everyone applying would be fresh out of college, so we let normal attire rules slide when we met with the applicants. But then one young woman came in dressed impeccably, and you knew she took time putting together her suit and was dressed to impress. This didn't look like the woman who would be answering our phones; this looked like the woman we could bring to clients' offices as part of the team. Before she even began to speak, we assumed she was smart, professional, and ambitious. And she got the job.

> —*KELLY WILKES*
> *ATLANTA, GEORGIA*

• • • • • • • • •

I WENT TO AN INTERVIEW WEARING A SKIRT that buttoned twice on the side, and I forgot to button one of the buttons. Before I had a chance to get to the bathroom to fix it, the interviewer entered the room and immediately stared at my skirt. I just smiled and pretended that was how it was supposed to look. After the interview was over, she told me I probably shouldn't wear that skirt to an interview again.

> —*K.M.*
> *ARLINGTON, VIRGINIA*

• • • • • • • • •

ALWAYS WEAR A SUIT TO AN INTERVIEW, even if the job won't require you to wear one. The difference in your appearance is amazing. Wearing a suit gives me more confidence.

> —*ANONYMOUS*
> *SAN DIEGO, CALIFORNIA*

I WAS ONCE INTERVIEWING a young lady for a job. She stood up mid-interview, adjusted her slip, and then sat down and continued speaking. Make sure your undergarments are in place *before* you enter the interview.

—*NANCY SHENKER*
THORNWOOD, NEW YORK

WHAT TO WEAR TO AN INTERVIEW

Dress professionally and appropriately for a job interview. My rule of thumb is to dress one step more formally than the style of clothes people generally wear at the place you are interviewing. If the dress code is formal, wear a business suit. If the dress code is business casual, dress slightly *more* formally than that. Do *not* wear flip-flops, jeans, low-cut tops, or T-shirts—unless, of course, you are interviewing to be a lifeguard or camp counselor. Remember that dress code, in addition to being variable by industry and company, is also variable by geography. The Northeast—particularly New York City—tends to require more formal business attire than Silicon Valley in California. Make sure you do a little research before your interview to find out what the dress code is. You want to make a good impression, showing your interviewers that you are an adult, ready to work in the adult world.

—*Ricki Frankel*

ALWAYS BE ON YOUR BEST BEHAVIOR when you are on a job interview. But also consider it your opportunity to interview the company. I had four job offers. I went with the one with the best salary. It was a good experience, but it wasn't the right fit for me. I've since learned that it is important to hold out for a work environment that you enjoy. It may not be the one that offers the best paycheck. In the long run, it will be worth it.

—BILLIE
CHICAGO, ILLINOIS

• • • • • • • •

"Prepare for a job interview like you're making a 30-second commercial of yourself. Make sure your story is clear, to the point, and flows smoothly from beginning to end. Most important, rehearse!"

—JEFF CELLIO
LAGUNA NIGUEL, CALIFORNIA

• • • • • • • •

BE UPBEAT, POSITIVE, and cheerful at your interview. Don't let any negativity slide into your voice or your body language. Paint a freakin' clown smile on your face for that hour and keep it there. It's contagious.

—LORNA MERKEIL
ELLSWORTH, OHIO

GRIN AND BEAR IT

Practice your answers to as many potential interview questions as possible. I had an informational interview with the CEO of a company. He had served in the Navy when he was young, and he was very salty and intimidating. Things were going OK until he asked me what I considered to be my biggest strength. Since I had never considered this question before, and since I actually had no strengths outside of the college experience, I struggled to come up with an answer before blurting, "My smile." Even as I said it, I could hear how stupid it sounded. The CEO just sort of nodded and frowned at me, and the interview was over soon after. I didn't get a job offer from him. You might have a great smile, but when an interviewer asks you about your greatest strength, go with something a little more business oriented and less sweet. Especially if the person you are talking to served in the navy.

—*J.A.*
ATLANTA, GEORGIA

I APPLIED MY MILITARY EXPERIENCE TO FINDING A JOB: Show up on time; make sure everything's crisp and polished and that you're not hung over. You've got to pay attention, get the person's card, send a thank-you, and always follow up. Good presentation has saved me when I wasn't as qualified as others. And no matter what, write notes in front of the interviewer. I do this. It doesn't matter if I'm going to use the notes; it's important for the potential employer to see that I care enough to write down what they are saying. Demeanor and attitude can count more than credentials.

—*NEIL*
TORONTO, ONTARIO, CANADA

THANK-YOU NOTES

Yes, you have to write a thank-you note after each interview. Do not agonize over the content; a thank-you note will not get you a job. Most people will have decided whether or not to offer you a job before you even leave the building, but occasionally, the lack of a thank-you note will be noticed. So, just do it, quickly, with good grammar and perfect spelling. Thank your interviewer for spending time with you, and briefly (in three to four sentences) make the case again about why you are qualified for the job. You may want to make a specific reference to something you discussed in the interview. If there is something you think you forgot to tell about yourself, and you believe it is important, briefly mention it. And reiterate your interest in the position. For most jobs in most industries these days, it is perfectly acceptable to send a thank-you email. Make sure you get the interviewer's business card so you have the right title and both snail and email addresses. And send it quickly—at least by the following day.

—Ricki Frankel

• • • • • • • •

AFTER ARRIVING HOME FROM A JOB INTERVIEW, the first thing I do is sit down and write thank-you letters to every individual I met with during my interview. And when I say "write" a thank-you letter, notice that I did not say "email" or "type" it. If you are really interested in working for them, nothing will make a better impression than the fact that you took the time to sit down and hand-write a note of thanks.

—Kenneth C. Riney
Dallas, Texas

JUST SEND THE THANK-YOU NOTE

Eighty-five percent of executives say that a post-interview thank-you note has some influence on the hiring decision.

THANK-YOU LETTER

Here's a template to give you an idea of what to say in your thank-you note:

Date

Name
Title
Organization
Address
City, State, Zip Code

Dear Mr./Ms. Last Name:

I want to thank you for taking time out of your busy schedule to talk to me about the _____ position with your company.

After speaking with you, I do feel that I would be a perfect candidate for this job. As I told you, I have experience in many of the areas that you seek, including _____. Also, after hearing about the responsibilities of the position, I'm very enthusiastic about the possibilities it offers.

Please feel free to contact me at any time if further information is needed. My mobile number is (555) 111-1111.

Thank you again for your time and consideration.

Sincerely,
Your Name

—Adapted from jobsearch.about.com

JOB-REJECTION LETTER

In a position to reject potential employers' numerous offers? If this happens, don't blow off the people who want to hire you. Instead, handle your rejection of them with a nice note. After all, you never know how your new job will work out; you might find yourself working for the people you rejected one day! Here's a simple job-rejection letter:

Dear Mr./Ms. Last Name,

Thank you very much for offering me the position of _____ with _____. I sincerely appreciate your taking the time to interview me. It was a difficult decision to make, but I have accepted a position with another company.

Again, thank you for your consideration.

Sincerely,
Your Name

Great Expectations: How to Start Your Job on the Right Foot

I t is often said that you never get a second chance to make a first impression; how you start off in your new job can set the tone for your career. Don't take this opportunity lightly! We asked career-minded people what they did to make the most of their first weeks on their first job. We also asked people what not to do. From flirting with the boss, to napping at lunch (and sensible things in between), here's a guide to launching your career.

HAVING A GOOD ATTITUDE is more important than the quality of your work. I've seen lots of smart, talented people get fired because they consistently come in late or are rude to their boss.

—*ROB SALTER*
MUNCHENGLADBACH, GERMANY

BUST YOUR ASS FOR YOUR BOSSES, WHETHER YOU WANT TO OR NOT!

—*ABBY HAGEMEIER*
LUBBOCK, TEXAS

HEADLINES
Best Advice and Top Tips

- Do your best at any task you are assigned, no matter how small—it will lead to bigger responsibilities.

- Do more than is asked of you and your boss will notice.

- Attend work parties, but be on your best behavior.

- Be careful about what you tell coworkers. Even something said in confidence can still get out.

- Keep a good attitude—it's as important as doing a good job.

Keep people in the dark about the true nature of your job. Even your boss, if possible. Then you will be thought of as a miracle worker.

—Anonymous
Alexandria,
Virginia

You LEARN YOUR JOB by just throwing yourself into it and doing it.

—Julie McKitrick
St. Louis, Missouri

• • • • • • • •

New PEOPLE SHOULD ALWAYS be flexible, be open-minded, and have respect for their peers. Learn from those who have been there before you; the people they call "the wise ones" in China.

—Maria
South Brunswick, New Jersey

• • • • • • • •

When I STARTED MY FIRST JOB, one shift a week, I made sure to show up on time and to stay late if necessary. When I ran into something challenging, I always asked questions. I also wrote down the answers to those questions so I wouldn't forget. All of this helped, specifically when another person doing the same job messed up. My boss got rid of that person and asked me to cover the shift.

—Liz Pope
Auburn, California

SUCK IT UP AND GO TO WORK PARTIES as much as possible. At my first job, there was a feeling that work parties were something of a requirement. I definitely went to some parties I didn't want to. But to be honest, I ended up having a good time at them, so maybe it wasn't such a bad thing.

—*ANONYMOUS*
BROOKLYN, NEW YORK

• • • • • • • •

WHEN YOU FIRST MEET your coworkers, say their name back to them: "Hi, John, nice to meet you." It helps to connect faces to names. Also, try to make mental notes about each person's workspace and obvious interests. Tom likes the Red Sox, Sue follows NASCAR, and Ann has a vegetable garden at her home. Remembering random things like that will help you associate names with faces and positions.

—*MEGAN*
SYRACUSE, NEW YORK

• • • • • • • •

WHEN YOU'RE STARTING OUT at your first job after college, expect to be thrown into the fire. Test yourself and let go of fear. On my first day of reporting for a public radio station, my boss told me, "Go cover this story." I had to interview legislators, but I didn't know what they looked like, and I had to approach people and say, "I'm sorry, I'm new. Can you tell me who you are and why you're here?" I learned quickly that way, and admitting that I was just getting started helped get people on my side.

—*JESSICA*
ALBANY, NEW YORK

Don't try too hard; you'll look cheesy.

—*ANONYMOUS*
OZARK, MISSOURI

ALWAYS LET YOUR BOSS THINK HE'S RIGHT. Mine will make mistakes and he'll scream at whomever. Everyone seems to have a problem with him, but I don't. He made me a manager and I got a raise.

—ANNA
WACO, TEXAS

· · · · · · · ·

Always say you know how to do everything, even if you don't. Ask someone else or Google it. Bosses love competence.

—KRISTI KAMERMAN
BATON ROUGE, LOUISIANA

I FLIRTED WITH MY BOSS and I got the cubicle that I wanted. I was seated by people I liked. If someone gave me trouble, I didn't have to worry about it. It wasn't like I was going out with my boss. I just made friends with him.

—K.R.
BELLEVILLE, ILLINOIS

· · · · · · · ·

GIVE YOURSELF TIME TO ADJUST to working full time. When I started, I was surprised at how exhausted I was each day when I got home. I'm an active person, but it took my body a while to get accustomed to the schedule.

—ERIN BEDEL
FOUNTAINTOWN, INDIANA

· · · · · · · ·

REMEMBER THAT EVERY EXPERIENCE you have is not worthless or devoid of value, though it might seem that way at the time. So many skills and experiences are transferable to other fields of work, and often employers look for people who have a broad range of experience because they bring new, original ideas to a workplace or organization.

—SALLY
ADELAIDE, AUSTRALIA

WATCH YOUR LANGUAGE. No matter how much you want to scream every expletive known to man at your frozen computer, the fastest way to get that "stupid kid" label is by swearing in the office. Granted, if your bosses do it or if your workplace is a more casual environment, you have a little leeway, but it's better to be conservative.

—*MEGAN*
SYRACUSE, NEW YORK

> Nothing impresses a new employer more than if you take initiative.
> —*NADIA*

• • • • • • • • •

" When you're new at a job, look around and see who the best workers are. Pay attention to what they're doing, figure out what makes them stand out, and then model your work after theirs. "

—*VI HOWG*
MINNETONKA, MINNESOTA

• • • • • • • • •

WHEN I GOT MY FIRST JOB, I showed up 15 minutes early every day to see if I could help out where needed, and I never asked for a day off. When I made it through the first year, instead of being offered one week of paid vacation, I got two weeks and three sick days.

—*ANDRE PARKER*
CHICAGO, ILLINOIS

Consider

FIRST JOBS FROM HELL

AFTER THREE MONTHS OF JOB HUNTING, I was offered an interview at a well-known salon. The job title: graphic designer and office manager. I figured, "OK, I can do the design stuff. I went to school for that, right? And as for office manager, what's a little phone answering and filing in exchange for rent money?" When I was interviewed by the owner, she dazzled me with glamorous stories of celebrity clients and international photos shoots. "I can do this," I remember thinking, "Hell, I *want* to do this!" I accepted the job with little pay negotiations or thought. After three months, I was in hell. I had done maybe two design projects, using my "valuable" time to instead buy lunches, answer personal emails, purchase sporting event tickets, and create book reports for my boss's 5 year-old daughter. There were no celebrities, not to mention a severe lack of photo shoots.

> —*LAUREL*
> *ATLANTA, GEORGIA*

● ● ● ● ● ● ● ● ●

AFTER WAITING TABLES FOR A WHILE AFTER COLLEGE, I found a job as a recruiter, and it was the worst job imaginable. I had to sit directly across from my boss, our desks aligned, and make about 300 calls daily. We had to be there at 7:30 a.m. and stay until our work was done, which was rarely before 6:00 p.m. The manager would make fun of what we were wearing, be rude to our clients, and be generally awful in some facet on a daily basis. One day, she took away our chairs and made us stand on our desk because our energy level wasn't high enough. The turnover was so bad it was funny. Most people didn't make it through the first week. Some people just didn't return from lunch the first day. We called them "lunchers." I worked there for eight months and had seniority over most of the office. My advice if you get into a situation like this? Get out as soon as possible.

> —*ANONYMOUS*
> *ATLANTA, GEORGIA*

FIRST JOBS FROM HELL AREN'T ALWAYS A BAD THING. I'd rather learn what doesn't work first than be unpleasantly surprised later in my career. I had the supervisor from hell, but I learned what to look for when interviewing and to look back on the red flags I should have paid attention to. I stayed at the job a year – in my profession it's frowned upon to leave before a year is out. I'm at my new job and it is fantastic, but I also learned a whole lot from that job from hell.

—*JENNIFER*
ALABAMA

. . . .

MY FIRST JOB TAUGHT ME about stress management, discipline, and to shrug off overly harsh bosses. No one likes their first job, but they are the most important since we learn so much after being thrown in the fire.

—*RYAN*
PHILADELPHIA, PENNSYLVANIA

. . . .

MY FIRST JOB OUT OF COLLEGE WAS HELL ON EARTH. They would say, "Leanne, you need to brush your hair when you come to work." And I had brushed my hair. One day I stretched in my office and my midriff showed because my shirt came untucked. A female partner walked by right then and told me I needed to tuck in my shirt and dress more appropriately. I would cry every day. There was always screaming and yelling. They eventually let me go. But sometimes the worst thing that happens to you could be the best thing. I got another job within a few months and I've been there ever since. My boss just took us all down to the beach for a weekend. I love it.

—*LEANNE*
ATLANTA, GEORGIA

ALWAYS KEEP YOUR COOL. If something goes wrong, don't show it. People react to your reactions. If you act frazzled and stressed out, everyone around you will definitely notice, and they might start to question your abilities. You can always freak out later in the privacy of your own home.

—ASHLEY
DALLAS, TEXAS

* * * * * * * *

There's no need to tell your older coworkers you went to the bar last night. Fib a bit and leave your wild side for your friends.

—KELLI
ATLANTA, GEORGIA

MAKE THE MOST OF YOUR FIRST disappointing job. After going away to college, I was set on getting a job that could help save the world and keep me intellectually satisfied. I found a job as a paralegal for the number-one intellectual property law firm in the country. I thought it would be interesting and good experience, because I had been studying law and policy in school. The first day at my job, I was shown my desk … in the basement. No windows. No sun. Only chipped beige paint and a lonely computer. I told myself it would be OK. At least I was getting paid. The firm moved to a new building four months after I started. I still work in the basement, but now most of the 40 or so other paralegals are also down there. I sit in a workroom with five others, and they are a lot of fun. My days are getting better.

—JACKIE
WASHINGTON, D.C.

* * * * * * * *

KEEP UP WITH CURRENT EVENTS and trends in your industry. Managers and higher-ups at my job talk about politics and what's going on in the world. When I was in school, I mostly just concentrated on partying and studying, but now I try to stay up to date by reading CNN.com and my company's newsletter.

—RICHARD JOCO
HOUSTON, TEXAS

THE KEY TO KEEPING A JOB and advancing in the workplace is doing more than is asked of you and more than is expected of you. Work more hours than the next guy; volunteer to do the jobs that nobody wants to do; ask your boss if you can attend training seminars in your field. All that stuff is priceless. They say that water finds its own level, and it's true. But make sure your level is higher than that of the other people who work with you.

—*K.F.*
CANFIELD, OHIO

• • • • • • • •

BOSSES LIKE THE EMPLOYEE who goes the extra mile. For instance, I noticed a glitch in our company's online ordering system and I pointed it out to my boss, who then called the people above him. It turned out that no one had noticed this before. The problem was fixed, and now my boss always mentions it to me. If you see something that could help the business down the line, take the extra step. Your boss will be glad that you helped him or her look good.

—*JOSH*
WEST PLAINS, MISSOURI

WHO NEEDS EMAIL?

In order to improve company communication, Scott A. Dockter, CEO of PBD Worldwide Fulfillment Services, launched "No Email Fridays" at his company. On Fridays, employees must pick up the phone or meet in person, Email use at the company dropped 80 percent.

SAVING FACE: FACEBOOK AND THE WORKPLACE

You know the game Six Degrees of Kevin Bacon? Well, it doesn't just work with Kevin Bacon. As you get older and more advanced in your career, you'll find that everyone is connected somehow. This is good and bad. Suddenly the guy in your poker group is helping you get an interview at his office. On the flip side, an ex's brother's wife could be your new boss. Ouch. But there is one thing you can control: your online image.

It's All in Whom You Know: Facebook is a social network, but that doesn't mean it can't be a professional network, too. If you use it right, it's a great way to keep abreast of what's happening in your industry or the field you want to enter. You can join professional groups and find out about events in the community.

If you're friends with someone who has been successful in your chosen career, do a little snooping on Facebook to find out what they're up to. People spend more time at work than anywhere else, so they tend to talk about it quite a bit on Facebook. This can give you a lot of insight. Just imagine: Someone you've met casually is pretty senior at a great ad agency in town where you'd love to work. He posts a status update that he's working double-time because two people have quit. What a perfect opportunity for you to send him a message letting him know that you would love to help out! You look friendly, eager and resourceful, and Facebook makes the interaction casual and timely.

Working 9 to 5: While Facebook can be helpful to you professionally, playing on Facebook or any other social networking site at work is a big mistake. Don't you wonder how busy your friend really is when she has time to update her status four times a day? Not only is it unprofessional; playing too much online makes it look like you don't have enough to do.

Time management is everything. Designate a time each day to visit your social networking world, so that you aren't tempted to log in all day. If you don't want to get to work ten minutes early to Facebook over coffee before your day starts, then give yourself a window at lunch. Believe us that your boss will not be happy to find you updating your profile during working hours. Resist the temptation! You can thank us when you get that promotion.

Status Updates for the Recent College Grad: Gone are the days of sharing absolutely everything that's on your mind. That Tuesday night happy hour may have been "kick-ass," but you'd be well advised to characterize it differently now that you are in the working world. The dumbest status updates we've seen for young professionals? Ones that make any kind of negative reference to work. How many times have you seen postings like, "Charlie is bored in this meeting," or "Amy cannot WAIT until Friday," or "Cameron just can't seem to get in to the work thing today." Not smart, guys.

As long as your profile is presentable and you know what you're doing, you can use Facebook to give you a little edge in your career. As with everything in life, just remember that people are watching!

—Elizabeth Lovett, Angie Mock, and Robert Rhu

DON'T GET ALL HELL BENT ON YOUR FIRST JOB.
Most college students leave after two years so
this will not be the job that defines you. I worked
in a retail store as a manager and hated it. I realized after three months it was not for me and
started looking right away to find a job on the
other side of retail in the corporate world.

—*ERIN BLACK*
PITTSBURGH, PENNSYLVANIA

66 Everyone is faking it. No one
really knows what they're
doing; it's who can fake what
they're doing the best. But
that's OK, because the
minute you think you know
everything, you've stopped
learning. 99

—*BECKY HOUK*
INDIANAPOLIS, INDIANA

BE IN TOUCH WITH WHAT'S GOING on in the world.
You'd be surprised how many conversations you
can start with your boss. I had a boss who I didn't
have anything in common with and didn't know
anything about. Talking about the news gave me
ways to stay away from the less-than-pleasing
small talk.

—*JAMESE JAMES*
DALLAS, TEXAS

DON'T SHOW UP LATE. Don't leave early. Don't take long lunches. Don't talk on the phone with or IM your friends. Don't spend all your time reading. Don't complain about anyone to anyone. Most of all, be professional!

—*ANONYMOUS*
SAN FRANCISCO, CALIFORNIA

• • • • • • • •

TRY TO STAY AT YOUR FIRST JOB long enough to really learn something so you can build up your résumé and not look unstable. It shows employers that you're not wishy-washy, that you actually care about the company and aren't just looking to make money by moving around. Stay put for a bit!

—*KELLI*
ATLANTA, GEORGIA

The workplace is not college. It's where you should start maturing.

—*J. L.*
SAN FRANCISCO, CALIFORNIA

ATTENTION: READING THE HANDBOOK IS GOOD FOR YOU

When you start your job, your company may conduct an orientation session with you. You'll receive a copy of the company's employee handbook, as well as any other written policies and procedures related to your job. You should take the orientation seriously and carefully review all of the information the company provides.

Although many people never read the employee handbook, you should; it is a gold mine of information. It probably will include the dos and don'ts of your employment and will inform you of the important policies and practices of the company, including on issues of harassment, discrimination, and other workplace misconduct.

—*Angela J. Reddock, Esq.*

WHEN YOU START A NEW JOB, you should not give 110 percent, wowing everyone with your capabilities and enthusiasm. Then you become the go-to guy (or girl). This happened to both my friend and me; we got tons of praise and good raises, which fed our egos. But as time goes on, you can barely keep up and will be working lots of overtime. Give 95 percent, and have a real life outside of work.

—*MIKE BLIZZARD*
CHICAGO, ILLINOIS

Consider

DON'T PUT THESE ON YOUR FACEBOOK PAGE

We know: You have some funny pictures of yourself that your friends would really appreciate. That doesn't mean you need to post them to your Facebook page. Especially now that you are in the real world. Below is a list of some pictures you should show your friends in person, rather than on the World Wide Web.

- Pics that show you obviously drunk or high.
- Pics that show you passed out and covered in a substance.
- Pics that show you TP-ing a house, stealing something from a rival frat or sorority, or engaging in any other even mildly illegal activity.
- Pics that show you doing cruel things to cows (or any animal, for that matter).
- Pics that show a part of your body that you would never show your boss.
- Pics that show a part of your significant other's body that they would never show *their* boss.
- Pics that show you with your tongue in someone else's mouth.

HAIR OF THE DOG?

We understand: You're a mature adult who's serious about your career. You don't have time to party like you did in college. Then along comes a Tuesday night with friends at the local pub and ... well, it seems like old times! Only now you have to rise and shine for work the next day. How will you get through it? Try these hangover cures from those who have been in your (sick) shoes.

TAKE A NAP AT LUNCH. One of the first things you should do when you start a job is find where you can take a nap if you really need one.
> —S.H.
> ATLANTA, GEORGIA

BC POWDER WASHED DOWN WITH A DIET COKE. BC Powder has aspirin and lots of caffeine in it. This, combined with the caffeine in the Diet Coke, helps a hangover. Also, as a preventative, take two ibuprofen tablets with a big glass of water prior to passing out/going to sleep!
> —KELLIE
> TAMPA, FLORIDA

THE BART SYSTEM NEVER FAILS: Bananas, Applesauce, Rice, and Toast. You'll be good as new.
> —KEITH LOBECK
> BOARDMAN, OHIO

IN THE MORNING, JUST LISTEN TO YOUR BODY. If it says, "Double Quarter Pounder with Cheese, two cigarettes, Mountain Dew, and a nap," obey. Give the hangover what it wants. This is no time to say, "We don't negotiate with terrorists."
> —J.P.
> CHARLOTTESVILLE, VIRGINIA

DRESS FOR SUCCESS

WHEN YOU START YOUR FIRST JOB AFTER COLLEGE, make an investment in your clothes. The rule of thumb is to dress as if you were already in the position you want to be in some day. Even if your office allows casual dress, you'll have a more professional attitude, and it will be one more thing that will make you management-worthy in the eyes of others. I've seen people get passed over for promotions because they were considered "not management material." The way they dressed was one of the problems.

—ANONYMOUS
SOUTH BEND, INDIANA

. . . .

MY FIRST JOB OUT OF COLLEGE, I worked in an office with three other people, and it was very casual. In fact, I'd wear shorts and a T-shirt to work, and so would my coworkers. The trick was that we all left suits in the closet, and when we rushed to get dressed for a meeting, it was like a scene from *Four Weddings and a Funeral*.

—N.J.
SAN FRANCISCO, CALIFORNIA

. . . .

THE SUMMER I GRADUATED FROM COLLEGE, I moved to Washington, D.C., and got a job. Although I turn purple with embarrassment every time I think of it, I wore a blazer every day and carried a briefcase to work! I thought I was the transformed Melanie Griffith in *Working Girl!* My $16,000-a-year job hardly required a suit. One day, a coworker, whom I deemed the pillar of maturity at age 32, asked me if I was interviewing elsewhere. I relaxed my work attire after that.

—ELIZABETH C.

I WORK IN A PROFESSIONAL OFFICE IN MANHATTAN, where men still wear suits during a heat wave and women wear heels through rain and snow. In order to survive, I wear comfy shoes, typically Reef flip-flops, during my commute to work, and switch shoes before entering the building. I learned the hard way by breaking a heel while walking home from the subway. Now I wear flip-flops regardless of how silly they look with suits.

—*N.L.*
NEW YORK, NEW YORK

FASHION RULES FOR CAREER WOMEN

- Always wear makeup to work. Don't wear too much or too little, just enough to give you some color.

- Women with long hair should wear their hair back because it looks more professional.

- If you have nice legs, always wear pants to important meetings. You want people to respect you for your brains, not your legs.

—*MELANIE*
MARICOPA, ARIZONA

ASK!

If this is your first job, you are probably coming straight from your senior year in college, where you were on top of your game. You knew the school, you had your friends, you were established. Suddenly, you are in a totally new situation of work, where you are expected to show up at a certain time every single day and do things you have never done before. You don't have experience to draw on, it's all new, and you are low man (or woman) on the totem pole. Depending on the situation, it can be a shock to the system. Don't worry; you are not expected to know everything. This is your opportunity to learn. Ask questions. Cultivate relationships with people from whom you can learn. Most important, when other people try to help you, don't resist them. Just because they are guiding you doesn't mean you aren't doing a good job. This is just your first job, not your last one; your task is to learn and grow.

—Ricki Frankel

ASK EVERYBODY EVERYTHING. You have a one-month grace period when people are willing to hold your hand. Sure, you want to look knowledgeable, but if you wait too long to ask questions, you could look as if you're not catching on.

—KELLY WILKES
ATLANTA, GEORGIA

• • • • • • • •

THE MOST IMPORTANT THING when starting out in a career, regardless of your field, is to act at all times honorably and with tremendous integrity. Never misrepresent yourself, your group, your product, or your company. Know that the relationships you make, even at the beginning of your career, are going to be important to you for years to come.

—JANE
MONTCLAIR, NEW JERSEY

JUST BECAUSE YOU'RE YOUNGER doesn't mean you have to take crap from other people. You have to stand up for yourself. I had a coworker who would give me all the worst work, piling it on. So I went to my boss and told him. And he respected me for it.

—*INGRID*
PATTON, PENNSYLVANIA

• • • • • • • •

" When you are just starting out, your motto should be 'Work harder, not smarter.' Of course, with more experience, that should change to 'Work smarter, not harder.' "

—*ANONYMOUS*
SHERMAN OAKS, CALIFORNIA

• • • • • • • •

MAKE SURE YOUR EXPECTATIONS and those of the person you're working for are completely in sync. Like all relationships, employer/employee relationships often take a bad turn when one party wants something and the other party simply isn't giving it. Be sure you really understand what your job entails, and touch base with your supervisor at least weekly to make sure that you understand both immediate and long-term priorities.

—*NANCY SHENKER*
THORNWOOD, NEW YORK

> Also: Be truly committed. Don't just act committed. EVERYTHING communicates!
>
> —*NADIA*

THE HALO EFFECT

Your reputation is everything in the workplace, and reputations are often made or broken in the first six months of a job. During this time, you can demonstrate your ability to learn, to apply yourself, and to work hard and do what it takes. If you establish a good reputation, you will likely benefit from the "halo effect"—the assumption by others that you are doing a good job. The halo effect doesn't mean that you can slack off, but it does mean that you won't have to prove yourself over and over.

After your reputation is established, it takes a while to change it, for better or for worse. That's great news when you have a good reputation: That's the halo effect. It's not good news when you don't have a good reputation. I have a friend who for years was late for everything—and not just five or ten minutes, but an hour or two. He worked on it, and for the last two years, he hasn't been late for anything. But still, people always assume he will be late, and they make jokes and comments about it. It's going to take some time for him to change his reputation. Your best bet is to create a good reputation for yourself in your first six months on a job. It will serve you well in the future.

—*Ricki Frankel*

Check your work. And check it again.

—*SARI KEMPE*
HOBOKEN,
NEW JERSEY

THE MOST IMPORTANT THINGS to do when you start your new job are 1) arrive early, 2) talk to and smile at everyone, and 3) do not gossip about others.

—*KAITY KROMPASICK*
FORKED RIVER, NEW JERSEY

• • • • • • • •

DO YOUR BEST AT WHATEVER TASK you're given, even if it's something you don't really enjoy. People will continue to trust you with more responsibility.

—*ERIN BEDEL*
FOUNTAINTOWN, INDIANA

Tough Assignment: Interacting with Your Coworkers and Boss

*R*emember friends? No, not the '90s TV show. Actual college friends that you hung out with, lived with, shared secrets with, took road trips with, created memories with. Well, now your waking hours are spent with a different type of friend. It's called a "colleague." Also, you now have someone to tell you what to do with your time, called a "boss." Dealing with these new people in your life requires a style of politics that's very different from figuring out whether your college roommate hooked up with so-and-so. But you have to learn to get along with them. The simple truth is, how you work with those around you could (and will) affect how successful you become. Check out these true tales from the workplace.

THE PEOPLE ARE WHAT TRULY MAKE one's work experience better, so reach out to your fellow colleagues and get to know them. It will make your time spent in the office more enjoyable.

—*K.S.*
NEW YORK, NEW YORK

BE FRIENDS WITH EVERYONE AT WORK, FROM THE MAILROOM PEOPLE TO THE RECEPTIONIST.

—*ANONYMOUS*
NEW YORK, NEW YORK

HEAD LINES
Best Advice and Top Tips

- An effective skill in any job: handling conflict. Learn it!
- Know that dating a coworker or boss comes with a lot of risk.
- A little office gossip is OK, but too much of it might get you fired.
- When drinking with coworkers, know when to say when.
- Creating a respectful, healthy work relationship with your boss should be a top priority.

If a coworker has a split personality disorder, know in advance which person-ality you are talking to.

—*D.*
ATLANTA, GEORGIA

DON'T GET TOO COMFORTABLE with your coworkers. I don't think you should talk about your personal life and give everyone your whole life story. Also, don't bring friends and significant others into the workplace. I want my coworkers to know me, but not to have too much information. One woman in our lab always talks about her guy problems, and it gets annoying. I don't want to hear it.

—*ANONYMOUS*
LOS ANGELES, CALIFORNIA

• • • • • • • •

YOU HAVE TO PUT YOURSELF on the level of every-one you meet. You'll meet someone who makes $400,000 a year, and someone who makes $20,000 a year, and everyone in between. You have to learn to have a common bond with them.

—*BRIAN*
ATLANTA, GEORGIA

I'VE HAD REALLY GOOD EXPERIENCES with bosses, and one of the reasons is because I give the boss all the power. It costs me nothing. And if someone feels like they have all the power, they are much more likely to give it away. I realized this when I watched the way I treated the boss and the response I got, and I watched the way other people treated the boss and the response they got. My response wins. If you give respect, you get it.

> —ANONYMOUS
> ATLANTA, GEORGIA

· · · · · · · ·

YOU'RE GOING TO COME IN CONTACT with a lot of people you don't get along with. You have to find that one thing that you have in common with them. At the end of the day, you can go home and deal with your real life. If you don't get along with a coworker, life will go on.

> —LAUREN BOWDEN
> FRANKLIN, TENNESSEE

· · · · · · · ·

YOUR SUCCESS AT YOUR JOB largely depends on the relationships you form there. If you are regarded as likable and easy to get along with, you'll have a much better chance of keeping your job. If you are widely regarded as charismatic, confident, and gregarious, you'll have a much better chance of being promoted.

> —S.D.
> MANCHESTER, PENSYLVANIA

ENGAGE IN ACTIVITIES WITH COWORKERS outside the office. The first place I worked, all the guys used to get together on the weekends to play flag football. I initially told them I wasn't interested, but I soon started picking up a vibe that told me that wasn't acceptable. So I gave it a try. I wanted to fit in. I hadn't played any form of football since junior high, but it came back to me pretty quickly. I found that playing football again helped me to lose some weight that I gained in college, and it was a real bonding experience with my coworkers.

—*ARIC MECHLIN*
WATTS FLATS, NEW YORK

• • • • • • • •

Forty percent of workers have dated a coworker. Thirty-one percent went on to marry that person.

I HAD A BOSS ONCE WHO DIDN'T LIKE confrontation. Instead of approaching me and telling me to my face that he might not have liked something I did, he would send me an email and copy others so everyone knew what was going on. Email is the wrong way to go about criticizing someone. It is embarrassing, it is impersonal, and it is a cop out. Praise, on the other hand, is something different. Email is one of the best ways to do it. You can email them and copy their supervisors and others who will then know of that person's job well done.

—*AMY*
RALEIGH-DURHAM, NORTH CAROLINA

• • • • • • • •

YOU'LL MAKE FRIENDS and get to know people as you go, so don't focus too hard on that at first. Make your work the best it can be, and you'll be respected by the others around you who value doing a job right.

—*J.B.*
MATTOON, ILLINOIS

HIT THE ROAD, JACK!

DON'T BE STUPID ENOUGH TO THINK THAT JUST because you tell a coworker something in confidence, it will not get out. I made the mistake in my very first job of making a joke about my boss's hair to a guy I worked with. I hadn't been there long enough to know if I could trust him. Not only did my boss find out about what I said, he found out quickly. He called me into his office later that same day to confront me about it. He didn't fire me, but our relationship was tarnished to the point that I eventually had to quit.

—*E.L.*
HARRISONBURG, VIRGINIA

. . . .

IF YOU'RE A DISGRUNTLED EMPLOYEE AND DISSATISFIED with your job, you shouldn't go into work and talk about how you're ready to leave. I had one coworker who constantly complained and even talked about what he would do in his next job and what date he thought he'd be gone by. He ended up getting let go before his planned date because management heard about all his complaining. Now I try not to gripe as much at work.

—*RANDALL S. WRAY*
MUNCIE, INDIANA

PEER-TO-PEER "WHINE-FESTS" are very common in any work situation. Try to limit the time you spend complaining about what's wrong with your job. It will only depress you (and take time away from doing a really good job). Plus, you don't want to get a reputation as a complainer.

—*NANCY SHENKER*
THORNWOOD, NEW YORK

DINNER WITH THE BOSS: ETIQUETTE 101

It's the second month of your new job at a large company, and your boss invites you to dinner with a potential client. You know instinctively that this is some kind of test to see how you handle yourself in a social situation, which makes you extremely nervous. What to wear, what to order and what to say are just some of the concerns you face.

So, how do you make this painless, and prove to your boss that you are a social asset? Let's start with accepting the invitation. Make sure your boss knows you are delighted to accept and feel privileged to be included (even if you are dreading it and wish you weren't).

Second, make sure you find out what the dress code will be. Most times, the answer is business casual. If that is the case and you are a man, wear a jacket over a crisp, well-ironed shirt and slacks. You can always take off the jacket if your host does. For women, especially if you are young, avoid cleavage, miniskirts or other clothing that is too revealing. Remember you want to be taken seriously, and while provocative dress may get you a date, it won't enhance your career prospects.

Always take your cues from the host of the event. When you are being seated, wait for the host of the evening to assign seating. If the venue is very formal, and the host keeps his jacket on, then you should do the same. If your host orders a starter and main course, then feel free to also order both. However, if your host only orders the main, then follow suit. Also, although it is tempting, do not order the most expensive item on the menu; rather, take the lead from the other guests.

As far as cutlery goes, always start with the pieces on the outside and work your way in. Smaller pieces are for starters and the larger knife and fork are for your entrée. Wait for the host to start eating before you do, and, even if it feels like you haven't eaten in days, take your time. Once you have finished eating, place your knife and fork parallel to each other on the plate – but do not scrunch your napkin over the top!

The rule for alcohol is simple: Keep it to a minimum. It's easy to behave graciously and in control when sober, but as we all know an "adult beverage" can lower our guard. This is where I have seen so many people inadvertently sabotage themselves. Keep in mind that everything communicates, and you should make it a point to keep that internal monitoring system switched on at all times.

This is also a chance for you to display your social skills, so ask intelligent questions. If you are at a loss, remember that everyone has a past, present and future, and you can frame your questions accordingly. Just make sure that you take an interest in the answers, but also that you don't cross boundaries and make your questions too personal.

If you follow these simple rules, your boss is sure to be impressed. Good luck!

—Nadia Bilchik

CORNERED BY A COWORKER

SOME OF THE PEOPLE I WORK with just want desperately to be heard. There are two in particular who are constantly interrupting each other's work to share personal stories. Whenever I feel myself getting sucked into their stuff, I smile politely and say I don't have time right now to hear a story, I'm on a deadline.

—*M.*
CONCORD, CALIFORNIA

• • • • • • • • •

THE PEOPLE WHO TALK ABOUT PERSONAL THINGS at the office must have no one else to talk to, or they just need to vent. If I'm on the receiving end of some tale involving PMS and bringing a dog to the vet, it's a drain of my time and energy. The storyteller has accomplished clearing her mind, however, and I guess she won't need to dump it on her husband.

—*B.*
HAYWARD, CALIFORNIA

• • • • • • • • •

MOST PEOPLE CAN RUN ON ONLY SO LONG without encouragement in the form of recognized discourse markers like "Oh, really?" or, "I know what you mean," or, "Fascinating!" I have no fear of being mildly rude to avoid hearing what I really don't want to know about what Joe Neighbor thinks about the Middle East or affirmative action.

—*BETTE CRAWFORD*
PHILADELPHIA, PENNSYLVANIA

• • • • • • • • •

WE HAVE A RECEPTIONIST in our office who is notoriously loud and loves to gossip. She also loves to snoop and cause trouble in general. When I first started my job, I attempted to be nice. Unfortunately, she is one of those people who twists things to make you look bad. I could say, "Good morning!" and somehow she'd make it look like I'd told her she was a horrible person. I just stopped talking to her unless there was someone else there as a witness.

—*ANGELA WILSON*
SPRINGFIELD, MISSOURI

IT'S IMPORTANT TO HAVE SOMEONE at work to whom you can direct questions. When I started my job, I latched on to the coworker who was closest to my age. She often used the word "dude" in talking to other employees, so I knew I would relate to her. I think it's important to have someone like that.

—*TAMI HARMAN*
MILPITAS, CALIFORNIA

HEADS UP: RECEIVING 'CONSTRUCTIVE' FEEDBACK

If you get some criticism from your boss, don't act like it's fatal. Take a deep breath. You'll be OK.

First, make sure you pay attention to the positives. Most people don't really hear positive feedback when they get it. Rather, they obsess over the negative, and they miss the big picture.

Second, evaluate the feedback. Don't get defensive—even if you don't agree with it, there may be some truth there. Get some understanding about what it means. Ask for clarification. Ask for guidance in addressing the issues. Think over what's been said and then develop an action plan to address the issues. Don't forget to go back to your boss, show him your plan, ask for input, and get his approval for it.

And most important, don't make it bigger than it is. Many people receive constructive feedback at work and go on to successful and fulfilling careers.

—*Ricki Frankel*

In a survey of workers aged 18 to 34, 31 percent say they prefer a male boss, and 29 percent say they prefer a female boss. The rest say it doesn't matter.

HAVING A COMFORTABLE working environment is especially important if you like your job. And if you can't get along with a coworker, just be as polite as possible. Act as though you like them. And when you get home, blow off some steam: Vent to someone about the annoying woman in the cubicle next to you, or your boss with the bad B.O., or the guy in your office who tries to pawn all his work off on you.

—B.H.
SEATTLE, WASHINGTON

• • • • • • • •

WHEN I WORKED FOR A CABLE TV CHANNEL, one of the show producers was a screamer and an abuser. I was supposed to get him on board with our very simple Web design templates, and he hated them. I called my boss, in tears, asking how I was going to deal with this guy and get my own job done. She gave me a piece of advice that has served me well ever since: Start with a common goal and work back from there. That producer was a jerk, but we did share the goal of publishing a website that would support and enhance the show. Every time he started to yell or I wanted to cry, I would remind us of our common goal and guide us back to the realities of what we could and could not do. It was difficult and awful, and I was so relieved when it was over. But the common goal approach has carried me through some difficult projects and earned me a reputation as a good leader.

—REGINA
LOS ANGELES, CALIFORNIA

HOW TO SURVIVE THE EVERYDAY

GO FOR THE OFFICE COFFEE RUNS as often as you can. Take orders for your colleagues; they'll love you for it, and it'll help pass the time.

    —*K.M.*
      BROOKLYN, NEW YORK

• • • • • • • •

ANYTIME I CAN GET AWAY FROM my desk and still be doing my job, it's a good thing, so I get involved outside of the office as much as I can. I enjoy my job much more with the change of pace. Having to sit at my desk and stare at my computer all day wouldn't make me happy.

    —*TRACEY GARNER*
      GRAND ISLAND, NEW YORK

• • • • • • • •

THROW THE BALL AROUND the office. But avoid the sprinkler heads on the ceiling.

    —*ANONYMOUS*
      TAMPA, FLORIDA

• • • • • • • •

I PASSED THE TIME AT MY OLD OFFICE by playing Ping-Pong. If your office doesn't have a Ping-Pong table, I would recommend the Internet, the all-time best time killer.

    —*HUNTER*
      TORONTO, CANADA

UNDERSTANDING PERSONALITY STYLES

Throughout high school and college, most people have the luxury of choosing who they hang out with. If you find a particular individual irritating, you can simply ignore them and not invite them to your party. On that level, life can be pretty simple.

In the real world of work, however, it's not so easy. When a coworker behaves in a way that is upsetting or hurtful, you can't necessarily walk away in the hopes that you will never have to deal with that individual again. Indeed, a huge part of the transition into the real world is handling interpersonal conflicts and developing the ability to work with people who you would definitely not choose as your friend.

First, know that you are not alone in this challenge. Second, it's natural to have a tendency to connect immediately with people who have a similar disposition, and fail to connect with people who seem different. For instance, an extrovert may find it challenging to connect with quieter, more reserved people. Equally, if you are very social and people-oriented, a coworker who is totally focused on work and getting the job done may at first appear cold and disinterested.

How do you overcome this to make the most of your career and life? By understanding personality types and how you can relate to them. A quote comes to mind: "We see the world not as it is, but as we are."

I have studied numerous "personality type" profiling systems, from Myers Briggs, to Berkman, to Herrmann Brain Dominance, to DISC. Whatever personality analysis you choose, the reality is that this is a complex, lifelong learning process that is unique to the individual.

But here a couple of tips to quickly assess a person's personality type:

- When meeting or working with someone for the first time, the first thing I observe is whether or not they more "reserved" or more "open." Are they more "formal" or more "casual"? You can tell this by how loudly or softly they speak, whether or not they shake your hand or hug you, etc.
- I listen to their language and ask myself this question: Are they talking in detail, very specifically? Or are they broad and big-picture in their thinking?
- I assess whether this is someone very similar to me in communication, or if I need to adjust my style accordingly.

I happen to be a very open, informal, big-picture person. I am challenged most when I meet someone who is much more reserved, detail-oriented and formal. It forces me to become conscious of toning down my naturally ebullient personality. I also take care not to ask or share too much personal information and keep it professional on the first meeting.

The key to all of this: Know yourself first. How formal or informal, open or reserved, detail-oriented or big picture are you? Once you know this, appreciate the qualities of the person you are communicating with and honor their style.

—*Nadia Bilchik*

ASK THE EXPERT: OFFICE POLITICS

Mention the word "politics" and many people tack on a negative connotation. But at work, politics usually describes how decisions get made and how things get done. Once you have three people in an organization, you have politics. If you are in a workplace that seems to have no politics, that just means that the politics there come naturally to you; it fits with your values and your nature, so you don't notice it. In any new organization or group you join, it is imperative for you to pay attention to the politics, or you won't know how to get things done. You can't avoid politics completely, so you may as well become a student of it and figure out how to work within the system with honor and integrity.

Here are some things to pay attention to:

- Who are the key decision makers? Are they in that role based on their titles or due to some other factor?
- How do decisions get made? Is there a clearly defined process, or does it seem to result from behind-the-scenes influence?
- Are some people more influential than others? What makes them so?
- How are people rewarded and on what basis? If there's no clear system for reward, try to figure out how it happens.

—Ricki Frankel

DO NOT ASSUME THAT ANYBODY who works in a cubicle beneath a flickering fluorescent light for 40 hours a week has a sense of humor. It is my experience that coworkers are tortured, embittered people who will be all too willing to read the worst into anything you say and actually believe you have a martian's pelvic bone hidden away in your desk drawer if you say it's so. They are dangerously happy to be gullible.

—*ANONYMOUS*
PHILADELPHIA, PENNSYLVANIA

. . . .

66 If you're not going to deal with people effectively at work, then you're not going to do it anywhere. Work is a microcosm of the real world. How you deal with it is a reflection of you. 99

—*T. S.*
ATLANTA, GEORGIA

. . . .

BE SOCIAL. YOU HAVE TO GO out at night with people you work with, if that's what it takes, for two reasons. One is to be friendlier with the people with whom you're spending your day. The other is to network. I started socializing purely for the friendship aspect, but then I met other people. At some point in your career, this investment typically comes back to help you.

—*ANONYMOUS*
PISCATAWAY, NEW JERSEY

SOMETIMES MY COWORKERS can get a bad attitude, and I'm tempted to get one back. But I just keep smiling and reminding myself that my life is beyond this job. Once 5 p.m. hits, they're out of my life, at least for the rest of the day.

—*BETH HARVEY*
CHICAGO, ILLINOIS

• • • • • • • •

I'VE ALWAYS FOUND THAT HAVING a good sense of humor, an open mind, and a positive attitude will get your coworkers to like you. But the crucial part is being a hard worker. Some of my coworkers spend the entire day surfing the Internet. People notice, and they resent that person for not putting in the same amount of work as the rest of the staff.

—*MICHELE*
ROCKAWAY TOWNSHIP, NEW JERSEY

• • • • • • • •

WORK IS A WEIRD THING. Every day, you go to the same building, the same floor, the same cubicle. It's like prison, in a way. You have to make it interesting. Talk to people by the water cooler about random things. Take a walk around your building. Go out for lunch.

—*GERALD*
CINCINNATI, OHIO

• • • • • • • •

THE BEST WAY TO SURVIVE the workplace is to meet as many people in the organization as possible, no matter what their level may be. You never know who may be hiding behind the suit.

—*ANONYMOUS*
NEW YORK, NEW YORK

TOOTING YOUR HORN

One common mistake is assuming that if you do a good job, people will somehow know it. That may or may not be true. It's important to figure out the best, most authentic, and natural way for you to let, if not the whole world, then at least your boss know what you are doing. If you don't know how to do that—and your boss hasn't been explicit enough—watch your coworkers. Ask for advice. Look for someone to emulate as a role model, and adapt his or her style to fit you. The more you can manage your relationship with your boss in a way that helps both of you, the better.

—*Ricki Frankel*

WHEN DEALING WITH SOMEONE who's been in the industry for about as long as you've been alive, it's impossible to stump them or teach them something about the profession. Instead, impress your boss with things that you've done and experiences that you've had. Any internship, special project, even community service can impress. Think of the things that you're really passionate about; passion and dedication tend to be impressive, especially to someone who may be concerned about a recent college kid's commitment level.

—MEGAN
SYRACUSE, NEW YORK

• • • • • • • •

IT HELPS TO MAKE FRIENDS with your coworkers outside of work. You'll work more efficiently together, and there's less stress because you're all friends. We were all friends at the last place I worked. It was a really good environment.

—CHATOYER HUGGINS
FT. LAUDERDALE, FLORIDA

Keeping my workspace neat impresses my boss; my messy coworker is constantly digging through piles of paper to get answers to the boss's questions.

—APRIL
CHICAGO, ILLINOIS

TO DATE OR NOT TO DATE

OFFICE ROMANCES ARE LETHAL. At first you think, "Wow, I don't have to waste time looking for a date in a bar, because there are people in my office I see 40-plus hours a week and whom I might be attracted to. I'll sleep with them!" But it's the same reason why some married couples choose not to work together: You see this person every day, and if you're in a relationship, you see him or her at night as well. "Casual dating" can get intense and dangerous pretty quickly.

—*ANONYMOUS*
SAN FRANCISCO, CALIFORNIA

• • • • • • • • •

I MET THE LOVE OF MY LIFE IN THE OFFICE. She sat across from me, and things just clicked. I used to put a cookie in her desk drawer every day because it was something no one else noticed. Make sure you don't give a damn about what others think and only about what makes you happy.

—*ANDREW*
EVANSTON, ILLINOIS

• • • • • • • • •

MY WORST EXPERIENCE WITH AN OFFICE romance wasn't even after a long relationship; it was after one date. The woman in question worked in an area of the office called "the fishbowl," where there were only women. I sat close to the fishbowl and had to walk past it dozens of times a day. The day after my date, every time I walked past the fishbowl, it would fall silent. Then all I could hear were whispers and giggles. For weeks, it was brutal. I got so paranoid that I considered quitting my job. You really might as well slam your hand in a drawer rather than date a coworker. You'll hurt some, yes, but the pain will be shorter-lived.

—*ADAM DREYFUS*
NEW CANAAN, CONNECTICUT

HOOKING UP WITH A COWORKER IS BAD, BAD, BAD. I hooked up with this guy for a few weeks. It wasn't a huge thing. But we had our fling and then it was over, and it left us both incapable of being friends.

—*B.*
ALBUQUERQUE, NEW MEXICO

· · · · · · · · ·

THERE'S A COUPLE IN MY OFFICE that are living together. At first, they were in different departments and on different floors, but then she came down to our department, and now I work with both of them. They are in the same room every day, and they go home together every day. Maybe they're good at separating home life and work life. There are some weird dynamics with it, but it's hard for me to say that people shouldn't date at work, because I see it working.

—*ANONYMOUS*
SAN DIEGO, CALIFORNIA

· · · · · · · · ·

I THOUGHT IT WOULD BE CUTE to secretly date a guy at work. We would be so friendly at work and nobody knew why, because we always denied our relationship. But after I was tired of him, he told me he felt uncomfortable being around me. He would avoid me, and when he couldn't, he would make petty arguments or complain about the way I was doing my job. Then there was no denying to my coworkers.

—*ZAKIA SIPP*
CHICAGO, ILLINOIS

DATING A COWORKER

Workplace romances are inevitable. You spend a lot of time with your coworkers, and it is an obvious place to meet potential romantic partners. Sometimes, office romances work out very well, and everyone lives happily ever after. However, sometimes they don't. I certainly would never advise you not to pursue a workplace romance if you feel the risks are worth the reward, but I do advise caution.

First of all, keep it private, particularly in the beginning. It is no one else's business, and workplaces are notorious for gossip. You don't want to be part of the rumor mill. Eventually, your colleagues will find out, but in the meantime, try to contain it.

Second, don't date your boss or someone in your management line (above or below you). If you feel compelled to see this person, do what you can to get out of the management chain—get a new job in the company, for example—otherwise, one of you is open to the possibility of sexual harassment accusations somewhere down the road. And, as quiet as you try to keep it, someone will always find out. You don't want people to speculate that the reason you got your latest promotion was because of whom you were sleeping with.

Third, if it doesn't work out, don't talk about it at work the way you might with a different break-up. You don't want to force people you have to see daily to take sides. After all, what if they don't side with you?

—Ricki Frankel

A FINE LINE EXISTS between building a good relationship with a supervisor and being a total suck-up. If you're a "boss's pet," you're sure to get grief from your coworkers.

—NANCY SHENKER
THORNWOOD, NEW YORK

* * * * * * * *

" Find out what your supervisors' pet peeves are—and don't do them. And in conversations, let them talk about themselves and what they like. Everybody likes to talk about themselves— everybody. "

—ALAN
MEMPHIS, TENNESSEE

* * * * * * * *

HALF OUR OFFICE JOINED a kickball league this summer. At first it seemed like an odd way to bond with coworkers, but it was great! I got to know others outside of the office; many of them aren't in my department, so they weren't ones I'd speak to on a normal day. It really helped us to support each other, and it was a great way to laugh with each other. No one could take it too seriously, so it didn't matter if you were terrible. We were adults playing kickball!

—KELLY WILKES
ATLANTA, GEORGIA

If someone yells at you, calling him "sir" sometimes helps.

—ANONYMOUS
ST. LOUIS, MISSOURI

HANDLING CONFLICT

YOU NEED TO BE ABLE TO ADAPT to someone else's style of communication. I've worked with people who like to stand up and have a shouting match; the person who shouted loudest won. I knew one guy who offered to take one of my partners outside for a fistfight to settle something. They never got out the door, but it was a tense moment. The best way to handle someone like that is to have your facts straight and stay calm. Sometimes you lose your temper, but staying rational is helpful.

> —*BILL*
> *BOSTON, MASSACHUSETTS*

• • • • • • • •

IN DEALING WITH PROBLEM COWORKERS, the straight-ahead approach is the best approach. Sit down with the person and say, "I want to work with you. I don't understand this. Is there something I've done?" Swallow your pride; it gets you nowhere. Focus on the prize: It's to enjoy your job and move up in your field. Allay a problem coworker's fears or concerns, and if you can't, go to your boss. I'm a big fan of getting problems out in the open, telling everyone what's going on. Give it a name, and it loses its power.

> —*ANONYMOUS*
> *ATLANTA, GEORGIA*

• • • • • • • •

I HAD A PROBLEM WITH ONE OF MY COWORKERS; I felt as if I was doing all of the work. But I hate confrontation more than anything, so I kept it inside for a long time and became more and more angry. Finally, I couldn't hold it in any longer, and I told my boss. My boss then realized how much work I was doing. It's my boss's responsibility to discipline us, anyway. And now, the coworker is doing her share and we are good friends. I just wish I had said something when it first started.

> —*K.*
> *PHILADELPHIA, PENNSYLVANIA*

I NEVER WAS A GOLFER, but that's a skill in the business field. If you take up golfing or if you're a good golfer, that can lead to a lot of contacts. Don't be a recluse. That's where I went wrong the first few years. I missed some advancement, I feel, because I didn't get my name out there.

—*ALLEN BARKLEY*
DALLAS, GEORGIA

• • • • • • • •

❝Sometimes I need to be a role model and a leader, and sometimes I need to follow. Knowing when to do each is an important skill to develop.❞

—*DAWN RODRIGUEZ*
PASSAIC, NEW JERSEY

BATTLING DISCRIMINATION

DISCRIMINATION EXISTS. Sometimes it is inadvertent, sometimes it is deliberate; it is never acceptable. Both federal and state laws protect applicants for employment from being discriminated against or harassed in any manner during the pre-hire and interviewing process. In the interview, discrimination can occur if the interviewer asks you inappropriate questions about your age, sex, race, color, national origin, ancestry, pregnancy, religion, disability, gender or sexual orientation. Discrimination occurs when answers to questions in any of these areas somehow keep you from getting the job or cause you to suffer some other adverse employment action.

—*The Editors*

MY MENTOR AND ME

WORK FOR THE SMARTEST PERSON you can find who will be willing to be a coach to you. I believe strongly in formal education, but I believe informal education is the single biggest shaper of your career. When I was younger, I started off in a consulting firm. My first year, we were working for a large automotive company in Brazil, and my supervisor gave me a key role. One of the things I had to do was give a presentation in front of our clients. I wasn't altogether comfortable doing it, so he spent time on a Sunday and coached me through the presentation. He gave me responsibility early on, and he gave me support when I needed it.

—BILL
BOSTON, MASSACHUSETTS

MY FIRST MENTOR WAS MY BOSS at an online advertising agency. When I was hired, I had no clue what I was doing. My boss guided me. He fielded all of my stupid questions and didn't get mad when I did something wrong. He offered a ton of constructive criticism and put me on the path to becoming successful. I found that very inspiring because I've had other bosses who don't take the time to sit down and really teach. If you're just starting out, learning and trying can be a very humbling experience. Try to pinpoint the person who will be patient and who can offer you the most guidance.

—J.L.
SAN FRANCISCO, CALIFORNIA

I WAS LUCKY WHEN I FOUND MY MENTOR at my first job out of college. One of the account managers liked me because we had a lot in common, and she took me under her wing while she was trying to advance her own career. She took the time to teach me the ropes. She would give me new and interesting projects and would help guide me and discuss my progress. She wanted to help me advance to the next level, and it worked: I was promoted within a year.

—ANONYMOUS
NEW YORK, NEW YORK

MY FIRST JOB OUT OF LAW SCHOOL was at a small boutique law firm. Because there were so few lawyers at the firm, I had the opportunity to work very closely with my boss. I tried not to kiss up to her. Instead, I put all of my energy into working hard and completing every task she presented to me. She told me that I made her life much easier. I believed that it was important to impress her with my legal knowledge and hard work, rather than with gifts and small talk. It's been 20 years since that first job, and my boss has moved to three different jobs. Once she was settled at each, she brought me in with her. We still work together, but now as partners.

—*ANONYMOUS*
LOS ANGELES, CALIFORNIA

WHEN YOU'RE THE YOUNG ONE in the office, you'll probably find that your older colleagues want to teach you, even when you know how to do the job. I learned that it's best to let go of my ego. My days go much smoother when I let someone tell me how I should do something rather than arguing that I already know how to do it. And I learned that it's good to be open to advice from coworkers, because I don't know everything.

—*KRISTIN*
STAMFORD, CONNECTICUT

SOME NEW WORKERS SIMPLY don't know the questions to ask advisors and mentors that will help them plan their career. I asked my mentors: How did you get into the industry? What exactly does your job entail? What does someone starting out in your industry need to know? What does someone starting out in your industry need to do? The guidance I received led me to my current position as an executive in an advertising agency.

—*MUHAMMAD SHABAZZ*
CHICAGO, ILLINOIS

TALKING TO THE BOSS

FIGURE OUT RIGHT OFF THE BAT how much you can joke around with your boss. Some bosses are great and like a feisty attitude. Others do not. You really need to find out, so you don't cross a line when you are trying to be funny.

—SARA WALKER

· · · · · · · ·

NEVER ARGUE WITH YOUR BOSS if you want to keep a job. Even if you are right and you resolve the problem, anytime a small thing happens at work, you are out the door.

—A.P.
CHICAGO, ILLINOIS

· · · · · · · ·

DON'T GO INTO A MEETING with your boss unprepared, especially when you are going to ask him or her for a raise or a promotion. It is essential that you think through the meeting beforehand so that you are confident and can answer any question that he or she might have. You don't get a ton of one-on-one opportunities like this, so it would be smart to really make the most of each chance.

—DAVID KARL
NEW YORK, NEW YORK

· · · · · · · ·

START BY ASKING YOUR BOSS if he has a few minutes to talk. Once you're "on," you should say something like this: "You told me yesterday my work is sloppy." (This shows you were actually listening.) "I heard you and would like to talk to you about how I can improve it." (This shows you care.) "I had a couple of ideas of things I can do to catch my own errors. For example, I can take an extra few minutes to proofread, and maybe hand my work over to Joe Colleague to read as well." (This shows you are a creative problem solver and a good team player.) "Do you have any other suggestions?" (This way, you are giving him a role in solving the problem, not just complaining about it.)

—NANCY SHENKER
THORNWOOD, NEW YORK

THE ODD COUPLE

I had a great job and loved my coworkers; then, they hired *him*: the most intolerable, disgusting guy I had ever met, and he was to be my partner. He was weird, impolite, critical, and abrasive. We literally shared an office, shared all accounts, and ran the department together. I am a very friendly and tolerant person, but after the first day, I knew I hated him. After the first week, I was plotting to get him fired. After the first month, I told my boss it was either him or me. But then something completely unexpected happened: I realized we were the perfect team. Because we were so incredibly different on every single level, we perfectly balanced each other. Our clients were well served because they had the creative and the practical, the traditional and unconventional, the front man and the man behind the scenes, the yin and the yang. We started racking up unprecedented successes. Don't get me wrong; we still would get on each other's last nerve. But in the end, we were a terrific team.

—KELLY WILKES
ATLANTA, GEORGIA

MAKE YOURSELF SEEM approachable to your coworkers. Doing little things such as saying "good morning" and "have a nice weekend" make a difference, and graciously accepting lunch invitations is a good idea, even if you're a shy person. I worked with someone who kept to herself, not even participating in conversations with the people around her. Eventually her coworkers stopped inviting her to social gatherings and didn't include her in conversations because they assumed she wouldn't respond.

—ANONYMOUS
NEW YORK, NEW YORK

Consider

...WITH THE BOSS?

WHEN DRINKING WITH YOUR BOSS, stay more sober than him. Drink less. Be a part of it, but don't lead.

—*EVAN*
ATLANTA, GEORGIA

• • • • • • • •

DON'T GET DRUNK WITH YOUR BOSS. He could say something that he shouldn't say. You could say something that you shouldn't say. And you think that, the next day, what you talked about at the bar won't come to work with you. But it doesn't quite work like that.

—*ALLEN BARKLEY*
DALLAS, GEORGIA

• • • • • • • •

IT'S A TRICKY THING TO DRINK WITH THE BOSS. I was at a conference with my boss, and one night I described an S&M club that I had visited years before. I went there as a journalist, of course, but I think he missed that part of the story. He was intrigued and asked me many questions about the experience. Since then, I try not to wear anything made of leather when I'm in the office.

—*A.S.*
NEW YORK, NEW YORK

• • • • • • • •

YOU KNOW HOW THEY SAY you should never drink more than your boss? Well, you shouldn't bet more than him, either. When I was first getting into restaurant management, my boss took my coworkers and me to Vegas. A couple of guys started showing off, throwing around ridiculous amounts of money. When the owner saw it, he simply said, "How much do we pay our bartenders? Obviously, they're making far too much."

—*T.J.K.*
WESTMINSTER, CALIFORNIA

I DO A LOT OF ENTERTAINING IN MY WORK. I try to stick to one cocktail, possibly two, per outing with clients and coworkers. It's important not to go over the line in a professional setting.
　　—*S.F.*
　　　TAMPA, FLORIDA

• • • • • • • •

DON'T EVER GET DRUNK WITH YOUR COWORKERS. I've seen people do stupid stuff. It's never good. You lose the respect of your coworkers. Be professional. If you're out on a Tuesday night with people from work, you still have to act like you're at work.
　　—*JUSTINE MOJICA*
　　　ATLANTA, GEORGIA

• • • • • • • •

WHEN DRINKING WITH COWORKERS, don't mention the stupid stuff that you did in college. Everybody does stupid stuff; don't bring it up. I think if you have any flavor in your personality, it will come through without saying specifically what you did.
　　—*EVAN*
　　　ATLANTA, GEORGIA

I DON'T HAVE THE BEST BOSS right now, but every time he's unbelievably insensitive and uncool, I try to remember the times I really messed up and he didn't say a word. He teaches me so much every day. That's what a boss is for. He's not there to hold your hand. He's there to make you the best at what you do.
　　—*RAY*
　　　ROCKY MOUNT, NORTH CAROLINA

MY BOSS IS A MICROMANAGER, and I have several strategies for dealing with him. First, I agree with everything he says, and then when he leaves, I do exactly what I think is the right thing to do. Second, I ask for his advice when I know exactly what he's going to say and it is exactly what I'd want to do.

—*S.L.*
SAN FRANCISCO, CALIFORNIA

. . . .

" When you screw up, open your mouth. No manager wants to discover a mistake for him- or herself. Even if it is bad news, it's best if it is brought to his or her attention. "

—*JANE*
MONTCLAIR, NEW JERSEY

GIFT-GIVING AT THE OFFICE

Movie tickets, a donation to a charity in someone's name, and magazine subscriptions are great gifts for coworkers and bosses. Clothing and personal toiletries (like body lotion) are too personal—as well as a bit weird.

THE GOLDEN RULE AT WORK

Remember the golden rule: Do unto others as you would have them do unto you. Respect for others in the workplace is vital. Be sure not to do or say anything to others that would offend them or make them feel uncomfortable. Respect the differences in and the diversity of your coworkers. In your first job, you are likely to work with individuals who have a range of experiences and backgrounds. You will work with people of various racial, ethnic, gender, religious and other backgrounds. The key for you is to embrace, or at least accept, these differences. Never treat others insensitively because of them.

If you need more incentive to do the right thing, do it because the law requires you to do so. As an individual, you can be legally liable for engaging in inappropriate conduct in the workplace against your coworkers, particularly conduct of a discriminatory or harassing nature.

—Angela J. Reddock, Esq.

I **LEARN AS MUCH AS POSSIBLE** about other departments within my company by being personable with my coworkers and asking many questions about their work. As a result, when a client wants something done that involves production, and I know from talking to the production people that it will take a certain number of days to do it, I can tell my client what to expect then and there, during our conversation, rather than telling him I'll call him back with the information. I'm more efficient, and I come across as being knowledgeable.

—MUHAMMAD SHABAZZ
CHICAGO, ILLINOIS

I'VE DEALT WITH A COWORKER who was a sniffer. I reported the sniffer to HR. I waited a year and a half to do this because I thought I was just being anal. Unfortunately, the sniffing got so loud and so frequent that it really started to interfere with my work. HR talked with him, and he hardly sniffs anymore.

—*J.L.*
    SAN FRANCISCO, CALIFORNIA

Technology, Work & Life: What You Need to Know to Get Plugged In

S ure, you're familiar with technology. In fact, you're probably much more tech-savvy than the managers now working above you. But that doesn't mean you know it all. In fact, using technology in a real-world job is very different from using it in a college dorm. From old-fashioned email to newfangled social networking, here are a few things to keep in mind – so that you can keep your respect on the job.

"REPLY TO ALL" ON EMAIL is the worst thing ever created. Some people make a quick joke or a snappy comment, they hit "reply to all," and it goes to the entire company. Then they get in trouble.

—KEITH
LONG ISLAND, NEW YORK

BE VERY CAREFUL WHEN OPENING EMAILS FROM FRIENDS WHEN YOUR CUBICLE IS WIDE OPEN.

—ANONYMOUS
TAMPA, FLORIDA

Keep emails short, because nobody really cares. An email is not a letter, so write a sentence and get to the point.

—*K.M.*
BROOKLYN,
NEW YORK

REMEMBER THAT EVERYONE is on Facebook now. I am Facebook friends with old professors and with people I work with on a daily basis for my job. I don't think you have to edit your personality completely – after all, even people in their 40s can recall their days of drinking out of red plastic cups – but be careful that your status or wall messages don't include negative comments about the place where you work. Also, beware of what people can find when they Google you. When I was 15 I filled out a questionnaire on a fan site for a comic strip, and when you Google me, that's the second hit. Even though it's not controversial, it is embarrassing, and I need to figure out how to take it down!

—*SHIRA PINSKER*
WASHINGTON, D.C.

• • • • • • • •

IF A JOB WATCHES OVER YOUR INTERNET usage like Big Brother, expect a bit of frustration - but plenty of productivity. Jobs that let you spend hours on Facebook and celebrity blogs catching up on the latest gossip can be a lot of fun, and usually indicate a laid-back, youthful environment. I started at a small advertising agency where it was fun: I could waste hours on Facebook, but I found my coworkers immature and no one took work seriously. I also didn't get paid enough. My current job is in Corporate America, and it's a bit daunting to know that people can watch your every move, but my daily grind is more fulfilling as I am able to see more substantial projects through to completion.

—*SHIRA*
PHILADELPHIA, PENNSYLVANIA

DON'T DELETE SENT EMAILS; you may need those for proof that you've been on top of things at work. This happened to me once; my boss challenged me, and I responded, "I have the email to show you I did that, ma'am!" That felt so good!

—*K.M.*
BROOKLYN, NEW YORK

It's ridiculously moronic to look like a slut on social networks. You're probably not going to get into any management positions anytime soon. Or ever. Promise.

—*AMBREEN HUSSAIN*
NEW YORK, NEW YORK

I JOINED FACEBOOK AFTER college and the craze never settled with me. To this day, I just try to compile more friends than my girlfriend (she has over 1,000). Here's the thing: Don't be defined by Facebook. While it's an invaluable tool to stay in touch with people without having the awkward conversation, don't be an idiot and start using every application ... and then making sure I know about it in the newsfeed.

—*RYAN*
PHILADELPHIA, PENNSYLVANIA

Lock your cell phone. You don't want any random pocket or purse dials.

—*KELLI*
ATLANTA, GEORGIA

I SENT AN EMAIL TO A CLIENT ONCE, and when I got a response back, I saw through the email chain that it had gone to six or seven other people in various departments. Fortunately, I'd taken the time to carefully craft that email, but it made me think of others that I'd been less careful with. You are committed to anything and everything you put in writing, and everything should be an accurate reflection of you as a professional. Err on the side of formality, because you never know where your email might end up.

—*ASHLEY*
IRVING, TEXAS

. . . .

ONE GUY AT A TECHNOLOGY JOB I had was using the company computers late at night to go to porn sites. I guess he thought he wouldn't be caught. But we have all the Internet logs at the corporate office, and he got fired. Don't use company computers for things like that. Everything is being watched.

—*CHATOYER HUGGINS*
FT. LAUDERDALE, FLORIDA

. . . .

ALWAYS, *ALWAYS* CHECK your attachments before you send them. Many times I've sent a similarly named document by accident, or I checked the attachment and noticed something that needed to be fixed that I had missed before. And at one point in your career, perhaps often, you will send an email referring to an attachment, and you will fail to attach anything. Then you will send a follow-up email that says, "Sorry! NOW it's attached! Need more coffee!" That's just the way it is.

—*J.A.*
ATLANTA, GEORGIA

EMAIL IMPRESSIONS

Sixty percent of business correspondence has grammar or spelling errors. Thirty-eight percent of employees have sent an email without the required attachment.

HANDLING EMAIL

THE ONLY WAY TO MANAGE MY EMAIL is to take care of my messages as soon as I read them, whether I send a response, save them to the correct folder, or delete them. If I don't handle my email this way, my messages can easily get lost. With so much email coming into my inbox all the time, a message that I mean to go back to can be buried in no time, and I won't find it again until I'm cleaning out my inbox.

— *TRACEY GARNER*
GRAND ISLAND, NEW YORK

IT'S IMPORTANT NOT TO PUT TOO MUCH personal information or pictures on social networking sites. Anything even slightly inappropriate could be used against you at some point, so try to keep things PG and as clean as possible. Also, limit your memberships to just one or two sites. It can be very distracting to be tempted to check so many of these at the same time, especially while at work!

— *KATIE*
NEW YORK, NEW YORK

JUST WHAT DO YOU MEAN BY THAT?

In a recent study, as few as 50 percent of email users grasped the tone or intent of an email message; most people vastly overestimated their ability to relay and comprehend messages accurately.

PRIVACY ON THE JOB? NO SUCH THING

As with their policy prohibiting personal use of emails and technology in the workplace, most companies let employees know that their electronic communications are not private and can be monitored as the company sees fit. Be careful not to engage in any communications with your coworkers, friends, or family that you would not want your company to see. You also want to be careful not to go to any inappropriate websites, which can get you in trouble with your company and with your colleagues.

Consider the following rules of thumb:

- Do not use company email to send jokes to your coworkers or others, particularly jokes of an offensive nature. You can be legally liable for sending such information if it is of a harassing or discriminatory nature.
- Do not go to pornographic or other inappropriate websites while at work or while using your company Internet or computers.
- Do not conduct your personal business over the company network or use company technology devices.
- Do not update your personal pages on MySpace or other personal websites utilizing the company network or property.
- Do not use the company network or property to gamble on-line.

There's a general principle here: When you are at work, focus on work. Find other ways to conduct your personal business and to engage in your personal hobbies and interests. Also, find other ways to engage your coworkers and to create a congenial, fun workplace. Sending offensive jokes and engaging in offensive behavior is not the way!

—Angela J. Reddock, Esq.

DON'T FORWARD MASS inspirational emails to everyone in your Outlook list, including your entire office and the company's offices in New York, L.A., and Tokyo. They get annoying, they can be insulting (especially if they reference religion), and it wastes time and valuable in-box space.

—*MEGAN*
SYRACUSE, NEW YORK

● ● ● ● ● ● ● ●

> " Don't use a Webcam, even in the off hours. The network administrators *will* see it and *will* post your boobs all over the Internet. "

—*ANONYMOUS*
SAN FRANCISCO, CALIFORNIA

● ● ● ● ● ● ● ●

SOMETIMES I GET CAUGHT UP in compulsive email checking, and I interrupt my work to check my personal account every few minutes. The only way to stop this is to take a walk around the building: outside if possible, but inside if the weather is bad. It's a terrible temptation when I'm not feeling motivated or absorbed in a work project. I have learned to listen to it as a signal that it's time to talk to a coworker or call my boss or start some other legitimate work activity that involves other human beings.

—*REGINA*
LOS ANGELES, CALIFORNIA

DON'T SEND ANYTHING IN A WORK EMAIL that isn't appropriate for the front page of a newspaper. And make sure you're sending email to the people you want to send it to. At our company, someone sent an email to an entire group, saying, "We're having problems with our system. We're working to solve it. Blah blah blah." One guy responded with something obscene. He knew the sender, and they were just joking around. If this guy had just sent it to his friend, it would have been fine. But he sent it to everyone. And he was fired that day.

—*JUSTINE MOJICA*
ATLANTA, GEORGIA

• • • • • • • •

DON'T FOOL AROUND WITH SOMEONE ELSE'S EMAIL or Instant Messaging. One a supervisor walked away from her computer without logging out. My friend and I used IM to send a coworker a message that said, "We need to make an appointment to discuss your dismissal." We thought it would be funny. It turns out, the coworker had been in trouble recently and actually thought he was being fired. He got really angry and confronted the supervisor. It was a real mess! My friend and I had to tell them what we had done. As you might imagine, they did not think it was funny. We got a note in our files.

—*CONNIE*
ST. LOUIS, MISSOURI

THIS IS YOUR BRAIN ON EMAIL

Email users suffered a 10-percent drop in IQ scores – more than twice the decline recorded by marijuana users – in a clinical trial with over 1,000 participants.

ORGANIZE YOUR EMAIL

Recognize that the in-box is not the ultimate filing cabinet and that the delete key is your friend. The in-box should be used as the temporary holding location for email that still requires action. If the email requires no additional action and does not have to be kept for future reference, it should be deleted immediately so that you do not waste time later rereading it and deciding what to do with it. If you decide that you need to keep it, file it. Create sub-files for your email. Subfiles could be organized by project, by person, or by topic; whatever method you select, make sure that the file-naming conventions that you use are specific enough for you to be able to retrieve the information when you need it.

—*Laura Leist*
Seattle, Washington

LET'S SAY YOU GET AN EMAIL from somebody who really stabbed you in the back or someone sends an email that really makes you mad, and now you want to come back at them really hard. Write the email, then walk away before sending it. Think about it. Let it settle. Then come back and reread it. You probably won't be sending that email, but it was good to get it out. So erase it and write a more conservative one that still gets to the point.

—*Allen Barkley*
Dallas, Georgia

• • • • • • • •

TRY TO REMEMBER THAT not everything has to be done online. Email is great, but it doesn't take the place of exchanging information over the phone or in person. Don't overly rely on it. I often find that I spend way more time answering emails than doing actual work. Unless something is truly urgent and cannot wait, then put answering it aside to complete important work tasks.

—*Katie*
New York, New York

11

Survival Skills: Adult Etiquette, Dress Codes & More

*S*ure, there's a good reason college students attend keggers, keep a basic wardrobe of t-shirts, shorts and flip-flops, and often fail to send handwritten "thank you" notes. In college, "low mainte-nance" is just how things are done. But in the real world, the kegger might transform into a black-tie soirée, which will require a differ-ent wardrobe, and even handwritten correspondence. And more. Yes, adulthood can be downright "high maintenance." With that in mind, here are tips on how to carry yourself like an adult.

YOU'RE AN ADULT NOW, so dress like one. Pitch the Green Day shirt with the cigarette burn on the sleeve. Same with those jeans with the rips in the knees. Two words: cotton Dockers. As far as underwear: Start over.

—V.S.
BOARDMAN, OHIO

GET THE BIG EMILY POST ETIQUETTE BOOK. IT'S GOT TEMPLATES AND SAMPLE LETTERS.

—A.H.
BROOKLYN, NEW YORK

HEAD LINES
Best Advice and Top Tips

- Being an adult means you should dress like one.
- Send handwritten thank-yous for gifts, promptly.
- When dining out, keep your language and your behavior in check.
- When sending any kind of correspondence, make sure you've spelled the recipient's name correctly.
- Keep money matters private—once you're out of college it's no longer appropriate to talk about how broke you are.

WHEN I WAS IN COLLEGE, I acquired my favorite sweatshirt at a Christmas social. It is warm, heavy-duty, and forest green. On the back, though, it has a picture of Santa Claus passed out with a bottle of whiskey and a plate of cookies. I wore it with pride for four years. I've been out of school for several years, and now my wife won't let me go near the thing. I accidentally wore it to the grocery store one day, and after a few curious and disgruntled stares, my wife made me hide it away. The moral of this story is: Drunken Santa sweatshirts are only cool between the ages of 18 and 22.

    —E.E.
      St. Louis, Missouri

• • • • • • • •

BEING AN ADULT MEANS not drinking too much at parties. It took me a little while to figure out that one, but it's important.

    —Amy
      Durham, North Carolina

IF SOMEONE CONTACTS YOU in any way—letter, email, phone call, whatever—reply to them. This is how adults operate. I absolutely hate it when I call or email someone and they don't get back to me.

—*C.E.*
HARRISONBURG, VIRGINIA

. . . .

"Remember everyone's name. It is the most important thing to learn in terms of etiquette. Take notes if you have to, and call people by their name every chance you get."

—*F.R.*
BINGHAMTON, NEW YORK

. . . .

DRESSING UP FOR BIG EVENTS: Jeans and a sweater are not dressy. Athletic shoes aren't dressy either, no matter how much they cost. When you're going to an event, it's always better to over-dress than to under-dress. Guys - always have a suit available. If you're on too tight a budget, have a shirt, tie, and blazer available. Girls - proper foundation garments are just as important as what people see! Going bra-less at formal events is not an option! Any good department store will be able to help you in that department. A simple black dress and pumps do not need to be expensive, and they'll get you through almost any type of event.

—*LAUREN*
ATLANTA, GEORGIA

Clean top to bottom whenever people are coming over. You actually feel better when it is done.

—*MATT*
LITTLE ROCK, ARKANSAS

WHAT TO WEAR TO ...

... A JOB INTERVIEW

Whatever you decide to wear to an interview, try it on ahead of time to make sure it's comfortable and appropriate when you are either standing, or sitting. Clothing should be a confidence booster, not a source of anxiety.

Men: A black suit, white shirt, tie of any conservative color or pattern (that Looney Tunes tie from middle school is out), black belt, black socks, and black shoes. Black is your friend; embrace it. Do not marinate in cologne.

Women: A black suit, white shirt, nylons, and black shoes. Traditionally, women wear skirt suits, but pants suits are acceptable, too. A word of caution: make sure your pants suit is age-appropriate; if you're 22, you don't want to look like Hillary Clinton. You can wear either comfortable, easy-to-walk-in heels no more than 2-inches high, or flats. Do not wear ballet flats, however. Pick something with a sturdy sole. Long hair should be swept into an attractive ponytail, chignon, or French twist. Jewelry ought to be minimal. Make-up and nail polish should be light or neutral.

... THE COMPANY BARBECUE

Most companies have dress codes, but relax them for informal events. However, this is not an invitation to wear your grubby sweat suit.

Guys: Shorts or casual khaki pants, t-shirt or polo with no underarm stains (or really any stains), and sneakers. Do not marinate in cologne.

Gals: Shorts or linen skirt no shorter than mid-thigh, or casual khaki pants, t-shirt or polo that does not expose your stomach or cleavage, and sneakers or sandals.

—Sarah Franco

I AM THE TYPICAL T-SHIRT and jeans person in my free time. But one of the biggest not-so-secret secrets is that the better you dress, the better your reputation is and the more respect others have for you. Don't overdress just to impress, but looking well put-together, groomed, and manicured goes a long way. From the first handshake to closing the deal, your contemporaries will notice.

—*RYAN*
PHILADELPHIA, PENNSYLVANIA

* * * * * * * *

I HAVE A JOB WHERE I get to wear what I want. It's a blessing and a curse because, hell yes, I'm going to wear flip-flops. It's a curse when I have to speak to a Very Important Person and try to be very important myself ... in flip-flops. That doesn't fly. I'm just about the last person to care about my own presentation, but other people will judge you for it. It's like high school. So, unless you're the coolest kid on the block or have a great reason, dressing like an adult (even if you don't feel like one) will earn you respect the second you go through the door. Sure, they'll find out later that you're an immature little twerp, but at least you're looking good.

—*ANONYMOUS*
ATLANTA, GEORGIA

* * * * * * * *

LADIES, YOU ARE NOT in college anymore. Don't wear tight or low-cut clothes. If you are not sure how to dress for work, err on the more professional, conservative side at first. Once you see how everyone else dresses, follow their lead. As a young professional I find it helps to dress up slightly more than your coworkers. This helps counteract your youth with professionalism.

—*RACHEL WIECK CUPIT*
NEW ORLEANS, LOUISIANA

Learn to tie a tie. Anybody who wears clip-on ties is simply a loser. You might as well wear a polyester suit.

—S.C.
HARRISONBURG,
VIRGINIA

WHEN YOU'RE LEAVING SOMEONE a message on an answering machine, leave your phone number. Your friends might not care, but businesspeople get annoyed if you don't leave your contact information.

—LIZ ASHBY
EUREKA, CALIFORNIA

• • • • • • • •

WHEN I WAS GROWING UP, if I didn't write a note for every gift I received, my mother would beat me. Write letters. And handwrite them. You can generate those cover letters on the computer, but definitely handwrite a thank-you letter.

—LEANNE
ATLANTA, GEORGIA

• • • • • • • •

" Keep family business private. You especially don't talk about money. When you are in college, everybody talks about how broke they are. But it's not polite conversation in the business world. "

—BETSY MILLER
MARSHFIELD, MISSOURI

• • • • • • • •

FIRST IMPRESSIONS MATTER. Go boutique shopping and find something unique. Boutique clothes have mostly exquisite and mature taste. Look like an adult by opting to pay more for something that leaves a lasting impression, especially for big events.

—AMBREEN HUSSAIN
NEW YORK, NEW YORK

WHEN YOU GET YOUR FIRST JOB and you have to dine formally for business, don't act like an uncouth slob, even if you are one. If you don't know which fork to use, there are plenty of etiquette websites that you can peruse. But if you get to the restaurant and you get confused, don't act flustered. Just pretend like you know what you're doing, even if you don't. It will be more noticeable to your dining companions if you stop to look around at which fork they are using than if you just pick one and go with it.

—*GINA LEMKE*
POLAND, OHIO

• • • • • • • •

ONCE, WHILE DINING WITH MY FRIENDS at a high-end restaurant, a waiter walked by carrying an enormous piece of cake. Without thinking, I blurted out, "Holy shit!" All I could think about was that there was no way one person could eat the whole thing! Later, my friend told me that everyone in the restaurant had turned to stare at me. When you go to a nice restaurant as an "adult," it isn't proper to talk—or curse—so loud!

—*ROBIN*
HARTFORD, CONNECTICUT

MISS MANNERS ON THANK-YOU NOTES

"The longer you put off this task, the longer the letter you have to write. It should not contain your paltry excuses but overwhelm them with gratitude for their kindness and enthusiasm about whatever you must have long since bought with their money."

One time I used the salad fork to eat the whole meal. I figured I was using the right fork at least part of the time.

—GINA LEMKE
POLAND, OHIO

IF IT COMES DOWN TO A CHOICE between being late and looking good or being on time and looking bad, go with the former. People will quickly forget about tardiness. However, an unseemly appearance will be remembered for a long time.

—B.M.
DRY RIDGE, KENTUCKY

• • • • • • • •

ALWAYS MAKE SURE YOU'VE SPELLED people's names correctly—in party invitations, thank-you notes, emails and memos at work. Nothing makes a worse impression than receiving something with your name misspelled on it. It shows a lack of respect and attention, and it essentially says, "I only halfway care about you."

—ERIKA
TALLAHASSEE, FLORIDA

• • • • • • • •

WHEN YOU ARE AT A FORMAL DINNER and the food is being placed on the table—particularly food that is for the table to share, like bread—never be the first to reach for it. I don't care how much anybody you ask would deny it; people always look down at the unfortunate soul who is the first to grab a roll out of the basket. Let someone else go first. Better yet, let everyone go first.

—RALPH DILUIGI
FLORENCE, KENTUCKY

• • • • • • • •

GETTING DRESSED FOR WORK in the morning can sometimes be a challenge. If I'm late, I might grab the pants I wore two days ago, thinking, "Will anyone notice? Can I get one more wear out of these before they go to the dry cleaner?" But what's the alternative to dressing creatively; wearing a uniform?

—STEPHANIE
FOSTER CITY, CALIFORNIA

EMAIL ETIQUETTE

As a member of the e-generation, you know how to email with the best of them. But as you mature, your electronic correspondence should mature as well. Check out these tips for guidance.

- Answer promptly
- Use a meaningful subject line
- Do not overuse "Reply to All" or the "cc:" field
- Avoid using Urgent, Important or High Priority options
- Make it personal
- Be concise; avoid long sentences
- Answer all questions, and pre-empt further questions
- Use proper spelling, grammar and punctuation
- Limit use of abbreviations and emoticons
- Do not write in CAPITALS
- Do not leave out the message thread
- Do not attach unnecessary files
- Do not use email to discuss confidential information
- Do not forward chain letters
- Do not send or forward emails that contain anything that might get you sued
- Read the email before you send it

—The Editors

I ALWAYS CALL SOMEONE THE NEXT DAY to thank them for inviting me to dinner or a party. I also send thank-you cards for all gifts that same week. And in business I send thank-you cards for prospects who took the time to meet with me. It is the single most effective way I could think of to be in good standing with people: friends, clients, and family. And it feels good to acknowledge and be acknowledged—so simple, yet so powerful!

—*KALYNA*
SAN FRANCISCO, CALIFORNIA

· · · · · · · ·

If someone is older than you, call them "ma'am" or "sir." Say "please" and "thank you." You catch more bees with honey.

—*LEANNE*
ATLANTA, GEORGIA

SINCE I'VE BEEN WORKING, LAUNDRY has taken on a whole new meaning. I have to wear nice professional clothes. That means I have to buy clothes that are either for work, or for both work and going out. It's pretty easy to find stuff that is versatile, and it saves you money if you buy a sweater or a shirt that can serve both purposes.

—*BECKY STRUBE*
BELLEVILLE, ILLINOIS

· · · · · · · ·

AT WORK FUNCTIONS OR OTHER EVENTS I try to tone my exuberant personality down and also not talk about all my college drinking stories ... at least right off the bat. I tend to take in the tone of the event or group and work from there. I don't want to be known as the 25-year-old Yankee egomaniac. That's not always the best first impression.

—*JENNIFER*
ALABAMA

THINGS YOU SHOULDN'T DO AT A HOUSE PARTY

What you do on your own time is your own business. But there will come an evening when you attend a house party where lines marking "your own time" are blurred – in other words, work colleagues and possible networking pals will be in attendance. That means you must put on your "I'm responsible and mature" face and act like an adult. For those who are still unclear about what this means, here is a guide to the specific, sometimes obvious things you should never do at these kinds of events.

Do not:

- Reenact, for everyone's entertainment, the Frank the Tank streaking scene in "Old School"
- Skinny dip, do drugs, guzzle alcohol, or puke in the bushes
- As a joke, be seen putting grain alcohol in the punch
- Have sex, even in a locked bathroom or bedroom. In fact, do not even engage in a make-out session in public view.
- Fight with a rival, or wrestle with a friend
- Play beer pong for more than one game
- Wear a beer helmet

—The Editors

LEARN TO HANDLE ALCOHOL. This is probably the one that has taken me the longest but you have more to lose now that you are out of college. You could lose your job (don't get too crazy at the office party or the happy hours). There are fewer people looking after you and you need to know your limits.

—ERIN BLACK
PITTSBURGH, PENNSYLVANIA

GOT IT OUT OF YOUR SYSTEM?

COLLEGE IS THE BEST TIME to get your mistakes out of the way. That said, I made a few mistakes that nearly killed me, so don't make those mistakes. Make the ones where you drink too much and hook up with someone you might be embarrassed to tell your friends about ... or when you just decide to go around the room slapping people in the face. I made that mistake in college too, and believe me: You won't be able to get away with that in the real world.

—*ANONYMOUS*
ATLANTA, GEORGIA

Wearing black
is always safe.

—*JENNIFER*
ALABAMA

AN INVALUABLE TOOL TO HANDLE LAUNDRY is a home-pick-up-and-delivery laundry service. I don't care if I sound like a yuppie or a suburbanite. It's worth the money and the time you save, and it's one more thing you don't have to worry about. My pick-up days are Tuesday and Friday. They pick the stuff up on Tuesday and bring it back on Friday. It is the best thing that has ever been invented.

—*AMY*
RALEIGH-DURHAM, NORTH CAROLINA

● ● ● ● ● ● ● ● ●

WEAR COMFORTABLE SHOES, either small heel or no heel. Many women like to look attractive at work, and heels can help. But if you're walking from cubicle to cubicle, floor to floor, going out for lunch, and standing up while making PowerPoint presentations, your best bet is to remain comfortable.

—*AUDREY PARKER-DAVIS*
CHICAGO, ILLINOIS

Nice Job: Going to Grad School Instead

Here you stand, on the precipice of a new life called Adulthood. Lying before you on the road ahead: a new place to live. A career. A love interest. And – what's this? You say you're considering a detour? You might want to go back to school to earn an advanced degree? There certainly are benefits to this path. There are drawbacks, as well. We asked others what motivated them to return to grad school and what advice they would pass along. Here's what another degree might get you.

THE BIGGEST CHALLENGES of grad school are overcoming the self-doubt of living in a studio apartment at age 30 with no savings, and having to constantly answer the question, "How many more years of school do you have?"

—KAREN
BOSTON, MASSACHUSETTS

COLLEGE IS ABOUT FINDING YOURSELF. GRAD SCHOOL IS ABOUT FINDING A JOB.

—D.M.
NEW YORK, NEW YORK

HEAD LINES
Best Advice and Top Tips

- Grad school can be an important tool for advancing your career.

- Taking time off between college and grad school can give you valuable work experience and make you more marketable in the long run.

- Grad school is a personal choice—think carefully about whether or not you want to spend more time and money on school.

- Don't be discouraged if you have to pay for grad school your-self—it's hard, but it can be done.

Try to pick something you enjoy. If you don't enjoy what you're doing, it's going to drain your spirit and your soul.

—*Warren
Oakland,
California*

I HAD AN EXCELLENT ACADEMIC experience in college, and it seemed odd to me that it was time for my education days to end. I didn't feel full or tired. Secondly, and more directly, I found out that a program existed that incorporated basically everything I did in college that gave me a warm fuzzy feeling. And once I interviewed, I was overwhelmed by the attitudes of the professionals in my program. They won me over. After that visit, any hesitations I had were erased. And I would be remiss not to mention that I majored in Comparative Literature in college. I mean, what else was I going to do with myself? Plus, um, they pay you to go to grad school a lot of the time, and then you leave with a master's degree instead of a severance package.

—*Amelia
Atlanta, Georgia*

SEEK OUT EVERY PENNY and every minute you can. I eked an extra two years of working on my dissertation thanks to some really obscure fellowships. I probably put more effort into turning over every possible stone to find that money than I would have if I'd just sucked it up and worked, but it was worth it just to delay the stress of finding a real job.

> —*ELLEN*
> *KIRKLAND, WASHINGTON*

. . . .

" Study abroad if you can. It will open your horizons. The best thing about grad school was the semester I spent in Ireland. I met my husband there, who was on a year abroad for his under-graduate program. "

> —*ANNE*
> *PARIS, FRANCE*

. . . .

FORGET GRAD SCHOOL. Take that job at Wal-Mart and spend some time volunteering in a profession that interests you. So many young people really have no idea what is out there in the world. They just know that they need more letters behind their surname, and they make rash decisions about what those letters should be.

> —*S.G.*
> *SEATTLE, WASHINGTON*

For a breakdown of the best graduate schools, visit the U.S. News & World Report rankings at: http://gradschools.usnews. rankingsandreviews.com

FIT IN TRAVEL WITH YOUR FIELD OF STUDY. I did my anthropology studies in Ecuador and then stayed to work on my dissertation there, too. I was there for years and probably spent what it would've cost to be in the States for only a few months.

—*M.G.*
ALAMEDA, CALIFORNIA

• • • • • • • •

MY LAW SCHOOL ROOMMATE and I said that we were not going to get involved in that hard-nosed, competitive culture. We attended class, we studied a lot, but we did not get involved in the "who can stay at the library longest" or "I have no time to eat because I have too much to study" rituals. We continued with our normal lives and incorporated school into that lifestyle. It is possible. And it is possible to maintain good grades at the same time. The two keys are your time usage and priorities. But I can guarantee that you will be happier if you avoid the drama, headaches, and mind games of grad-school competition.

—*ZACH*
DALLAS, TEXAS

TOP 10 BUSINESS SCHOOLS

1. Harvard
2. Stanford
3. Northwestern (Kellogg)
3. (tie) University of Pennsylvania (Wharton)
5. Massachusetts Institute of Technology (Sloan)
5. (tie) University of Chicago (Booth)
7. University of California, Berkeley (Haas)
8. Dartmouth (Tuck)
9. Columbia
10. Yale

GENERALLY SPEAKING, my grad school professors could be divided into two groups: those who worked for the university full time (code for *lack of real-world experience!*) and seemed bitter, negative, and discouraging; and those who taught a class or two each semester as adjuncts. They were awesome. These people typically had extremely successful professional careers (one had written for *Sports Illustrated* for more than 20 years) and seemed to genuinely want to help and support the students. Get to know the adjuncts early, because they'll make terrific and powerful mentors later.

—SHANNON HURD
HIGHLANDS RANCH, COLORADO

• • • • • • • •

DON'T TAKE GRAD SCHOOL FOR GRANTED. You will never again be around so many bright people. Incompetence will rear its ugly head once you hit the outside world.

—JEANIE
MINNEAPOLIS, MINNESOTA

• • • • • • • •

THE BIGGEST BENEFIT OF GRAD SCHOOL is the opportunity to really hone in on something that you want to study. It gives you more time to really concentrate your studies, and I think it also allows you more time to form a better-educated worldview. I really grew up quite a lot in those two years. Sometimes when you're older and focusing on a subject you can take a much more in-depth approach than someone would who was more of a novice to the process of learning.

—JULIA
NEW YORK, NEW YORK

The worst thing about grad school was looking at the under-grads and knowing how easy and fun they had it without realizing it.

—MATT
SAN CARLOS, CALIFORNIA

IS GRAD SCHOOL FOR YOU?

Graduate school can be a great opportunity to take your education to the next level, and to add to your credentials; a graduate degree can give you an edge throughout your career. However, if you're headed back to school just to avoid a tough job market, or working, think again. It's a temporary fix, and going to grad school is a big step. Here are some key questions to ask yourself:

Since college, have you learned more about what kind of career you want (and don't want)?

Having worked in a job or two after college will serve you very well as you consider graduate school opportunities, as it will give you real-world insight. That insight will help you better evaluate what sort of career you really want, as well as what additional education you want or need.

Have you had any experience in the industry that is the likely "end game" at the conclusion of grad school?

For instance, if you're planning to go to law school, have you interned or worked as a paralegal at a law firm? Don't go into a graduate program blindly – have an objective. Your goals may change, but having one will help to keep you focused.

Are you still learning a fair amount in your current job, or has the learning curve flattened?

If you're still learning a lot, you may want to consider sticking around for a while, especially if you want to continue working in that field after graduate school. Learn what you can, and then apply to school as the learning curve flattens.

Also, consider seriously how a graduate degree will make you a more valuable worker, and weigh this against the "opportunity cost," which includes the cost of grad school, cost of the time committed and lost wages.

—Shannon Duff

I **SUGGEST WORKING FULL-TIME** and attending a part-time graduate program. This option gives you the best of both worlds upon graduation. By the time you complete your graduate program, you'll have about three years of real world work experience under your belt AND a master's degree. This will put your résumé at the top of every stack.

—LINDSEY
ATLANTA, GEORGIA

CONSIDER GRAD SCHOOL CAREFULLY. I applied to med school. When I went to the interview, they told me that this would be my entire life for the next six years. They actually told me that it was a commitment more serious than marriage, and that I should expect to have no life in the meantime. It was really informative. I decided it wasn't what I wanted, and my fiancée decided it's definitely not what she wanted!

—JASON T.
CHAPEL HILL, NORTH CAROLINA

If you're going to go to grad school, just make sure you understand that it's not an extension of undergrad. It's the real deal.

—JON SHAM
COLLEGE PARK,
MARYLAND

I **WAITED FOR A COUPLE OF YEARS** after undergrad to get my MBA. I didn't know anything about business after undergrad, so I got a job in the corporate world. I think it would be difficult to learn about business if you didn't get out and experience business first.

—BECKY HOUK
INDIANAPOLIS, INDIANA

The best advice I can give anybody about going out into the world is this: Don't do it. I have been out there. It is a mess.

—*Russell Baker, 1995 commencement speech at Connecticut College*

I GOT MY DOCTORATE BECAUSE I needed to be taken seriously as a woman in a field that is very male-dominated. I would never be as financially secure and as professionally respected if I hadn't done it.

—*Mel Miller*
Brisbane, Australia

• • • • • • • •

GET A GRADUATE ASSISTANT JOB within the college or with a professor/advisor. This really helps you take full advantage of your degree because you are able to work with the professors to better understand and appreciate graduate school.

—*Micah Karber*
Silverton, Texas

• • • • • • • •

IF YOU'RE GOING TO GRAD SCHOOL, just make sure you understand that you don't have to go right now. It's not the end of the world if you take a couple years to decide where to go.

—*L.F.*
New York, New York

TOUGHEST LAW SCHOOLS TO GET INTO

1. Yale
2. Harvard
3. Stanford
4. Columbia
5. University of Pennsylvania
6. Northwestern
7. University of California, Berkeley
8. University of Chicago
9. University of California, Los Angeles
10. University of Texas at Austin

GRAD SCHOOL: PRO AND CON

The downsides of grad school: You're not a part of the student body the way you were in undergrad. If you have any sort of teaching role (and often you do), you immediately have very specific and very serious stipulations to follow regarding your conduct with students. Essentially: no going to the popular campus bars. You live in an odd in-between world. And while I was in school, living off of a stipend and spending my nights writing about theory, my friends with jobs were going out 3-4 nights a week, using real paychecks to finance their fun, and living in the cities I missed and/or envied.

But then: I got summers off. My working friends did not. And while I still had pangs of jealousy for nine months out of the year, for three I was able to recharge and feel like a 20-something, rather than a reviled old student. Plus I got to say snooty things like, "I'm pursuing my master's in..." – which helps when you're down.

—AMELIA
ATLANTA, GEORGIA

I CHOSE GRAD SCHOOL because I didn't think the training I received for my undergraduate major (English) would lead me to the kind of life I would like to live, mostly because I didn't want to be an English teacher or professor. What I learned is that you can afford to major in something in college that interests you, but may not directly lead you to a career. For example, I majored in English but instead am pursuing a career in journalism.

—JON SHAM
COLLEGE PARK, MARYLAND

I CHOSE A CAREER that required a Master's degree, so I decided to pick all the big cities I could see myself in, and apply to all of the schools within those cities. When I got into George Washington University in the heart of D.C., I knew that's where I had to be. It was a REALLY hard decision though, because I had to pay for 100 percent of my graduate tuition, rent, entertainment, etc. I mean, are you kidding me? I thought that was so unfair considering my college tuition was free! But it was the best decision I could've made. Not necessarily for the school, but for leaving my comfort zone and making a life for myself somewhere else. I could no longer rely on anyone but myself to make that life, and I'm SO glad I did.

—*JAIME SCHULTZ*
WASHINGTON, D.C.

DEALING WITH REAL-WORLDERS

IGNORE THE PEOPLE WHO MAKE FUN of you for still being in school. My siblings kept asking things like, "When are you going to cut the umbilical cord?" It was especially hard. I finally learned to just ignore them. I figured that my parents were the ones who were supporting me, and they were fine with it.

—*JULIANA GOODWIN*
SPRINGFIELD, MISSOURI

• • • • • • • •

ANYTIME ANY OF MY FRIENDS would tell me that I was just avoiding work by staying in grad school, I'd tell them, "Yep, and you're just jealous." I think a lot of them would have done the same thing if they could have afforded it, and their comments were just sour grapes.

—*J.G.*
JAMESTOWN, NEW YORK

COMMON REASONS FOR CHOOSING GRAD SCHOOL

Job Market: Fact: Grad school applications go up when the economy tanks. Students figure they can bide time, earn a higher-level degree, and receive more money when they graduate (again) and the job market clears.

Career Goals: Many grad students spent some time in the real world to get their career bearings – and realized they would be better off (would advance quicker and/or earn more money) with a graduate degree.

New (or More Specific) Interests: Grad school allows/forces students to focus on a single area of expertise – good for those with a passion for specific pursuits.

Teaching: Some students who want to teach in college need an advanced degree, and sometimes more than one. Others assume that with a graduate degree, they can always fall back on teaching if they don't find another preferable job.

Doctor, Lawyer: Want to be one? Grad school is, of course, the only way to get there.

—The Editors

YOU SHOULDN'T GO TO GRAD SCHOOL if you simply feel that it's the next logical step for career advancement. You should only pursue grad school if it's something you truly crave.

—*KATRINA*
NEW YORK, NEW YORK

FUN WITH(OUT) MONEY

IT SUCKS LIVING like you are really, really poor, especially when it is because you are actually really, really poor. At one point during my Master's program my wife and I had $7 total to our name. When I told her, she hyperventilated and I tried to do the paper bag thing (for real). But then the next check came, and it got better after that.

—*BRENNAN*
ATLANTA, GEORGIA

IT CAN BE A LITTLE TRYING being in grad school and having friends that are not. Your "real world" friends are getting paid to work, while you are paying to work hard in school. It can be socially difficult sometimes when you really don't want to blow your money on another fancy Friday night outing with your friends who are getting paychecks.

—*KATIE*
ATLANTA, GEORGIA

WEIGH SERIOUSLY THE BALANCE between the cost of grad school and the benefits of grad school. I knew going into it that finances would be a big burden, but I worked while going through school and just told myself that I'd have to find a stellar job afterward to help me with my loan payments. It was a big gamble. What if I didn't get a good job after I graduated? What would I do then? I did the math and found that I'd have to find a job that paid about $90,000 a year in order to live comfortably and make my loan payments. It was a risky decision, but so far I feel that it's under control.

—*KATRINA*
NEW YORK, NEW YORK

IF YOU'RE GAINFULLY EMPLOYED before grad school, save as much as possible while you are looking into your options. Otherwise, the best way to finance grad school is to become a teaching assistant. Also, be sure to factor your living expenses into your student loans. And don't be afraid to ask for help if you have relatives who are available and supportive.

—*L.F.*
NEW YORK, NEW YORK

YOU CAN PAY YOUR OWN WAY if you have to. My parents told me that I had to pay for my Master's myself. I looked at the cost of school per credit hour. I worked 40 hours a week and saved everything I could and kept my money for school separate. On the first day, I was able to buy my books and pay in full for my first nine credit hours. That was very gratifying.

—*ANONYMOUS*
KIRKSVILLE, MISSOURI

GO TO GRADUATE SCHOOL if your undergraduate degree is in a field where further education is extremely useful, extremely profitable, or accepted as necessary. Many of the science fields, for example, expect their graduates to continue past their undergraduate work, and the employers in those fields expect the same thing. You are not going to graduate with a degree in chemical engineering, like I did, and expect to walk into a company like DuPont and get a high-paying job. Those companies expect that they won't see you on their doorstep without at least a master's degree in hand.

—*OMAR REINOR*
FLORENCE, KENTUCKY

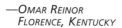

IF YOU ARE HAVING TROUBLE CHOOSING between two options for a career path, consider what you want in the long run. I was having trouble during my last two years of undergraduate school deciding what to do with my life: going into medicine versus getting a Ph.D. and eventually teaching. I ended up thinking about which path would have more options in terms of lifestyle, income, and intellectual stimulation down the road. I picked medicine, thinking I would be able to choose down the line what field of medicine I wanted. It was the right decision for me.

—*R.H.*
LITTLE ROCK, ARKANSAS

WHAT Ph.D. *REALLY* STANDS FOR

Well, this isn't *really* what it stands for – but humor helps the Ph.D. survive:

Patiently hoping for a Degree
Please hire. Desperate.
Potential heavy Drinker
Pathetic homeless Dreamer

SEE YOU NEXT DECADE

It can take about nine years to complete a doctoral dissertation in English, as students are forced to juggle teaching, making money, and writing.

MAKE GRAD SCHOOL A PERSONAL CHOICE. While my friends graduated college and jumped into careers, marriages, and "adult lives," I took a couple years off, stayed busy, and considered my options. I decided on medical school, applied, and was accepted. The decision never felt 100 percent right; I felt good about it slowly, week by week, month by month. Now I am graduating medical school and am really happy with my choice.

> —A.F.
> NEW YORK, NEW YORK

• • • • • • • •

I WENT TO GRAD SCHOOL RIGHT AWAY, and it was the best time to do it. You've already got the momentum and the discipline school requires. You have fewer obligations, financial and otherwise, at 22 versus working for 10 years and going back to school at age 32. I know if I had waited, I would have never gone back.

> —JOHN BAKER
> KENNEDY, NEW YORK

THIS IS ONLY A TEST

I'M APPLYING TO LAW SCHOOL. Getting ready for the LSAT is like preparing for a big final. For people like me, who have been out of school for a couple of years, there's a certain amount of mental rust to shake off before tackling a test like that. The nice part is that there are no other classes or exams to study for when you're in that situation, so the preparation is a little less frantic. It's best to sign up well in advance and give yourself a few months to get ready.

—*JESSE AMMERMAN*
CHICAGO, ILLINOIS

I WENT TO LAW SCHOOL AFTER TAKING a few years off. I found myself a little out of touch with many of the students who had gone straight from their undergrad to law school. In hindsight, however, it was an excellent decision because my previous work experience combined with my legal education made me very marketable in the competitive field of entertainment law.

—*ANONYMOUS*
TORONTO, ONTARIO, CANADA

• • • • • • • •

TAKE GRADUATE CLASSES ONLINE. I never had to set foot on a campus or deal with parking nightmares. Plus (and this is a little-known fact), for most online master's programs, you don't have to do a thesis.

—*S.A.*
LAKE FOREST, CALIFORNIA

THE RIGHT STUFF ...

You've heard grad school is tough. But applying to grad school, and getting in, can be an arduous process in itself. It has been known to take potential students well over a year to complete.

Here are the basic things you'll need to do just to get in:

Study for, and do well on, the relevant standardized entrance exam (GRE, LSAT, GMAT, etc.). Look at the test schedules. The tests are offered only a few times a year. And don't put off studying – scores weigh heavily in your application.

Decide where to apply. There are thousands of grad school programs with hundreds of specializations. Where do you want to devote your studies?

Get Letters of Recommendation. Got a favorite professor or an impressive family friend who will say nice things about you? Get it in writing.

Write application essays. Make your essays sing. You're not in college anymore.

Send in applications. Each school has its own application deadlines and instructions. Make sure you get them right!

Interview. Some schools want to meet you in person before offering you a place in their institution.

Paying for it. Assuming you're not getting a full ride, what will you do to make ends meet? Where will you live? Can you handle this lifestyle for an extended period?

Decide on your school. Assuming you're accepted, where do you want to go? Factoring in financial numbers and program specifics, which school is offering the best overall opportunity?

—The Editors

GRAD SCHOOL: THREE REASONS

1. I felt like I was so much younger than everyone else in the office that I didn't get much respect.
2. Immediately after graduating from college, I realized how much of a haven school really is. I went to a small college, and I decided I wanted to see what the whole big-school-college-town thing was like.
3. Perhaps the biggest reason: I was a year removed from college, and I already felt like I was in *Office Space*. I was ready to beat a printer with a baseball bat to the tune of "Damn It Feels Good to Be a Gangsta." In sum, I decided to go to grad school out of a selfish interest in refusing to grow up and out of a search for inspiration.

　　—SIMON
　　　GAINESVILLE, FLORIDA

IF YOU ARE GOING INTO A PH.D. PROGRAM, be sure to do your research on the programs you apply to. Know which faculty you want to work with, program requirements, and funding opportunities. You are committing at least the next five years of your life to this program, so make sure you find a good fit. Once you get there, just remember that the first year is the hardest. And it isn't possible to read everything they tell you to read. The faculty knows this. Read the things that interest you personally first, and just get through as much as you can. Save a little time to have a life, or you will get burned out in no time.

　　—LESLEY
　　　ATLANTA, GEORGIA

IN THE SAME BOAT

WHEN YOU'RE IN GRAD SCHOOL and you see your friends from high school and undergraduate studies who are getting married, having children, and working, it is at first difficult to relate to them since they seem to be achieving more than you. However, after you settle into the rhythm of going to school again, and you make new friends who are at the same phase of their lives as you are, it becomes easier for you to get adjusted. It's also nice to have friends who are pursuing higher degrees because usually you all will have a lot in common.

> —*JULIA*
> *NEW YORK, NEW YORK*

TAKE SOME TIME OFF after completing your undergraduate degree. During that time, try working a few different jobs in areas that you are interested in. Also, take a few classes in the field you are thinking of entering. This will give you a better sense of the field you think you want to specialize in. It is very likely that you will be able to determine if you actually will benefit from an advanced degree if you begin with these steps.

> —*DAN WILLIG*
> *QUEENS, NEW YORK*

• • • • • • • • •

GRAD SCHOOL IS A GREAT TIME to really assert yourself in a professional way in your intended career field. For example, I studied to be a classically trained singer, and in grad school I began to get myself solo singing opportunities in area churches, museums, and concert halls, which allowed me to really start to make a name for myself.

> —*JULIA*
> *NEW YORK, NEW YORK*

IF YOU ARE GOING TO GO TO COLLEGE for four years, you might as well go the distance and go for one more. The additional work and money are more than made up for by the increase in earnings that a master's degree will get you. I'm a teacher, and in our union the salary increase for those with a master's degree compared to those with a bachelor's degree averages about $10,000 a year. In some fields it can be even more lucrative.

—*PERRY O'MALLEY*
HARRISONBURG, VIRGINIA

Consider

• • • • • • • •

IF YOU GO TO A LARGE UNIVERSITY for your undergraduate degree, do the opposite for your grad work and go to a small college. Or vice versa. You will be exposed to different ways of thinking on the same subjects.

—*LONNIE PRETNOS*
CAMPBELL, OHIO

EMBRACE THE OPPORTUNITY

I never quite understand those folks who get bored with their dissertations or drag themselves through awful paper topics every semester. If you find yourself complaining about your work when you are in graduate school, you only have yourself to blame for not asking intriguing questions. If you ask good questions, you will love what you do. But you have to have the guts to ask really important questions, things you really care about (touchy subjects like religion or politics, or things like love or beauty or violence or oppression or truth), and then you will want to work every day.

—*BRENNAN*
ATLANTA, GEORGIA

FRINGE BENEFITS

ONE OF THE BIGGEST BENEFITS to graduate school: taking advantage of student resources. I would regularly visit the career center to ask for guidance on my résumé. I interned for a different company every semester. Ultimately, this led to a job after graduation and helped me to build a professional network.

—*DAN WILLIG*
QUEENS, NEW YORK

• • • • • • • •

THE BIGGEST BENEFIT OF grad school is that you get longer holidays and summers off!

—*ERICA*
WASHINGTON, D.C.

IF YOU GO BACK TO SCHOOL after a period of "real life," you'll find that your point of view has changed. You'll be more demanding of the courses, the professors, and of yourself. You'll want to really get something of value for your time and effort, not to mention your money.

—*N.*
BROOKLYN, NEW YORK

• • • • • • • •

I WAS STARTING TO FEEL a bit stuck and bored with the type of work that I was doing as a graphic designer. I really wanted to advance my skills and knowledge of the industry and felt that going to grad school was the best way for me to do that. Take some time to work in the real world before making the decision to go to grad school. It's a huge commitment and is significantly more intense than college.

—*KATIE*
ATLANTA, GEORGIA

Food for Thought: Cooking Basics

A *mong the many things you learned in college: how to make*
macaroni and cheese, which late-night pizza establishments
offered the best deals, and the benefits of a college meal plan. But
now you're an adult, and part of being a grown-up is steadily
improving your kitchen skills. You don't need to become an Iron
Chef who can whip up a gourmet étouffée out of beans. But you
are going to be eating for the rest of your life, and you might as well
start eating healthy and even learn to impress friends with a dish
or two. Read on for starter culinary advice.

I LEARNED HOW TO COOK BECAUSE of Darwin; if I
didn't learn how to use the George Foreman, I
was going to starve. After that, just experiment.

—*RYAN*
PHILADELPHIA, PENNSYLVANIA

**LEARN HOW TO
COOK! AT LEAST
THE BASIC THINGS.
IT WILL SAVE
YOU MONEY.**

—*BARAK*
TEL AVIV, ISRAEL

HEADLINES
Best Advice and Top Tips

- Prepare your kitchen with the basic equipment needed for cooking.
- Cook with friends. It's a great social outlet and you can learn from each other.
- Build your recipe book slowly.
- Don't be afraid of casseroles.

SINCE I INITIALLY HAD NO IDEA how to cook, I have always suggested to my lady friend that we cook dinner at her place. I allow her to choose the recipe and I offer to go to the grocery store to pick up the ingredients. This way, you get to know your date better while you both learn to cook at the same time. Add in some wine while cooking and you got your self a bonafide date that's teaching you to cook.

—*SANDERS MCCOWN*
ATLANTA, GEORGIA

YOUR MEALS HAVE TO ACCOMMODATE the pace of your life. I ate a lot of Ramen noodles in college, as well as spaghetti and frozen dinners—anything that I could make quick. Now I try to use fresh vegetables and eat healthy. But because of work and school I still like to have something quick to make. So I make a big batch of food on Sunday. I refrigerate it, and that is what I eat throughout the week.

—*VERONICA*
SPRINGFIELD, MISSOURI

THE FIRST TIME I EVER BAKED A CHICKEN, I didn't see the little paper piece in the bottom of the package so that went into the oven with the bird and set off the smoke alarm. Buy *"The Joy of Cooking"* because it gives you all the basics. Watch plenty of cooking shows, too. Even if you don't know what they're talking about, or if you don't like the recipes, you can still learn techniques. It's one thing to read in a book "sauté the onions" and it's another to see it being done properly.

—*LAUREN*
ATLANTA, GEORGIA

• • • • • • • •

IF YOU ARE NEW TO COOKING, start with simple recipes. I really enjoy using a Crock-Pot. They are not expensive and there are many recipes out there that are really good and easy to make. I have a busy schedule so it is nice to put every-thing together the night before and then start it when I leave for work. When I get home every-thing is ready for me to eat and I have leftovers.

—*RACHEL WIECK CUPIT*
NEW ORLEANS, LOUISIANA

• • • • • • • •

There is NO shame in five nights of Boca Burgers and Bobili Pizzas!

—*SHIRA PINSKER*
WASHINGTON, D.C.

I'M STILL LEARNING HOW TO COOK, and it helps if you have friends that will cook with you. I started a cooking group with friends and we try to do something every month or two. One person hosts and decides the theme, and everyone brings a dish and the recipe. We've had letter or color themes (for Valentine's Day in February, everyone made a dish with something red or pink in it), eth-nic themes (Mexican, Italian, etc.), and it's so fun!

—*JAIME SCHULTZ*
WASHINGTON, D.C.

YOUR FIRST KITCHEN

*W**hether you hate to cook, love to cook, or are somewhere in between, you do need to eat. If you eat take-out food all the time you'll go broke. If you eat ramen noodles all the time, you'll die of malnutrition. You'll just have to use that kitchen.*

It doesn't have to be your parents' well-equipped, haute-cuisine establishment. The fact is, you don't need a lot of fancy (expensive) equipment to turn out delicious, nutritious meals. Here's a list of the basics you'll need in order to cook for yourself.

TIP: You can find many of these items at tag sales and Salvation Army stores. Cast iron is easily refurbished, takes light maintenance, but lasts forever and is well worth it.

EQUIPMENT

- ❏ 1.5 or 2-quart saucepan
- ❏ 6-quart saucepan
- ❏ 10- or 12-quart soup or stock pot, each with a lid to fit
- ❏ 10" Cast-iron skillet
- ❏ 6" Cast-iron skillet
- ❏ 6" Chef's knife
- ❏ A paring knife
- ❏ A cleaver
- ❏ A few long-handled wooden spoons
- ❏ Long-handled slotted spoon
- ❏ Long-handled ladle (8 oz.)
- ❏ Spatula
- ❏ 1-Quart Pyrex measuring cup
- ❏ Set of dry measuring cups
- ❏ Set of measuring spoons
- ❏ Colander
- ❏ Mesh strainer
- ❏ Can opener/bottle-cap opener/cork remover
- ❏ Vegetable scraper
- ❏ Pyrex baking dish, preferably square or rectangular, 4-quart capacity

❏ 1 or 2 baking sheets

❏ Metal roasting pan

❏ Potholders and/or oven mitts

APPLIANCES

❏ A really good blender ("good" means a heavy-duty motor and a glass container. Put this on your Christmas wish list.)

❏ A toaster-oven (instead of a toaster)

UPGRADE

❏ Hand-held mixer

❏ Small food-processor/ chopper

❏ Non-stick cookware (requires plastic implements instead of metal)

❏ Microwave oven

❏ Omelet pan

PANTRY

❏ Salt

❏ White vinegar

❏ Cornstarch

❏ All-purpose flour

❏ Canned chopped tomatoes

❏ Canned chicken broth

SPICES

❏ Whole peppercorns and pepper grinder

❏ Small quantities of dried:

  ❏ Oregano

  ❏ Thyme

  ❏ Basil

  ❏ Cinnamon (ground)

  ❏ Parsley

  ❏ Chicken bouillon, cubes or powder

BY THE TIME I GRADUATED COLLEGE, I had three "quality" meals in my recipe box: taco salad, chicken stir-fry and, being from St. Louis, I could grill some of the best pork steaks. During the week, I lived on cold cuts, macaroni and cheese, and chips and salsa. But during the weekends, especially when people would come over, I would break out one of my special meals. One of my favorite memories was cooking on a little five-gallon drum a neighbor of mine had turned into a grill. I could only grill one pork steak at a time, and it took forever, but it was fun. After a while, I learned to experiment with cooking. And now, six years later, my recipe box has about six "quality" meals in it—one for nearly every day of the week.

—*E.E.*
St. Louis, Missouri

• • • • • • • •

"Every time I go home, I try and learn one new recipe from my mother—one at a time is about all I can handle."

—*Jennifer*
Alabama

• • • • • • • •

I LIKE TO USE THE CROCK-POT AND MAKE A MEAL that will last for days, so I don't have to cook every night. Also, I have found that meals.com has some good recipes. My favorite source of recipes is to ask my friends because I know they will be good.

—*Carri Jobe*
San Antonio, Texas

FANCY COOKBOOKS ARE NOT ALWAYS THE BEST.
The best ones we have purchased are these cheap
Idiot guides to cooking. We picked up three not
too long ago: one for slow-cookers, one for low-
carb meals and one for five-minute appetizers.

—MATT
LITTLE ROCK, ARKANSAS

* * * * * * * *

TRY TO EAT FRESH AND COOK FRESH. On the
Internet you can find cooking recipes that are
under 30 minutes. My favorite chef is Rachael
Ray. There is lots of flavor in all of her meals.
Enjoy creating and trying new things. Cooking
is a lot of fun, especially when you share your
cooking with friends.

—BRANDI DICOSTANZO
DALLAS, TEXAS

* * * * * * * *

CASSEROLES, CASSEROLES, CASSEROLES! They are
easy, tasty, and make for great leftovers.
Also, invest in those big bags of frozen, skinless
chicken breasts; you can make anything with
those. Bake them in the oven for 30 minutes or
grill them. Cut them up for salads or just serve
them with some vegetables. They are healthy
and easy.

—ASHLEY
DALLAS, TEXAS

PUTTING THE F-A-T IN FAST FOOD

A Big Mac has 485 calories and 21.5 grams of fat. A single slice of
Domino's pepperoni pizza has 324 calories and 12.65 grams of fat.

7 MEALS AS QUICK (AND NEARLY AS CHEAP) AS MAC 'N CHEESE

Sunday: Angel Hair Pasta with Shrimp and Spinach: Cook 1 package of angel hair pasta according to the directions on the box. While the pasta cooks, sauté 1-1 1/2 pounds peeled, de-veined, and frozen large shrimp in 3 tablespoons of olive oil for 4 minutes on medium-high heat. Remove shrimp from pan and add 1/2 cup chicken broth and 2 tablespoons lemon juice. Add drained pasta, shrimp, and 6 cups chopped spinach. Heat until spinach wilts. If shrimp and spinach are not your cup of tea, try cherry tomatoes, goat cheese, and fresh basil instead.

Monday: Cream of Broccoli Soup: Heat 1 chopped medium onion and 4 cloves of garlic in 1/4 cup of water or chicken or vegetable stock. When the onion is tender, add 4 1/2 cups chicken or vegetable stock and 1 1/2 pounds broccoli. Bring to a boil and then simmer on low heat for 10 minutes. Pour contents into a blender and puréed. An immersion blender works even better! Return puréed broccoli to the range and add 1/4 to 1/2 cup of milk and salt and pepper to taste. Mix well and serve in bowls.

Tuesday: English Muffin Pizzas: Slather each half of an English muffin with jarred tomato sauce and sprinkle with grated mozzarella. Add your favorite toppings and toast in a toaster oven or regular oven for a few minutes.

Wednesday: Gazpacho: Toss 4 cored tomatoes, 1 peeled cucumber, 1 red bell pepper with the stem and seeds removed, and 1 or more tablespoons of vinegar to taste into a blender. Pureed until smooth. Serve in bowls with a teaspoon of oil drizzled on top. Great with crusty bread!

Thursday: Burritos: Sauté mushrooms and red peppers. Meanwhile, spread warm refried beans on a flour tortilla. Add mushrooms and red peppers. Cover in chopped lettuce, tomatoes, salsa, and a bit of sour cream. You can also add corn or grated cheddar cheese. Fold in the bottom of the tortilla and roll up the sides.

Friday: French Onion Soup: Sauté 2 medium onions sliced thin and 4 tablespoons dry sherry or red wine for 5 minutes, or until onions are tender. Add 4 cups beef broth and 1 teaspoon Worcestershire sauce. Bring to a boil and then simmer on low heat for 10 minutes. Serve in a bowl with a slice of toasted French bread and grated parmesan cheese on top.

Saturday: Mac 'N Tom: This is even easier than Mac 'N Cheese! Cook pasta according to the directions on box. Drain and return pasta to pan. Pour in jarred tomato sauce. Sprinkle with grated cheese.

—Sarah Franco

PLAN OUT ALL OF YOUR MEALS at the start of each month. I actually write them on a calendar and post them on the refrigerator. My sister teases me about being so anal, but it's really helpful.

—LISA
NIXA, MISSOURI

. . . .

ALWAYS, ALWAYS ASK sales assistants at fine grocery stores about what would pair well with what. They are trained to answer these kinds of questions. Some of my best and favorite dishes came from those simple interactions. So don't be afraid to ask a butcher for suggestions on how to cook a specific kind of meat that you want, for how long, what spices to put in, and suggestions for vegetables to pair with it.

—AMBREEN HUSSAIN
NEW YORK, NEW YORK

THE BEST ADVICE FOR COOKING IS SIMPLE: Just do it. And by that I mean, pick out a recipe for something deliciously enticing, and as long as you have all the tools you need to make it, putting it together is just a matter of following directions. So many people don't cook because they claim they don't have the skills or time, but there are so many easy and quick meals out there. Getting ingredients is simple, fun, and you can always ask employees at grocery stores for help getting those difficult-to-find items. Another great thing to do is to gather recipes from family members or friends for dishes of theirs that you love. I started with a binder full of my mom's recipes and it's provided a great foundation for my recipe collection and cooking skills.

> —*KATIE*
> *NEW YORK, NEW YORK*

• • • • • • • •

Until you understand how to cook, watch the *Food Network* for ideas.

—*BRANDI DICOSTANZO DALLAS, TEXAS*

ONE OF THE MOST IMPORTANT things about learning to cook is having the right equipment. You don't need anything fancy, but you do need a sharp knife, a nice big pasta pot, a deep sauté pan, a rugged cutting board, and your regular miscellaneous tools that come in handy. Keep a well-stocked pantry. Read menus. Examine how chefs pair ingredients and which flavors complement each other. Be a couch potato for a day and watch *Food Network*. The most important thing is to experiment. Don't be afraid to pair new ingredients and try it out. After a while, you'll know which flavors work well together and which don't. It's a learning process, and once you overcome it, you'll be able to whip up any dish in no time without sweat or fret over the outcome.

> —*ERIN MCCORMICK*
> *MIDDLEBURY, VERMONT*

Red Alert: Cars, Credit Cards & Other Money Matters

F*ew experiences say "real world" like balancing your checkbook. Now that you're paying your own bills, it can be disheartening to see how quickly the cash disappears. There are those student loans to pay off, cool clothes to buy, and rent to pay. And wouldn't it be great to dump that old junker for some new wheels? Can you afford to do all this and still have money for Friday nights with friends? Before you head down the road to Chapter 11 (that's bankruptcy, not a previous section of this book), cash in on this chapter for financial advice you can't afford to pass up, - including a special section from the American Institute for Economic Research!*

I'VE HAD MORE FUN and more luck when I haven't planned for things. Except in financial matters. It's too stressful not to have a plan with your money.

—*MICHAEL ALBERT PAOLI
TORONTO, ONTARIO, CANADA*

BUY THE CHEAP BRAND OF EVERYTHING.

—*WENDY
ALLENTOWN,
PENNSYLVANIA*

HEAD LINES
Best Advice and Top Tips

- When buying a car, get pre-approved for financing from your bank — you'll get a better interest rate than if you finance through the dealer.
- Set a monthly budget—and stick to it.
- Pay more than the minimum on your credit cards.
- Try to use credit cards only for emergencies.
- Keep enough money in your savings account to cover at least one month's expenses.

PAY OFF YOUR STUDENT DEBT and any loans that have higher interest rates, as soon as possible. I recently inherited money from my family and wrote a check for $20,000 toward my student loan debt. It felt really good and really odd to write a check for that amount!

—*RANAI*
SAN FRANCISCO, CALIFORNIA

SINCE I DON'T HAVE AN ACTUAL RETIREMENT account, and since Social Security may not exist in 40 years, my current approach to retirement planning is a little thing I call the state lotto.

—*JESSE AMMERMAN*
CHICAGO, ILLINOIS

BUYING THOSE BOOTS BEFORE YOUR TRIP to New York City is *not* an emergency!

—*MICHELE*
HOLLY, MICHIGAN

I GOT A CREDIT CARD that has no annual fee and an awards program. For every dollar I spend, I earn one point. Points can be redeemed for anything: cash, gift certificates, travel. Every time I charge something (and I charge everything I can), I automatically deduct that amount from my check register. That way, when the bill comes, I know I have enough money to pay it in full. Doing this, I've managed to build up enough points in a year to earn a free airline ticket. Plus, I have no debt and an excellent credit rating.

—*SHANNON HURD*
HIGHLANDS RANCH, COLORADO

"If you have to borrow to buy it, you can't afford it!"

—*SHANNON*
LAS VEGAS, NEVADA

I READ SUZE ORMAN'S BOOK *The Money Book for the Young, Fabulous, and Broke* and I found it so helpful. I was so confused by things like 401(k) and IRAs and retirement, and she makes everything clear. While everyone's situation is different, I think it is important to strike a balance between "enjoying yourself" and sticking to a budget. The cliché is "you're only young once," and if you forgo lots of fun activities because of budget, you'll never remember this time of your life! But you don't want to be constantly stressed because of debt hanging over your head.

—*SHIRA PINSKER*
WASHINGTON, D.C.

8 EXTREME WAYS TO CUT YOUR BUDGET IN HALF

1. **Channel Your Inner Julia Child:** Dining out can eat up a lot of your budget. For what one person spends in a restaurant, you could purchase and cook the ingredients to feed about four people. And – contrary to popular belief – cooking is not difficult, especially if you invest in *Joy of Cooking*, which explains everything in detail. (Also, see Chapter 13.)

2. **See You Latte:** I love lattes frothed to perfection as much as the next person, but coffee shop java is an expensive habit to fund. Home-brewed coffee is much cheaper.

3. **Life Unplugged:** It's no secret that Internet service provider fees are steep. If your local library or coffee shop offers free wifi, partake of the bounty!

4. **Go Local:** In the digital age, we've become accustomed to shopping online. Although this method is very convenient, shipping charges can add up quickly. Try human interaction for a change and support your local business owner.

5. **Ditch the Car:** Between monthly loan payments, insurance premiums, and gas, vehicles can be a significant drain on your bank account. Why not try public transportation, biking, or walking instead?

6. **Think Outside the Box:** Television has clearly rotted your brain if you don't know that what you pay for on cable is available for free, or almost free, on the Internet. You can find full episodes of many of your favorite television shows on YouTube, Hulu, or the television station itself, such as Comedy Central or MSNBC. If you can't find it there, you can find it at Netflix for a small fee.

7. **Can You Hear Me Now?:** Welcome to the 21st Century. Get a cell phone and ditch the landline. All the cool kids are doing it.

8. **Consume Less:** Before you make a purchase, ask yourself, "Do I *really* need this?" Be honest. Nine times out of ten, you don't really need it.

—*Sarah Franco*

I HAVE TWO LAST PIECES OF ADVICE. First, being pre-approved for a credit card does not mean you have to apply for it. And lastly, the best career advice I can give you is to get your own TV show. It pays well, the hours are good, and you are famous.

—STEPHEN COLBERT
2006 COMMENCEMENT SPEECH AT KNOX COLLEGE

• • • • • • • •

NO MATTER HOW POOR YOU ARE, you'd better have enough money to buy your mother a birthday present. The first year I lived alone, I was plumb broke and didn't even get her a card. I stupidly thought she'd understand because she knew I was struggling to find work. But she was really hurt by that. I guess I could have borrowed the money. The next year I was working, and I went all out for her birthday. I even had a special cake made for her. But I never forgot the look in her eyes when I showed up empty-handed that first year. Find a way to show Mom how much she means, no matter what.

—TIMOTHY QUIGLEY
INDEPENDENCE, KENTUCKY

NOBODY IS TOO GOOD to go out and flip burgers. When I was trying to start my own business, I did whatever I could to make money. I was determined not to ask my parents for money, even though I know they would have gladly helped. If you want to be an adult, you have to learn to make it on your own.

—*BETSY MILLER*
MARSHFIELD, MISSOURI

. . . .

"When doing your taxes for the first time, do it on paper, not electronically. Use Form 1040EZ or Form 1040A. Those are the easiest tax forms to fill out. They are very user-friendly. I felt very comfortable the next year after getting through that first time. "

—*A.D.*
HARRISONBURG, VIRGINIA

. . . .

I'VE GIVEN UP ONE OF MY FAVORITE HOBBIES, shopping, because I live in New York and have to try to save. Now, if I want to go shopping, I decide to get one thing instead of a million.

—*MARA*
NEW YORK, NEW YORK

TO SAVE YOURSELF SOME CASH, you have to learn to do some stuff on your car. Nothing major. But if you can change your oil and your wiper blades and burnt-out lights and even your brakes, you can really save compared to going to a garage for all that stuff. If you don't know how to do it, experiment. You're smart; you'll figure it out.

—*MELANIE SPLANE*
YOUNGSTOWN, OHIO

• • • • • • • •

GET FINANCED THROUGH YOUR BANK FIRST, so you can walk into the dealership with a check. It's like paying cash, which gives you a lot more negotiating power. Plus, it's cheaper because dealerships try to screw you with their financing.

—*S.A.*
LAKE FOREST, CALIFORNIA

• • • • • • • •

POCKET AT LEAST 12 PAYCHECKS without having to pay rent. I moved out of my parents' house and in with friends before I had a job. At the time I decided that living with a bunch of friends was worth living off of my savings. However, the more months I paid rent without bringing in any sort of salary, the more I regretted my decision. Especially when I looked at my friend who decided to live at home for a year, with a good job, and she was able to take big trips and buy things like a new computer and great clothes with the money she saved. After three months I finally secured a job, but it took me a while to build my savings again.

—*SHIRA*
PHILADELPHIA, PENNSYLVANIA

THE RIGHT FOOT?

The average college graduate owes nearly $20,000 in student loans.

THE BASICS OF BUDGETING

IT IS VERY IMPORTANT to make a budget. By writing down your expenses and your income, it becomes clear how much you have available to spend on entertainment or savings. Once you have created a budget, I would then go through your bank statement and see if your budget is an accurate reflection. You may be surprised to find that you spend more than you think you do on certain items. It is important, once you realize your budget, to stick to it.

—*RACHEL WIECK CUPIT*
NEW ORLEANS, LOUISIANA

• • • • • • • • •

SET A BUDGET AND STICK TO IT. My husband and I budget every month. We put our money into three categories. Fifty percent goes to necessities, 25 percent goes to 'wants', and 25 percent goes to savings. If we exceed the amount set aside for necessities, then it comes out of "wants". The whole goal is to save that 25 percent. It has worked really well. I save every receipt. If we exceed our budget for the month, the next month, we go without.

—*ANONYMOUS*
KIRKSVILLE, MISSOURI

• • • • • • • • •

BUDGET, BUDGET, BUDGET. At the top of the column, write down the amount you bring home AFTER taxes and other deductions from your paycheck. Then subtract everything else. At the top of your list should be rent, food, gasoline, and student loan payments (and car loans, if you have one). Don't forget to set aside some savings - you'll need money for a down payment on a house or car. Also, if you get sick, the medical expenses could crush you. Then you can start thinking about discretionary items such as entertainment and (expensive) clothes. You need a positive number at the bottom of the column - otherwise, you're in trouble. Do NOT depend on your credit cards. The interest will crush you!

—*LAUREN*
ATLANTA, GEORGIA

UNDERSTAND THAT ISSUES like banking and insurance are not black and white. Those organizations have some wiggle room in terms of who they do business with and what kinds of rates they give. With that in mind, it's important to go meet these people in person when signing up to use their services. Don't do it over the phone. When I did that, I made sure that I looked my best. I figured if I walked into the bank where I would be doing my banking for the next several years wearing leather pants, I would not get the same service as if I walked in wearing a nice business suit. First impressions are important. And with car insurance people, keep in mind that as a young adult you are a high risk to them to begin with. So you want to look as mature as possible when you meet them, to alleviate some of those fears.

—*PAM WAXTER*
KEEZLETOWN, VIRGINIA

. . . .

I DON'T THINK I'VE EVER BOUGHT CLOTHES if they weren't on sale, and I rarely use my credit card. I made a conscious decision not to have credit card debt in my life, so I will only purchase something if I know I can pay for it.

—*MARIANA*
SAN FRANCISCO, CALIFORNIA

. . . .

DON'T ASK ME ABOUT FINANCES. I don't balance my checkbook. I thank the banking god for overdraft protection. Your guess is as good as mine when it comes to my checking account balance, but I also believe that you can't take your money with you, so spend it while you can enjoy it.

—*JENNIFER*
ALABAMA

I WENT THROUGH A PHASE of saving like crazy. I felt this strange panic if I didn't have enough money in my savings account to leave the country and go somewhere amazing at the drop of a hat. This is a hard time in your life to deny yourself instant gratification. But man, it can pay off in the long run.

—*F.S.*
CHAPEL HILL, NORTH CAROLINA

CREDIT CARD COMPANIES CAN BE DECEIVING. It's kind of like being stranded at sea. Just when you're about to max out one credit card and miss out on that trip to Vegas, along comes another credit card company to throw you what appears to be a life vest in the form of an application for another credit card. It's not until you apply for your first car loan or home mortgage years later that you realize what they threw you was not a life vest, but an anvil. How do you stay afloat? Tread water. Stop living beyond your means.

—*KENNETH C. RINEY*
DALLAS, TEXAS

ONCE YOU START WORKING AND GETTING a regular paycheck, you have to do at least two things with the money. First, set a certain amount that you will put in a savings account no matter what. Second, set an amount that will be your 'mad money'—money you can spend any way you want without feeling guilty. The key is sticking to the set amounts, no matter what. If your mad money for the week is gone and your friends want to go out, then you have to show some self-control and stay in.

—*SHERRI LAWTON*
HARRISONBURG, VIRGINIA

WITH MY FIRST JOB, I made the mistake of not having enough federal tax withheld from my pay. When it was tax time, I didn't have the money to pay my taxes and had to borrow from my parents. I was so embarrassed. You probably won't be making a fortune with your first job, so be sure to have extra money withheld. If you don't see it, you won't miss it, and it can make things easier for you come April 15.

—*MINDY HILDENBRAND*
HARRISONBURG, VIRGINIA

• • • • • • • •

DON'T EXPECT TO GET THE BEST APARTMENT and car out right of school. Once you're in debt, it's so hard to climb out. If you stay out of debt, you can work your way into something great.

—*BRODIE*
SITKA, ALASKA

• • • • • • • •

I HAVE ALWAYS COOKED MY BREAKFAST, lunch and dinners. I save at least $150 a week from that. One meal to cook is around $3-$5. Buying lunch is no cheaper than $10. Only once a week do I wine and dine.

—*AMBREEN HUSSAIN*
NEW YORK, NEW YORK

• • • • • • • •

AS SOON AS I GOT MY FIRST JOB, I went credit-card crazy. It's so easy to do. Shoes were my weakness. I eventually got in so deep that I had to cut the card up to keep myself from using it. I was like an addict.

—*LEAH GERSON*
ZIRKLE, VIRGINIA

Pay down more than your minimums! I wish I did that more.

—*KALYNA*
SAN FRANCISCO,
CALIFORNIA

HELL ON WHEELS

TO DIVERT MY ATTENTION AWAY from the overall price of the car, my salesperson kept asking me over and over what monthly payment I could afford. He got me so focused on lowering my payment that I didn't even realize I was being suckered into paying $30,000 for a car that's worth about $20,000. Watch out for this tactic!

—*D.S.*
DENVER, COLORADO

. . . .

MOST BANKS WILL REFUSE TO FINANCE you for more money than a new car is actually worth. So, if your bank turns down your loan request even though you have great credit, but the dealer is saying, "Oh, we'll make it work if you finance through us!" this is a huge red flag. This happened to me, but, at the time, I was too naive to know what it meant. I wanted the car so badly that I accepted the dealer's financing offer and ended up paying the sticker price of $16,000. Unfortunately, I found out a couple of weeks later that the car was only worth about $8,000.

—*R.W.*
FORT COLLINS, COLORADO

. . . .

WITH CAR INSURANCE, DON'T GET ANYTHING except liability insurance. Everything else is a scam. I only pay about $200 every six months for car insurance. Think about it: If you look at your lifetime, how many car wrecks do you actually have? The full coverage doesn't pay for itself.

—*RICH*
ANN ARBOR, MICHIGAN

. . . .

WHEN BUYING A CAR, you've got to be willing to walk away, because sometimes that's the only way to get what you want. The dealership was trying to charge me an extra $150 handling fee, and I said forget it and turned to leave. Suddenly, the guy started chasing me down. Guess what? They waived the fee.

—*RANDY FREITIK*
PEORIA, ILLINOIS

WHEN BUYING CAR INSURANCE, SHOP AROUND. You can check quotes on the Internet for just about every company out there. Or you can call them. I just changed my coverage about a year ago, and I'm now paying about $300 less a year than I was for the exact same coverage. That would probably pay for one Saturday night at a strip club.

— *SHEILA MANNING*
KEEZLETOWN, VIRGINIA

• • • • • • • •

I BOUGHT MY MOST RECENT CAR FROM A BROKER. Car brokers do everything for you: You tell them exactly what you want in terms of make, model, year, condition, and price, and they go out and find it. They have access to cars that are going up for auction, and cars whose leases have just expired, so they can find you a really good deal. They will even negotiate the car loan, take care of registration, and deliver your vehicle to you. I know they probably tacked on a fee to the overall price, but I didn't care. The bottom line is I ended up with exactly the car I wanted, did no legwork, and still paid less than I would have if I'd gone to a dealer.

— *SAJIT GREENE*
UTICA, NEW YORK

• • • • • • • •

I WANTED A CAR that reflected professionalism, and I ended up leasing. You can get into leasing with a lower monthly payment than purchasing. You don't have to worry about repairs or depreciation. You just pay your monthly bills, and at the end of the lease period, you go get a new car. Since I've been out of school, that's worked the best for me.

— *CHRISTOPHER*
HAVERTOWN, PENNSYLVANIA

REMEMBER THE ACRONYM EMILY: Early Money Is Like Yeast. It grows and grows. The money you put away in your twenties will be a huge pot of gold for your future. For many people, an automatic savings plan that deducts from their paycheck is the least painful option. Think of it as one CD and two grande cappucinos a week. You can do it!

—N.
BROOKLYN, NEW YORK

> "Set aside time to do your finances every week. Go to a café. Order your favorite drink. Take 45 minutes to make sure you've got everything in order. You will sleep better at night and have more fun when you go out."

—J.A.
ATLANTA, GEORGIA

USE CREDIT CARDS FOR EMERGENCY ONLY, and stick to that. Don't shop for everyday items with them; it only gets you into more debt and more trouble. Your credit rating is *very* important, even if it doesn't seem so important when you're young. It can haunt you for a long time after you screw up!

—BECKIE
SEATTLE, WASHINGTON

BUYING A USED CAR

It's common knowledge that as soon as you drive a new car off the lot, you lose 15 to 30 percent of what you paid for it. As someone who is just getting started in your financial life, this is a good enough reason to buy something used. You'll pay less, get a better "drive off the lot" deal, and feel better about yourself.

That said, watch out for car salesmen trying to unload a junker. Here are some tips to follow so that you'll wind up with the best car for your money:

❑ Once you find a car you like, have an independent mechanic inspect it. This usually costs around $100, and it could save you thousands in future repairs if he spots something wrong with the car.

❑ Have the dealer show you the car's inspection history. If they won't show it to you—or say they don't have it—consider that a red flag.

❑ Write down the car's Vehicle Identification Number, or VIN, and run it through a national database such as CARFAX. You'll get the car's full history, including odometer readings, accidents, and sales.

❑ Read the warranty and make sure you understand what is covered and what is not.

❑ Bottom line: never buy a car without sleeping on the final offer first. No matter what a salesman tells you, you can always come back tomorrow.

—The Editors

INSURE? YOU SURE?

HEALTH INSURANCE IS A LARGE PART OF WHY I avoid the doctor. I've found that health insurance companies truly exist to not help you. I've been more or less cheated by nearly every health insurance company I've been affiliated with.

—I.B.
INDIANAPOLIS, INDIANA

• • • • • • • •

DON'T BEAT YOURSELF UP ABOUT NOT HAVING HEALTH INSURANCE. If I could afford it, I would, but I'm a musician. I'm not going to give up what I love for a job with benefits. Instead, I eat really well. I'm a vegetarian, I eat organic produce, I work out, and I laugh a lot. I think that helps a person not get sick.

—KAMI
CAPE COD, MASSACHUSETTS

• • • • • • • •

IF YOU HAVE ACCEPTED A JOB that has health, dental, and vision insurance, use it. There is a reason it is called a "benefit." I look at it as money that is available for me to use if I choose to use it. I get $125 every two years to put toward contacts or glasses; I'm an idiot if I don't take advantage of that. Also, don't get off a schedule of going to the doctor or dentist, because, much like a gym, it becomes easier never to go back. I skipped two years of visits to the dentist, and it is going to cost me more in the end, with more drastic procedures and pain.

—JAMES RINEY
FORT WORTH, TEXAS

INSTEAD OF GOING ON A TRIP, I took the money I received for graduation and paid off my credit card. They warned us in college about the pitfalls of credit-card debt. I decided that I didn't want to start out with that hanging over my head. I had one credit card, and I cut it up after I paid it off. That was a good day.

—*SUZI MACK*
BENTON, MISSOURI

• • • • • • • •

WHEN THE STATE SAYS they want their student loan money paid back by a certain time, they mean it. Don't figure that you'll be able to skate around that or extend that loan forever. They will get serious on you. I had a hard time finding a good job after college, so I had a hard time paying the loan back. They gave me an extension, but when I fell behind again, they took my entire tax return check one year to get their money. It still wasn't enough. I made payments to pay it off. Those guys play hardball.

—*JASON HAMES*
DRY RIDGE, KENTUCKY

• • • • • • • •

IT PAYS TO PAY OFF DEBT, especially when you make just enough to get by. What is starting to help me pay it down is switching credit card companies. Look in the mail for credit card offers that give you zero percent interest for 12 to 16 months. I asked a financial adviser about this, and he said that as long as you have an OK credit score, this won't hurt you to do every year or so. Just keep shopping for the zero percent interest until you can pay it off.

—*JERALYN*
AUSTIN, TEXAS

OPENING A BANK ACCOUNT

These days, you can easily open a checking or savings account by walking into any bank with proof of address, age, and personal identification. You can also sign up over the phone or through online banking sites. But you want to make sure you're signing up for a bank that's right for you. Here are a few standard questions to consider when you open an account:

❑ What is the monthly fee for the account, if any?

❑ Is the account FDIC-insured? (Make sure they answer "yes" to this; it means you'll get your money back if the bank goes bust.)

❑ What is the fee for using an ATM machine that belongs to another bank?

❑ Do I have to keep a minimum balance? And what sorts of fees apply if I go below the minimum?

❑ Is there a limit to the number of transactions I can make in a month? What sorts of fees apply if I go over that limit?

❑ What rate of interest do I get on my savings account?

—The Editors

A LOT OF FINANCIAL BOOKS will tell you that you need six months' worth of salary in the bank as a cushion in case you lose your job. Who can have that kind of money in the bank when they're just out of college? As a recent grad, you need to just concentrate on paying off any debt. If there's anything left over after your bills, put that in savings. But don't kick yourself if you're not financially stable by the time you're 25.

—MICHELE
HOLLY, MICHIGAN

START CONTRIBUTING TO YOUR 401(K). I wish I had done that sooner. I know I still have plenty of time before retirement, but I kept thinking it would lower my paycheck. Then I sat down and did the math. I realized that since the money comes out before taxes, my check was actually only $2 less each time. That's a very small sacrifice to make to know I'm building something for my future. Basically, I see a 401(k) as sort of free money, where your employer is willing to match it. It's one of the best and easiest things to take advantage of.

—*RANDALL S. WRAY*
MUNCIE, INDIANA

> My financial planner says, save 10 percent of every paycheck ... and you will never have to worry about the future!
>
> —*NADIA*

* * * * * * * *

YOU SHOULD ALWAYS KEEP ENOUGH money in your savings account to last you at least a month. You never know when you will find yourself out of work. I ended up quitting my first job after about a year when my boss asked me to do something that I thought was unethical. I was unsure for a while if I was going to be able to collect unemployment or not. Luckily I had a nest egg tucked away to sustain me. Otherwise I would have had to move back in with my parents.

—*BILL STUDENA*
FLORENCE, KENTUCKY

* * * * * * * *

IT STINKS NOT BEING ABLE TO GO OUT and buy everything I want, but I am determined to stick to a budget. My weakness is eating out. Now, I make myself go home and find something in the refrigerator to eat. I save up for special occasions to eat out with friends. It's paying off, because I'm finally starting to build my savings account.

—*TAWNY WHITE*
SPRINGFIELD, MISSOURI

10 MOST EXPENSIVE U.S. CITIES

1. New York, NY
2. Boston, MA
3. Juneau, AK
4. Anchorage, AK
5. San Diego, CA
6. Philadelphia, PA
7. Los Angeles, CA
8. Fairbanks, AK
9. Ann Arbor, MI
10. Seattle, WA

BE SMART. Don't party five days a week because you will go into debt quickly and your work life will suffer. If you are going to a club, "pre-game" before, knowing they overcharge. And don't go binge shopping; rather, shop when you have to. This way, you'll have enough cash to play adult kickball and get hammered on Pabsts in the process. Two birds, one stone.

—*RYAN*
PHILADELPHIA, PENNSYLVANIA

• • • • • • • •

OVERDRAFTING IS AWFUL, so I recommend balancing your checkbook/debit card. Don't rely just on online banking statements or checking your account online. A lot of times things don't post in time and this can get you in trouble – i.e., overdrafting. Keep a running balance in a book yourself.

—*KELLI*
ATLANTA, GEORGIA

• Special Section •

Money Matters 101: Practical Post-Graduate Financial Advice

by R.D. Norton, Ph.D.

Excerpted from the book,
Start Here: Getting Your Financial Life on Track
Published by the American Institute for Economic Research

Table of Contents

I. HOW TO PAY YOUR BILLS ON TIME

Being fiscally responsible is a hallmark of being an adult. Paying your bills, and paying them on time, keeps you a customer in good standing, keeps you from incurring late fees that can dig a deeper hole for you, and keeps the electricity on.

Good intentions alone won't keep you in the black instead of the red. You must live within your means to avoid incurring a lot of debt. But you also must be *organized*.

Simple Steps to Bill Paying

The first trick to paying your monthly bills on time is to put them all in one place, by themselves, where you can find them. The second trick is getting into a set pattern of paying.

Step 1. When a bill arrives in the mail, put it in the designated place. Some people find that a shoebox works. Others prefer the 31-day cardboard trays that let you arrange bills by the date they are due. Whatever works for you is fine. Even a plastic bag will do.

Step 2. Get in a rhythm. Should you pay bills together, once a month? Or are you more comfortable paying a solitary bill as soon as it shows up in the mail? Or is there a happy medium, such as paying them once a week, on Saturday mornings, say? None of these tactics is right or wrong. The only requirement is that you keep track of when payments are due so that you can avoid late fees and other inconveniences.

Step 3. Consider paying on line—either by regular practice, or as a backup. If you somehow overlook a bill (or have been away traveling or simply slammed by an overloaded schedule), it helps to be able to go on line and make a payment that day, through a transfer from your checking account or on a credit card.

Step 4. Consider setting up automatic payments. Some people prefer to "automate" their monthly payments to the max by using either on-line or regularly scheduled electronic funds transfers from their bank accounts.

The benefits of this four-step drill are huge. For one, it makes you a responsible, organized bill-payer who never falls behind. For another, making payments on time, you build up your credit record. In addition, paying your bills in this orderly fashion gives you a reality check on your monthly payments—and whether you are spending more than your income.

How Much Is in Your Checking Account?

It used to be easier to balance a checkbook. All you had to do was write down every deposit made and every check you wrote. True, you also had to keep track of your ATM withdrawals. But that just meant holding on to the ATM receipt and entering it into your checkbook as a reduction in your bank balance.

All that was before people started using debit cards to write "instant checks" for payments large and small, right down to drugstore or newsstand purchases of a dollar or two.

The problem is that three different kinds of actions may overwhelm your fragile checking account. The checks you write, the ATM withdrawals you make, and the debit-card transactions all reduce the checking account balance. The simple—and crucial—solution is to *write down every transaction.* Keep the receipts not only for ATM withdrawals but also for all the debit-card payments you are racking up. Then set a time every day, perhaps in the evening when you're home and going through your wallet, to enter the deductions in your checkbook.

II. PAPERWORK YOU MUST KEEP— AND PAPERWORK YOU CAN TOSS

Your monthly bills aren't the only paperwork you have to keep track of. Some documents you need to keep on file in a safe place because they are vital records for you. But the good news is that much of the paperwork you have to manage can be tossed almost immediately. Now, some people are very organized, and can probably find gainful employment as clerks, if that's their desire. They are good at keeping records and putting documents in a place where they can be readily retrieved. But most people are not, either because they're not organized by nature, or they just
don't feel it's worth the trouble.

Let's say you're in the latter group, not really excited about neatly filing away receipts and credit-card bills. In that case, what is the bare minimum of pieces of paper (or computer records) you need to hold on to?

Here are five categories of paperwork—from stuff you can toss almost right away, to material you need to keep filed permanently for your own protection:

1. **Disposables.** These are items you can typically throw away without regret: routine bills that have been paid, including utility and phone bills and food receipts such as from groceries and restaurant meals.
2. **For tax purposes.** Hardcopy bank statements, in case of a tax audit, plus the previous seven years of tax returns. Meaning: If a return is more than seven years old, you can throw it away.

3. **"Semi-permanent papers."** Insurance policies in general: what you are paying and what they say they will provide, should it come to that. Loan agreements—the terms of how you are to repay a loan, and what will happen, say, if you repay the loan early. Warranties for products, so that if a gadget (or a car) goes wrong, you will have the piece of paper that says it has to be paid for by the seller.

4. **"Forever papers."** These include a birth certificate, college transcripts, diplomas, marriage certificates, a current passport, a Social Security card.

5. **For homeowners (and renters).** A home inventory of assets (preferably backed up by video) is essential, so that in case of fire, flood or other disaster, your home-insurance policy claims can be substantiated.

Speaking of fires, floods, and disasters, where should your records and documents be stored? Whatever is worth keeping is worth protecting, perhaps in a fireproof safe at home. Copies of legal or financial documents and agreements can be left with a lawyer or in a safe-deposit box in a bank, as backup.

III. TEMPTATIONS: CREDIT CARDS, DEBIT CARDS, ATMS

Your friends are planning a spring trip to the Bahamas, and you're dying to go, but your funds are short. It's all you can do to scrape by each month.

But there is a way you could swing the airfare and lodging: by whipping out the plastic. Even though you're paying off a hefty balance on your credit card already, you still have enough left on the limit before maxing out. Some of your friends tell you they're using their cards themselves. You're sorely tempted; you tell yourself you'll whittle away at the bill after you get back, and it will all be worth it. Who wants to stay behind in your same old town when everyone else is off partying in some exotic locale?

Credit cards are a necessary evil. On the one hand, they encourage shortsighted behavior and overspending. On the other, they are all but indispensable for such basic transactions as renting a car. What's more, when using credit cards for transactions, laws are in place to protect you from credit-card errors and even fraud. If you buy something with a credit card and it turns out to be defective, you probably have a better chance of getting your money back than if you had paid in cash.

This chapter looks at decisions as to when to use a credit card. We discuss some of the safeguards for credit cards and compare them to the less secure alternative of debit cards. We also alert you to common "gotcha" tactics banks frequently use to hit ATM and debit-card users with stiff overdraft fees.

The Road to Ruin?

Credit cards pose two special temptations. One is the cards' easy availability to college students. The other is the low minimum monthly payment requirement.

Ironically, college students with little income often have a simpler time getting a credit card than many other individuals seeking credit for the first time. Card companies court students, regarding them as potentially high-earning, long-term customers with good repayment records—especially since parents are likely to pay the bills if their children don't.

According to a recent study by the Sallie Mae Foundation, 84 percent of college students have a credit card, compared to 67 percent in 1998. These students carried an average of $3,173 in debt, excluding student loans.

In some unfortunate (and by no means rare) cases, such lingering debts may cause the first step toward a debt cycle that can overpower recent college graduates. In this scenario, those who are financially strapped sometimes obtain cash advances on one credit card just to make payments on other card accounts.

This situation often involves a sad downward spiral for the cardholder. The borrower ends up devoting a significant portion of after-tax income to paying credit-card interest and other charges—income, in other words, that cannot be spent on regular living expenses, much less put away in savings.

What this ultimately means is that, in exchange for what turns out to be a relatively brief acceleration of consumption, the debtor has a permanently lowered standard of living.

Perhaps the greatest risk of credit—and one that all too many credit-card holders in our society have showed they are willing to assume—is the mass of debt that builds quickly with slow repayment. Making just the minimum payment each month on a credit-card balance will stick you on an endless and frustrating financial treadmill. If you were only to pay the 2 percent minimum payment on a $5,000 balance on a card with an APR (annual percentage rate) of 11 percent, it would take more than 23 years (and $3,979 in interest payments!) to pay it off. In contrast, if you were to increase the monthly payment to $250, the balance would be paid off in 23 months at an interest cost of $549.

College Debt

Then there are the student loans—the dead elephant in the living room. This is one of the biggest obstacles to financial freedom that people in their twenties face today. Recent college graduates are said to carry an average of $20,000 in college debt (not including what may be accrued by those who go on to graduate school).

Realistically, then, college debt and credit-card debt, together, can add up to a veritable mountain of financial obligations, just as you are trying to get started in your career.

As if the typical debt burden you leave school with were not enough of an obstacle to financial freedom, a recent book exposé on college loans suggests that just as with credit cards, lenders are just waiting to pounce when you make a late payment. In *The Student Loan Scam: The Most Oppressive Debt in U.S. History—and How We Can Fight Back* (Beacon, 2009), author Alan Michael Collinge, founder of the grassroots organization StudentloanJustice.Org, charges student-loan companies with a litany of abuses that he contends cry out for reform.

All we can add here is that the double whammy of student loans and credit-card debt is likely to dominate the budgeting decisions of many recent graduates.

What follows is a framework on how to handle credit and debit cards—so that you do not take on any more debt than you have to.

Pay as You Go?

The financial crisis and recession of 2008-09 seem to have led many people to change their thinking—and habits—regarding credit cards. Along with frugality in general, cutting back on credit-card usage began to seem fashionable. This twofold shift has meant spending less, and using cash or debit cards more.

Not surprisingly, using your credit card less will tend to make it easier for you to cut down on your buying. "With cash, your spending ability is limited," Paula Peter, a professor of consumer behavior at San Diego State University, told *Wall Street Journal* writer Jennifer Waters in a timely article published in January 2009. (The article was head-lined, "Yes, You Can Live with Less Plastic.") A related point is to make specific plans for what to buy before you shop, rather than just cruising the mall, ready to shop on impulse.

In practice, shifting away from credit-card purchases requires people to use ATMs or debit cards more often. Both options tap directly into check-ing accounts. An ATM withdraws cash, while a debit card draws down the balance for a specific payment. So long as you request when setting up your account that no "overdrafts" on your account be honored, the net effect will be to pay as you go. (More on this point in a moment.)

Weaning yourself off of frequent, large and/or spontaneous expendi-tures with your credit card means you'll reserve paying with plastic only for a few specific purchases, with a view to paying off your entire credit-card balance every month. That way, you can build a credit history while avoiding the interest costs of carrying a big fat balance from month to month.

When would paying with a credit card make sense? One example might be paying for airplane flights or other big-ticket items, espe-cially where frequent-flyer miles or other rewards programs are in play. This allows you to build up rewards points over time, while still waiting until the end of the month to pay the card balance off in full.

Another example is making an unexpected or emergency payment (such as if your car dies on you) that might otherwise wipe out the balance in your checking account. Your objective in this scenario would be to pay off the balance in as few months as possible—both to minimize interest costs and to get you back on the pay-as-you-go wagon.

Take Charge of Your Checking Account

There are several drawbacks to this pay-as-you go approach. One is that debit cards provide less consumer protection than credit cards in the event of a disputed payment. Another drawback is that when you use your debit card to rent a car or check into a hotel, the business may put a *hold* on your checking account for more than you end up paying, making your available checking account balance temporarily smaller. The result is to make overdrafts more likely— even where there is enough money in your account to cover all your payments!

And now for a rather ugly truth: Banks *want* you to overdraw your checking account. Banks have developed surprisingly nasty arrangements to get you to do this, so that they can hit you with penalties and fees. Banks put a different spin on this. Their pretext is that they provide you, the customer, with a cushion against insufficient-funds penalties. The reality is that banks position themselves to gain much more in fees. By one estimate, such fees added up to $17.5 billion in 2007. This is a high-stakes game.

The way the game works is that with all the checks you write, ATM withdrawals and debit-card payments you make, you may lose track of your account balance. Suppose you make an ATM withdrawal or a debit-card payment, not realizing your account is low or empty. Instead of blocking your transaction, the bank may then honor the overdraft and charge high fees ($35, say, for each incident). Moreover, some banks require repayment of the "loan" and the penalty fee within a few days; additional fees kick in for any delay.

The solution is within your reach. Make sure that when your checking account is empty, your bank will reject both ATM withdrawals and debit-card payments. Simply by requesting a zero-overdraft privilege, you can avoid a potential cascade of overdraft fees and lateness penalties. By the way, this issue comes under the heading of "courtesy overdraft policies." Don't be fooled by the jargon; "courtesy" has nothing to do with it!

IV. YOUR CREDIT SCORE— AND WHAT TO DO ABOUT IT

So you're finally ready to bite the bullet and get yourself a newer car, one that doesn't leave a small puddle of oil every time you pull away from the parking spot. You research on line for a good late-model used car. You know that quality will cost money, but you figure you can handle a loan from a bank or other lender as long as the annual percentage rate (APR) isn't too high and the monthly payment is not too steep.

You've never applied for a loan other than a student loan before. Now you're about to learn what your financial report card really is. It's a four-letter word: "FICO."

FICO stands for Fair Isaac Corporation, a company that gathers and processes statistical information about your credit history. Fair Isaac is at the top of a three-layered pyramid of info-gathering agencies: lots of local credit bureaus, three national credit-reporting companies, and Fair Isaac—the ultimate authority that assigns a numerical grade to your credit-worthiness.

Imperfect though FICO and other credit scores are, they can determine whether you can get, say, a mortgage loan, or how much your car loan will cost. FICO scores range from 300 to 900, with few below 500 or above 850

How Lenders Score Credit

Traditionally, creditors classified risks according to the three "C's": character, capacity, and collateral. *Character* refers to how hard a borrower will work to make sure a loan is repaid. *Capacity* refers to the borrower's ability to repay, as measured by assets and discretionary income. *Collateral* is whatever the lender can claim (by repossessing a car or foreclosing on a house) if the borrower cannot or will not pay. Needless to say, considerable guesswork went into evaluating the three C's.

How do credit raters measure these variables today? You have a credit record with three national credit bureaus: Equifax, Experian (formerly TRW), and TransUnion. From their data, Fair Isaacs calculates your FICO score. Then most lenders either rely on your FICO score directly or use an "application" or "customized model" to evaluate your credit worthiness. The application or customized model combines the FICO score with data from your loan application to derive a composite score. Either type of score falls into a numerical range, indicating the risk level of a loan. The higher the score, the lower the perceived risk.

How is your basic FICO score calculated? Among dozens of possible variables, FICO scoring relies on five factors, giving most weight to your credit history:

Credit payment history (35 percent of the FICO score). This record is probably the single most important measure of a borrower's character. Credit bureau reports contain information on delinquent payments on credit cards and loans. They look at the past seven years, and no further.

Creditors examine how serious, recent and frequent your late payments have been within the seven-year reporting period. For example, if you missed the date when a bill was due and made a 30-day late payment, it would not be as troubling as a 90-day delinquency. However, if a credit report shows that you've made several 30-day late payments in recent months, your application for a loan would probably be viewed as a greater risk than someone with a 90-day delinquency several years ago. Finally, if a pattern of late payments (even minor ones) emerges, spread across a credit history, a lender would be concerned about your ability to repay the loan.

Level of debt utilization (30 percent). Applicants who are at or close to their credit limits will generally lose points in a credit-scoring system. Statistically, borrowers who have "maxed-out" on their credit lines pose more of a risk to lenders. (Keep that in mind if let your credit-card balance get out of control.)

Length of credit history (15 percent). The more years of credit experience you have—meaning, taking out loans, having a credit card or buying on credit—the better you will score in this category.

Number of new credit applications (10 percent). Each time you apply for credit, it gets posted to a credit report as an "inquiry." Too many inquiries (usually four or more in a six month period) will cost you points on a credit score, since people who apply for credit often have poor repayment records. In the past, consumers who have shopped around for a car or home loan would get multiple inquiries listed on their credit reports, even though they were, in effect, seeking only one loan. Credit-scoring systems now try to correct this misinterpretation by treating all applications for a car or home loan made within a seven-day period as a single inquiry.

A good mix of credit experience (10 percent). Having several major credit cards, as well as installment credit such as a car or student loan, will improve your credit score. Your ability to secure credit from a variety of reputable lenders indicates your credit worthiness. (On the other hand, a loan from a finance company—as opposed to a bank or major credit-card company—may count against you, since such lenders tend to work with riskier clients.) One note of caution, though: Because of the wave of personal bankruptcy filings and loan defaults in recent years, many creditors actually may give fewer points for possession of five or more credit cards.

To sum up: The old-school "three-C" method of rating your credit relied more on a personal judgment call, while today's credit-scoring systems analyze a lot more data, going back seven years, to determine the likelihood that you, the borrower, will repay a loan.

How to Raise Your FICO Score

Here's some good news if you're worried about ending up with low FICO score. If you handle your finances carefully, you can boost your score. Under "payment history," for example, www.myFICO.com advises you to pay bills on time and make good on missed payments as soon as possible. In regard to "amounts owed," you should keep credit-card balances low and pay off debt rather than shifting it from one account to another. As for "length of credit history," people with only brief credit histories are advised not to open too many accounts right away. Tips regarding "new credit" include a reminder that you are free to monitor your own credit report. When it comes to types of credit use, you are advised to have several credit cards and several installment loans (for example, car loans), and to keep current with your payments on all of them.

Credit Reports: How to Correct Errors

Local credit bureaus across the nation assemble and disseminate millions of consumer credit reports annually. Most of them store and distribute credit reports through one of the three national systems mentioned earlier. These are Equifax, Experian and TransUnion. Fortunately, borrowers have access to the same information as the lenders.

This means that you can review your credit reports to see if any errors have been made that could unfairly lower your FICO score. The Fair and Accurate Credit Transactions Act of 2003 says that you can order a copy of your credit report from each of the three national credit bureaus for free, every 12 months.

You can obtain your free reports online at www.annualcreditreport.com, which was created for this purpose by the three national credit bureaus in 2004. *This is the only online source for your credit record recommended by the Federal Trade Commission.*

While other advertised sites may look and sound similar, their offers of your "free" credit report usually involve the purchase of some other product for a price. You don't have to buy anything when ordering from annualcreditreport.com. As to your FICO score, it can be obtained free at www.myfico.com (although you may be asked to sign up for a service you can then cancel).

Table 1: Estimated Letter-Grade Equivalents to FICO Scores in 2008

FICO score	Letter grade
760-850	A+
700-759	A
660-699	B
620-659	C
580-619	D
500-579	F

Source: Don Taylor, "Dr. Don issues his FICO letter Grades," www.bankrate.com.

Table 2: Rate and Payment Contrasts for High- and Low-Score Borrowers

Annual Percentage Rate, 36-month auto loan	FICO score 15 year home-equity loan (monthly payment)
760-850 4.76 %	$1,587
620-639 6.35 %	$1,867

Note: Based on prevailing interest rates, March 2, 2009.

Source: "The higher your FICO credit score, the lower your payments," www.myfico.com.

You can order all three free reports at once, which may help you clean up any errors in preparation for taking out a new loan. Or you could space the three reports out over the course of the year, just to keep tabs on whether there are any suspicious listings creeping on to your records—a red flag for identity theft.

What if an error has been made in billing that may jeopardize your credit score? The Fair Credit Reporting Act provides borrowers some protection against erroneous and outdated credit information that could jeopardize your chance to borrow money. It gives the consumer the right to contest the items in a report that are inaccurate or outdated. The credit bureaus are required to look into your request in a timely manner and report any corrections, to clean up your record.

V. ABOUT CAR INSURANCE

Every state requires at least a minimum level of liability insurance, in case you injure another person or damage someone else's car or property. According to the Insurance Information Institute, the average car owner spent $817 on auto insurance in 2006 (the latest year with statistics available). Those who purchased "full" coverage (that is, a combination of liability, collision, and comprehensive insurance) paid $937, on average, in premiums. Let's consider how much coverage in each of these three main types—liability, collision, and comprehensive— you should carry.

Liability insurance. First, and as noted, liability insurance is legally required for drivers in every state. It protects the owner of an automobile from claims for injury to people and damage to property as a result of an automobile accident. When you register a motor vehicle, the state generally requires proof of such insurance. Even the careful driver needs this coverage. The degree of coverage afforded varies in policies issued by different companies, and the minimum amount of coverage required to register a vehicle varies from state to state.

The amount of liability coverage required to register a vehicle is often grossly inadequate when you consider the vast sum you may be legally liable for in the event of a serious accident. The mandatory minimums may be as little as $15,000 coverage for death or injury to one person, with a $30,000 aggregate limit of damage for death or injury to all persons to whom the owner becomes liable in a single accident. (Such amounts are described in the jargon of the insurance industry as "15/30 limits.") The cost of this insurance varies with the locality; the kind and model of car insured; the age, gender, and qualification of the operator; and the principal use of the vehicle.

The additional premium charged for increasing the amount of coverage is proportionally small compared with the increased protection gained. For example, increasing the coverage to 100/300 ($100,000 per person and $300,000 per accident) might only double the premium from its statutory minimum.

The insurance policy you buy states the limit of the insurance company's liability. You are responsible for any legal liability in excess of that amount. The risk of loss is substantial, and automobile accidents happen even to careful drivers. It is advisable to carry at least 100/300 "bodily injury coverage." An alternative way to get higher bodily injury coverage for automobile accidents is with an "umbrella policy" for personal liability, which offers liability coverage for home and car together at generally reasonable rates (say, $200 for $1 million in coverage).

Collision insurance. Collision coverage is included in most policies to insure against damage to or loss of the automobile itself. Such collision coverage usually is subject to a deductible, which is the portion of any claim that the owner must pay himself before the insurance company pays anything. Coverage for damage incurred in a collision is costly, often accounting for well over half of a motorist's auto insurance premium.

Collision coverage can raise insurance costs sharply for new or luxury cars. It can come as a shock to a younger buyer who has paid a premium for a fancy set of wheels to find that higher insurance costs also enter the picture, effectively raising the monthly car payments.

One way to reduce the cost of collision insurance is to increase the amount of the deductible to $500 or even $1,000, from the more usual $200 or $300, so that only a relatively major accident will result in a claim for collision damage. However, that would mean that the cost of most mishaps would be paid by the owner out of pocket.

This brings up a related issue. Many companies raise the premium or even drop the insured person as an account if the person has certain number of claims of any sort. So you should think twice before filing claims for small mishaps.

Comprehensive insurance. A comprehensive auto policy gives protection primarily against loss of a vehicle from fire and theft. But it also includes protection for loss due to practically any other hazard (except collision), including windstorms, tornadoes, hailstorms, floods, and acts of vandalism. The additional cost of such comprehensive coverage over the premium for plain fire and theft coverage is nominal. Insurance companies grade geographical locations according to the number and severity of the accidents occurring in each. These factors determine the premium rate for any single location.

"No-Fault." Incidentally, a number of states have "no-fault" automobile-insurance statutes. There are substantial differences in these laws among the states, but the common feature is that victims of an automobile accident who suffer bodily injury must recover their financial loss from their own insurance company rather than from another party. No-fault statutes in some states also apply to property damage losses. The no-fault feature applies to losses of specified amounts or less. Recovery for losses above these amounts must be made under the usual provisions of insurance and law. Ask your insurance agent if there are such laws in your state, and how they work.

Renting and Car Insurance

What about when you rent a car? You may not need the insurance that car-rental agencies offer, which tends to be expensive. So before renting a vehicle, check with your own insurance agent to find out whether you need to purchase the insurance the car-rental agent is obligated by law to offer you. Either way, make sure you are covered. The same dangers (liability and collision) you face when driving your own car are also present with a car rental.

A third option for insurance on a rental car is the offer some credit-card companies make. If you pay for the car rental with a given card, you may receive free insurance from the card company as part of the transaction. In sum, you should have the broadest possible insurance coverage and be sure that anyone else authorized to drive the vehicle is properly licensed and qualified to drive under the terms of the policy.

VI. TYPES OF INSURANCE COVERAGE

Unlike liability insurance for your car, health-related insurance is seldom if ever required by law. But you definitely need medical and disability insurance. So this chapter is intended to help you figure out what coverage works best for you, given the costs.

For most young people out in the workforce, health-related insurance coverage depends largely on employer benefits. This is notoriously the case for health insurance, and it tends to be true for disability insurance as well.

Life insurance is also a benefit some employers provide. In some cases, you will want to supplement such coverage. For the unemployed, of course, the task gets more formidable: how to maintain (and pay for!) continuous coverage between jobs.

In any case, even when younger workers have jobs, they may be tempted to go without health-related insurance. But accidents can happen. So can unexpected but costly illnesses—which can afflict even "young and healthy" people.

Consider the 28-year-old New York City woman who worked as a receptionist and didn't want to pay for insurance. That was fine until she experienced stomach pain that would not go away. It turned out she had diverticulitis (which, like other kinds of tummy aches, can be difficult to diagnose—opening the door to various expensive tests). The bill for her 46-hour stint came to $17,398. As she put it, "I could have gone to a major university for a year. Instead, I went to the hospital for two days." (Alanna Boyd, quoted in Cara Buckley, "For Uninsured Young Adults, Do-It-Yourself Health Care," the *New York Times*, February 18, 2009.)

The good news is that you may not need life insurance yet.

Life Insurance

To be real, the question here is this: Is someone near and dear to you dependent on your financial support, and would that person suffer hardship if, against all odds, you died. If so, you might want to consider taking out a life-insurance policy naming this person as a beneficiary.

On a similarly somber note, if no such dependent needs your financial protection, the only life insurance you might require would be for "final expenses," which is a nice way of saying burial costs.

If your goal is to protect loved ones against the loss of your income, you are probably best served by a straight *term insurance* policy. As the name implies, the premium (cost) purchases coverage only for a specified period ("term"), such as 20 years. Crucially, term insurance is renewable for additional term periods (possibly at higher premiums) *without a medical examination*. Otherwise, you could lose the ability to get life-insurance coverage if your health fails (which is increasingly likely the older you get), just when you would most need it.

The premium for each renewal period depends on the policyholder's age at the time of renewal.

In other policies, variously known as *whole, permanent, or universal* life insurance, the premium is larger than a similar amount of term insurance would be for someone of the same age, but the premium's rate remains the same as long as the policy remains in force. The initial excess premiums (the cash value of the payments you pay for the policy above the cost of insurance) are invested by the insurer.

The bottom line: You don't need it. There are better ways to invest your money.

What you will need, once you have financial dependents, is a term life insurance policy that pays from four to 10 times your annual income. If your employer does not fully provide that coverage, you will need to go out into the marketplace and shop around. Your advantage will be your youth. A 30-year-old non-smoker, for example, should be able to get 10-year term insurance paying a death-benefit of $100,000 for about $200 a year.

Disability Insurance

Despite the sound of it, disability insurance is not medical insurance. Instead, disability insurance benefits are designed *to replace earnings* in the event that the insured person is physically unable to work. In most instances, a worker who is severely disabled by accident or disease will be covered by Social Security, with monthly payments determined by the worker's prior earnings and the number of dependents. ("Severely disabled," in this instance, indicates impairment so extensive that you cannot perform *any* substantial gainful work for at least 12 months.) Other types of income supplements may be available, but most are inadequate. For example, workers' compensation policies, which most employers must carry by state law, will pay only in the event of an accident or injury sustained on the job, and the benefits tend to be low.

A good disability policy is a worthwhile investment. The most common flaw in personal-insurance programs is *a lack of balance between disability insurance and life insuranc*e. Many people who have adequate life-insurance protection carry little or no disability insurance. Without adequate disability insurance, a loss of income because of protracted sickness or injury may be financially devastating.

Unfortunately, unless offered by your employer, disability insurance can be expensive. You should have coverage equal to 60 percent of your income. If you earn $50,000, this would suggest $30,000 in coverage, which might run as high as $1,000 per year if purchased individually.

Health Insurance

A survey from the Kaiser Family Foundation found that 13 million young (19-29) adults had no health insurance in 2007. This was

29 percent of the 45 million uninsured Americans that year. More recently, the issue has heated up during the Subprime Recession because younger workers who lose their jobs may be especially likely to forego coverage.

Let's consider six scenarios for workers and non-workers:

1. **You have a job.** The cost of your health-insurance policy will vary depending on the type of plan, how much your employer contributes toward coverage, and the state you work in. According to another survey by the Kaiser Family Foundation, in 2008 monthly health-insurance at mid-sized to large companies averaged nearly $400 a month for individual coverage and over $1,000 a month for families. The employee-paid share of these policies averaged $64 a month for individual coverage and $248 a month for families. In some states, of course, the figures ranged higher.

2. **You've just lost your job, and your former employer provided health insurance.** You can continue coverage under COBRA (an acronym for a law Congress passed in 1985: The Consolidated Omnibus Budget Reconciliation Act). If you enroll in COBRA within two months of leaving your job, you can continue your coverage for 18 months. The problem with COBRA has been its expense, since unemployed workers had to pay for the entire premium, including the portion that the employer had paid before. This can easily exceed $500 a month just for individual coverage.

3. **You lack employer coverage, perhaps because you are self-employed.** It generally is difficult and expensive for a person to purchase basic health insurance on his or her own, directly from an insurer. But it can be done. The problem is that such individual plans are costlier than group plans as a rule, because group plans benefit from the pooling of risk.

4. **You are not working and have child dependents under age 19.** You may be able to take advantage of a nationwide program called the Children's Health Insurance Program. CHIPS is designed for

those who are not eligible for federal Medicaid and who have limited or no health coverage. For a small monthly premium, the program provides benefits such as hospital care, physician services, prescription drugs, and drug-treatment services. States have different eligibility rules, but in most states, uninsured children 18 years old and younger whose families have incomes below a specified threshold are eligible. For more information, visit the U.S. Department of Health and Human Services website: insurekidsnow.gov.

5. **You're interested in remaining covered by your parents' health insurance.** Some states have extended the age for which 20-somethings can be covered by their parents' health insurance. Health insurance under this category used to be open only to students, and only up to age 21. More recently, eligibility has been extended to non-students, and the age when parents can still list their children as dependents for this purpose has risen to 26 in some states. To learn more, contact your parents' insurance carrier.

6. **You trust in fate.** Millions of Americans lack any health insurance. They are known in the insurance industry, perhaps unfairly, as the "young invincibles"—a term that implies a conscious decision not to spend precious money on health insurance that they believe they will not need.

For some members of this optimistic group, going uninsured will amount to a de facto "catastrophic coverage" policy, one in which the emergency room is the solution to a catastrophe. By law, staffs in emergency rooms must treat the seriously sick or injured, regardless of the patients' ability to pay. But this isn't exactly a foolproof plan for the uninsured, because massive debt can follow.

The information in this section was excerpted with permission from *Start Here: Getting Your Financial Life on Track* by R.D. Norton and the American Institute for Economic Research.

About AIER

For over 75 years the American Institute for Economic Research (AIER) has offered unbiased research to the general public. Our research is conducted by eminent economists and scholars and provides timely and incisive analysis of contemporary issues. AIER has been featured nationally in such publications as the Wall Street Journal, Money.com, CNN, Investor's Business Daily, The Christian Science Monitor, USA Today, Miami Herald and on Fox Business News TV shows.

For as little as $39 a year for the online version and $59 for the print version, you will receive a year's worth of publications providing insight and education on the economy and personal finance. The support of our members helps our mission of providing nonprofit, noncommercial general economic education.

AIER does not accept gifts from private foundations, commercial interests, or government. We depend, instead, on support from individual members and donors who value the importance of the independent economic perspective we offer.

About the Author

Dr. R.D. Norton is a senior fellow and research advisor at the American Institute for Economic Research. He is the author or editor of a dozen books on economics and finance and holds a Ph.D. from Princeton University. He was formerly Executive Director of the Eastern Economic Association and an economics professor at the University of Texas at Dallas, Mount Holyoke College, and Bryant University, where he had an endowed chair in business economics.

To purchase a copy of *Start Here: Getting Your Financial Life on Track*, please visit the AIER Bookstore: www.aier.org/bookstore.

Others: Parents, Roommates & Friends

B y some estimates, 60 percent of college graduates return home after graduation. Whether they can stand to stay longer than a month is a different issue. As you'll read in this chapter, dealing with your parents after college can be a challenge. If you're living with them, you'll inevitably have rules to follow. If you live away from them, you'll need to keep in touch and set boundaries. And speaking of boundaries: Enter the roommate. Assuming yours is not psycho, there are still some trials that await you as you try to carve out a new life for yourself while sharing cramped space with someone else.

THE FRIENDS YOU HAVE in high school are your true friends. The friends you have in college are good friends. The friends you have at work are usually just acquaintances disguised as friends.

—*JACKIE EDMONDS*
WILLIAMSTOWN, KENTUCKY

DIFFERENT PLACES EQUALS DIFFERENT PEOPLE AND NEW CONNECTIONS.

—*BRIAN*
NEW YORK,
NEW YORK

HEAD LINES
Best Advice and Top Tips

- Call home once a week. Your parents (or at least your mother) will appreciate it, and they might leave you alone other times, too.
- If you live with roommates, make sure you each have your own space.
- To make new friends, and have fun with old ones, throw a house party.
- Join groups and sports teams (kickball, anyone?) to meet new people.

TRY TO REMEMBER THE THINGS your parents taught you. When I was first living out on my own and I faced a moral question, I would always stop and wonder what my parents would think about my decision. Would they approve? Those answers aren't always going to make you happy, but more often than not they will be the right things to do.

—JONATHAN GRESH
POLAND, OHIO

KEEP IN TOUCH WITH YOUR PARENTS. My mom has always been my best friend, and when I moved out three years ago I had horrible separation anxiety. Talking on the phone once a day with her helps tremendously.

—AFFTON BOEHLE
ST. LOUIS, MISSOURI

THE BEST THING YOU can ask prospective roommates is what television shows they like to watch. You can learn a lot about people this way. Someone who loves nothing but horror movies and slasher films might be someone to avoid. You don't want to be involved in a yearlong lease with someone who turns out to be an escaped mental patient.

—*BENNY TADFORD*
YOUNGSTOWN, OHIO

• • • • • • • •

IT IS GOOD TO KEEP IN CONTACT with your parents because they enjoy it, and usually there is a good meal waiting for you at home. Give a call to say you're OK. Or if you're in their area, drop in from time to time to catch up and eat well.

—*LOUIS HAGMAN*
SEATTLE, WASHINGTON

Don't live with a friend, but find an apartment in the same building as a friend. That way, you're not alone, but you have your space.

—*SHARON HAROWITZ VANCOUVER, BRITISH COLUMBIA, CANADA*

• • • • • • • •

YOU MUST CONSIDER your roommate's needs and expectations. You can't simply enter a roommate situation and think, "I'll stay the same and hope it works." There's going to be compromise and you have to know that going in.

—*MUCI*
TORONTO, ONTARIO, CANADA

• • • • • • • •

LIVE ALONE - IF YOU CAN AFFORD IT. It's so nice to not have to worry about disrespecting or getting in the way of a roommate. Living somewhere where you don't have to worry about being up all night disturbing anyone else, or having someone else's activity bother you, is valuable.

—*KATIE*
ATLANTA, GEORGIA

5 THINGS YOUR MOTHER WANTS TO HEAR

Look, call your mother, OK? We understand that you're independent now and you don't need someone to fret over you or give you a guilt trip. But a call *to* your mother might – just might – fend off five calls *from* her. And we're not telling you to lie to your mother; but here's what she's hoping you will say when you do call her. (And you *will* call her, right?)

1. You're eating really well. In fact, you might have gained a little weight. Cooking a healthy breakfast in the morning and dinner at night is really, really fun. Of course, it doesn't compare to Mom's cooking!

2. Vitamins really make you feel better. Why, since you've been taking your vitamins you've been filled with much more energy. Even your doctor, during your recent check-up, said you're healthy as can be. So did your dentist!

3. You're having trouble deciding which of the many social engagements you're going to attend this weekend. So many people like you and want you around! And you're so lucky that all of your friends are so smart and creative and drug-free.

4. The person you are dating is so good to you. Why, just the other day this person washed, folded and put your clothes away, then made you some soup. Just because!

5. Keeping up your appearance with a nice haircut and a respectable wardrobe really does make a difference in how you feel about yourself and how others treat you. Thanks, Mom! You were right!

—The Editors

PEOPLE ARE LIKE DOGS; they need to be trained. Your parents think you are irresponsible. Could it be your $100 tab at the bar and you subsequently asking them for money to cover rent? Listen to your parents so they can train you.

> —J.
> *WASHINGTON, D.C.*

Consider

• • • • • • • •

66 Don't expect your roommate to be a family substitute. He or she may have a very different idea of what a household is...of what a home is. 99

> —N.
> *BROOKLYN, NEW YORK*

• • • • • • • •

APPRECIATE HOW YOUR RELATIONSHIP changes with your parents. When I was in college, I was much more dependent on my parents to help me make the right choices and decisions. They were the ones giving me advice on life issues. After college, things began to change. I moved out to start a life of my own. As I became more experienced in life, I became more independent. I also found that when I spent time with my parents, I was formulating friendships with them. I have experienced some things they haven't and have been able to give them advice on certain things. I love to share with my parents as well as learn from them.

> —*CHERI*
> *MUNCIE, INDIANA*

Check This Out!

LIVE ON YOUR OWN AFTER GETTING A JOB. I wanted independence, and living with a roommate felt too much like college. I didn't want to have to depend on anyone else or worry about someone else not paying their share. It was hard, but it was worth it.

—*WENDY*
ALLENTOWN, PENNSYLVANIA

• • • • • • • •

66 Living alone is the way to go. I have a three-bedroom place for just my dog and me. There is so much less hassle. If there's a mess to clean up, it's my mess. If the music is too loud, I can turn it down. 99

—*T.J.K.*
WESTMINSTER, CALIFORNIA

• • • • • • • •

DON'T LIVE WITH A GOOD FRIEND and don't live with a complete stranger. It's best to live with someone you're connected to and that you know but that you're not that close with. If you live with a good friend, you run the risk of losing the closeness of the friendship and starting to see the person as a roommate who occasionally does annoying things.

—*VERONICA*
TORONTO, ONTARIO, CANADA

ROOMMATES HELP YOU GROW. I didn't have roommates for three years in Japan, so I lived in isolation, slowly going mad with my quirks and tendencies. It wasn't until I moved to Toronto and had roommates that I experienced that mirror: a chance to have all my weird traits reflected back at me. Suddenly, my quirks became apparent, and it forced me to reevaluate how obsessive I had become in my own little environment.

—*DARCY BELANGER*
SHERWOOD PARK, ALBERTA, CANADA

* * * * * * * *

TAKE THE HELP YOUR PARENTS OFFER YOU. I saw so many of my friends try to be tough and tell their parents to bugger off when they were really still kids who didn't know how to handle the world yet. I did the opposite. I went home to live with my parents twice after I moved out. I asked for advice; I asked for money. And now I am closer to my parents than most people I know. It's good for me and for them. We are still a family.

—*SARAH*
WEST HARTFORD, CONNECTICUT

* * * * * * * *

AFTER YOU MOVE OUT, make sure you call home at least once a week. Don't do it for your dad; he probably won't even realize you're gone. But do it for your mother. Believe me, she'll be missing you and thinking about you all the time. I used to call my mom late every Sunday night. I could hear the sparkle in her voice across the phone lines. Take the time to pick up the phone and make her day.

—*HENRY ANDERSON*
BOARDMAN, OHIO

IF YOU DECIDE TO MOVE in with the opposite sex (just as friends) make sure you know what you're getting yourself into. I had roommates all through college, and not once did I have a problem with any of them. I moved in with a girl, and it was the hardest thing to deal with in my life.

—*BRANDON*
DALLAS, TEXAS

* * * * * * * *

BE WARNED: You no longer live in a dorm and, sad and harsh as it may seem, not everyone may be trying to become insta-best friends with you in time for homecoming. Reserve the intimate details of your home life or love life for friends who really have earned your trust and demonstrated authentic interest (even if you have hung out a few times). Also respect other people's choice to do the same without feeling dissed.

—*T.M.*
ATLANTA, GEORGIA

THREE'S A CROWD

I had three roommates after college, which was less than ideal at that stage of life. It was fun at times, but I truly wanted my own space that didn't require sharing a bathroom, getting angry with roommates that didn't clean up after themselves, or having to come home to guests that weren't your own friends. That type of college-style living quickly gets old in the real world, and after a long day of work during your first year out of school all you want to do is come home to a nice haven that you've set up for yourself. I definitely would recommend sharing a living space with just one person or just getting a place of your own after college. You'll be able to take better care of yourself and be a happier person overall.

—*KATIE*
NEW YORK, NEW YORK

6 KEYS TO A HEALTHY ROOMMATE RELATIONSHIP

Clean Up After Yourself: This goes beyond the standard expectation of washing dishes, vacuuming, and picking up your laundry. Pay attention to other places where you might leave your "debris." Check the shower drain for tangles of hair, the sink for gobs of toothpaste, and the bathroom counter and mirror for signs of spittle. Save those bad habits for when you're married.

Eat Your Own Food: If you want to upset your roommate, eat what she was planning to have for dinner. Go ahead. I dare you.

Share the Domestic Duties: Set up a plan so the same person is not always the one to clean the bathroom or take out the recycling. Put the plan in writing so there will be no arguing and no excuses for not having done a particular chore.

No Exiling: In college, you may have asked, or told, your roommate to spend the night elsewhere if you had your significant other over to visit. This will not go over so well in the real world.

No 'Sexiling': A male cousin of mine once used the deodorant of his female roommate (not his girlfriend). He failed to understand why she was upset over this. If you want to borrow or use something of your roommate, ask first. If he or she says no, respect his or her wishes.

Don't Be Passive Aggressive: If your roommate frequently does something that bothers you, don't let your anger build up. Let your roommate know in a respectful manner. Use those "I Messages" your guidance counselor taught you about in the fourth grade: "I don't like it when you . . ." Chances are, your roommate will be happy to change to keep the peace.

—Sarah Franco

DON'T LET YOUR PETER PAN FRIENDS, the ones who will never grow up, interfere with you moving on and getting an adult life. I had a couple of buddies who still wanted to go out and party three nights a week even after I had gotten my first accounting job. They were living at home and sponging off their parents, so it was no big deal to them. I didn't want to hurt their feelings or lose their friendship, and I didn't want them to think I was a wuss, so I continued to go out with them. But having to get up early the next day and make myself presentable for life in the office really took a toll on me. I know some days I looked less than ready to work. My boss never said anything, but I think he knew what was up. When you have adult responsibilities like a job, you have to act like an adult. Even if your friends won't.

> —*A.M.*
> *ELLSWORTH, OHIO*

• • • • • • • •

IT WAS REALLY EASY TO MEET FRIENDS in Chicago. We would go to the bars in Lincoln Park to watch basketball and football. We met a lot of people that way. I also met other young people through work and by playing volleyball at the Social Club of Chicago.

> —*ANONYMOUS*
> *NEW YORK, NEW YORK*

• • • • • • • •

MAKE SURE THAT YOU LEARN THINGS from your friends. I used to make friends without considering what they could teach me or how they could help me grow. My new friends have all have shown me complete generosity, compassion, and empathy.

> —*TAI DAVIS*
> *PALATINE, ILLINOIS*

I'VE ALWAYS HAD AN UNDERSTANDING with friends who live far away: If we lose touch, and you find yourself back home, *get in touch!* Don't feel ashamed if you haven't written or called in months or years. The longer the time spent not seeing someone, the more involved and fun it is when we finally get together. It's like when you wait forever in a restaurant and you get hungrier with every passing minute. By the time you eat, the food tastes so much better!

> —ADAM SHALABY
> TORONTO, ONTARIO, CANADA

• • • • • • • •

IF YOU WANT TO STAY IN TOUCH WITH PEOPLE, you have to work at it. It doesn't happen magically. I still get together once a year with a group of friends that I met in college. Every year we move the location of the reunion near a different one of us so that person does not have to pay to travel. If you can afford to do something like our annual reunion, then do it. Nothing beats seeing your old friends in person.

> —JANE TABACHKA
> GREEN MOUNT, VIRGINIA

• • • • • • • •

AFTER COLLEGE, I was living in St. Louis but worked for a consulting firm, so I was constantly placed in cities in which I didn't know anybody. At times, it was pretty lonely. I went out with people whenever I could—they didn't need to be good friends, just people from work or neighbors. This helped me meet other people in the area. I also took some classes. The experience was great because it got me out and introduced me to new people, and I learned something in the process.

> —JEFF
> SAN FRANCISCO, CALIFORNIA

OBJECT: FUN

WE'RE KNOWN FOR HAVING REALLY GREAT GAMES, like the "No Game," when no one can say the word "no." You start off by saying something like, "So, Sally, did you kill anyone on the way to the party?" And Sally might say, "Thank God, not this time." We don't want our parties to be about networking—we just want everyone to be laughing. We want people to leave the party sore from laughing so hard.

> —KAMI
> CAPE COD, MASSACHUSETTS

• • • • • • • •

HAVE A THEME FOR YOUR PARTY. Sometimes I'll get together with my girlfriends for a house party. One time it was a cowboy theme—the food, the attire, the music. Another time, it was about baking and "getting baked." We had a good time at that one. Themes help create a fun party atmosphere right off the bat.

> —MICHELE
> HOLLY, MICHIGAN

• • • • • • • •

IF A PARTY IS FEELING SORT OF LAME, there's always Twister.

> —J.A.
> ATLANTA, GEORGIA

• • • • • • • •

FOR A PARTY, TWO WORDS: fancy cheese. Just make sure you can pronounce the type when your guests ask.

> —JENNIFER
> SEATTLE, WASHINGTON

WHEN THROWING YOUR FIRST ADULT PARTY, you are most likely going to have to stay within a tight budget. At times like this, Wal-Mart and Target are your best friends. You can throw an excellent "adult-looking" party for under $100 (depending on the size of the guest list). Wal-Mart or your local grocery store usually has a great selection of finger foods, beverages, and sweets. Target can supply all of your decorations, napkins, and plates. For background music, burn some of your favorite party songs to a CD.

—*ASHLEY*
DALLAS, TEXAS

AFTER A COUPLE OF YEARS AWAY FROM SCHOOL, if a party is just the same as it was in college, that's kind of depressing. Be careful how you act. You can give off a real "Frank the Tank" vibe.

—*JESSE AMMERMAN*
CHICAGO, ILLINOIS

AT FIRST, THE MAIN DIFFERENCE between parties before and after college was that you didn't have to pay for a cup at the door. Now, I attend dinner parties and enjoy myself much more with a small group. We laugh, talk, eat, drink, and there's a lot less puking the morning after. It still happens sometimes, but not *every* time.

—*ANONYMOUS*
SAN DIEGO, CALIFORNIA

TAKE A CHANCE ON SOMEONE. I met my one very good friend, David, in the park. I was reading a book about how Judaism was like Buddhism, and he had read it, and we started talking. I'm pretty sure he was interested in me romantically; he asked me out. Sometimes you meet a guy who likes you, and you think maybe you're better off as friends. But you never know, so you go out on a date. I'm glad I did. If I hadn't gone out with David, I would have never ended up being such good friends with him. And after he introduced me to the people he knew, I suddenly found I had a whole new circle of friends.

—REBECCA SHENN
NEW YORK, NEW YORK

• • • • • • • •

HOW TO COMMUNICATE WITH YOUR PARENTS: Therapy seemed to work. I figured out how to talk to them.

—ANONYMOUS
SITKA, ALASKA

• • • • • • • •

DON'T SEND MASS EMAILS TO YOUR FRIENDS. It's impersonal. Some of my friends will write a huge email about what's going on in their lives and then send it to something like 20 people. When I read them, I realize I'm usually like 10th on the list. So what am I supposed to do? Am I supposed to write them something back that's specific to them? Or should I send a generic response and address it to 20 other people?

—BECKY STRUBE
BELLEVILLE, ILLINOIS

I PLAY TENNIS AND BASKETBALL. It's a great way to meet friends and get exercise. It's also a good way to get a date; you automatically have something in common.

> —JAMES
> NEW YORK, NEW YORK

• • • • • • • •

TAKE TIME TO DEVELOP YOUR HOBBIES, your creativity, and your spirit. I stopped trying to meet people and followed my passions—writing, art, and music—and the people just showed up in the strangest of ways. Finding my passion was the best way to meet new people.

> —MARK LINDEN O'MEARA
> VANCOUVER, BRITISH COLUMBIA, CANADA

• • • • • • • •

WHEN MEETING PEOPLE, it's your outgoingness and daily activities that matter, no matter your location. If you went to the gym every day in your old city, and you met a bunch of people there, then chances are you're going to work out in your new city, too, and you'll find friends at that gym.

> —JEFF CELLIO
> LAGUNA NIGUEL, CALIFORNIA

• • • • • • • •

TO HANG OUT WITH OLD FRIENDS and make new ones, have a party at your house or apartment. Invite everyone you know through evite.com and encourage them to bring a friend or two. All you need after that are drinks, music, and some food. You'll hang with your good friends and meet new ones. Parties are the best way to socialize—much better than being at a bar.

> —J.A.
> ATLANTA, GEORGIA

> The best way to create atmosphere is to dim the lights, and use lots of candles!
> —NADIA

INGREDIENTS FOR A GROWN-UP PARTY

When having your first adult party, make something that actually involves a recipe, instead of soup mix and sour cream or jarred cheese in the microwave. You can still rely on good old chips and salsa, but also try a more complicated hors d'oeuvre, a multi-ingredient dip or a dessert that doesn't come out of a box. If you expect people to bring something, say so (a polite way to do this is to say, "Bring something to share"), but have a base of drinks (a 12-pack of beer, a bottle of vodka) and food on hand. Make sure you have either bought ice or made a bunch of it ahead of time. Have plenty of mixers available (ginger ale, some kind of cranberry juice, a citrus-based juice, and Coke are good basics).

Clean out your fridge. Clean the bathroom (yes, the bathtub too—someone will inevitably look in there) and empty *all* wastebaskets. Have a container set aside for bottles and recycling. Make sure a bottle opener is handy. Cut up some limes and put them in a bowl near the bottle opener. Empty the dishwasher.

Light some candles. Make a CD mix or put everything on shuffle so you're not jumping up and down to change discs all the time. Introduce all your guests to each other. Remember you are the host, not the life of the party, but have good conversation tidbits ready (movie trivia, news items, good news about a common friend) for awkward moments. Offer to refill drinks; don't rely on guests to simply help themselves. And save the rubber Nixon mask and the piñata for Halloween.

—*T.M.*
ATLANTA, GEORGIA

MY HIGH SCHOOL GIRLFRIENDS and I try to meet up somewhere at least once a year for fun weekend trips. We may not know every detail of each other's lives like we used to, but there's a strong bond and a sense of comfort when we're all together. We know we'll always be there for each other.

—*ANONYMOUS*
SAN DIEGO, CALIFORNIA

● ● ● ● ● ● ● ●

66 Make friends wherever you go. Friends are what keep you going through any transition. You feel more loved and more popular when you keep running into familiar faces. 99

—*KALYNA*
SAN FRANCISCO, CALIFORNIA

● ● ● ● ● ● ● ●

THERE ARE FRIENDSHIPS meant just for college. I was disappointed to learn that a few of the friendships I had initially deemed as everlasting fizzled out shortly after graduation. College is a time filled with fun, experimentation, life lessons, studying, achievement, and pursuit of goals. A few of my friends were perfect companions in college, but they never grew past the times of partying and financial dependence on their parents. In other words, they still have a lot of growing up to do.

—*M.H.*
RICHMOND, INDIANA

WHEN LIVING WITH SOMEONE, make sure they know that the Snickers bar in the fridge is yours. Once, I was at work all day, thinking about eating that Snickers bar in the fridge when I got home. But when I got there, you guessed it—my roommate had eaten it. She even thanked me!

—*MICHELE*
HOLLY, MICHIGAN

· · · · · · · ·

66 I strike up conversations everywhere. You never know who you'll meet. The other night I met a nice couple sitting at the bar. We ended up having a great time and exchanged numbers. 99

—*ROBIN VELLIS*
CLARKS SUMMIT, PENNSYLVANIA

· · · · · · · ·

WHEN YOU'RE ON YOUR OWN, you discover things about yourself. I've realized that I can survive on my own—no parents, no boyfriend. Just me and a restaurant job and a tiny studio apartment in the city. This place is crawling with people like me, and making friends is effortless. I've also learned how fluidly people enter and exit my life, stopping momentarily and then passing by. I expect a lot more of this to come.

—*JESSICA*
SEATTLE, WASHINGTON

KEEP AN OPEN MIND. I have one friend that I met in a very unique way. My ex-boyfriend and I remained friends after we broke up. A few years later, I met my ex-boyfriend's live-in girlfriend, and she and I totally hit it off. It sounds odd, but it actually makes sense to click with your ex's partner: You probably have a lot of the same qualities.

—*JENIFER MANN*
CASTRO VALLEY, CALIFORNIA

• • • • • • • •

STAY INVOLVED. In college you get really involved because there's stuff to do. When you leave college, you think there's nothing to do because your friends have moved away. But get involved with a church or community organizations. You'll be as busy as you were in college. I've got so many things I do: church, choirs, freelance writer, harpist, athletics. There's tons of stuff going on.

—*JENNIFER HUBER*
INDIANAPOLIS, INDIANA

• • • • • • • •

LATELY I ONLY MAKE FRIENDS when I feel a strong and organic connection. The new relationships I've entered have been natural. I haven't had to make too much of an effort to solidify the friendship.

—*NICHOLAS WEISS*
SAN FRANCISCO, CALIFORNIA

• • • • • • • •

SEEK THE PEOPLE YOU have something in common with. Adult friendships are segmented. The married people group together, the parents group together, the single people group together. It's just because you have more in common. We all evolve and want to talk about what's big in our lives.

—*BECKY HOUK*
INDIANAPOLIS, INDIANA

FINDING NEW FRIENDS

WHEN I MOVED TO NEW ORLEANS for a fellowship at Tulane University, I was scared because I didn't know anyone in the city. What I ended up doing was going on "friend blind dates." I asked everyone I knew if they had ANY connections in New Orleans, so I was literally going to lunch with the cousin of someone's friend from camp. However, it was through one of these friend blind dates that I met a girl who instantly became one of my closest friends. I then became very close with her friends. I am going to her wedding in a few weeks.

> —*SHIRA PINSKER*
> *WASHINGTON, D.C.*

• • • • • • • •

I SUGGEST JOINING A SPORTS TEAM such as soccer, flag football, kick ball, or ultimate Frisbee. They have leagues in every city and do not necessarily require athletic skill. It is a fun, great way to exercise, and a great way to meet people.

> —*RACHEL WIECK CUPIT*
> *NEW ORLEANS, LOUISIANA*

• • • • • • • •

BEING NEW TO A CITY, you really have to put yourself out there. I knew a handful of people at first, and we just went out to different places and tried different scenes and little by little our group grew. I recommend joining different clubs or organizations based on your interests. The organizations I joined really helped me make new friends and kept me busy.

> —*CARRIE*
> *ATLANTA, GEORGIA*

• • • • • • • •

I SOUGHT OUT NEW FRIENDS by joining groups like Junior League, which is dedicated to training women volunteers. I also got involved in our church. Volunteering for a cause that you care about is great because you automatically share a common interest.

> —*ALISON BRAWNER*
> *SPRINGFIELD, MISSOURI*

I MET ONE OF MY BEST FRIENDS from a new city on MySpace. I wasn't creepy about it, but I searched for people my age in town and messaged that I was new in town, blah blah. Of course we NEVER admitted to other folks how we met, but I got to become friends with her whole group, which instantly helped me adjust to a new place.

—*JENNIFER*
ALABAMA

• • • • • • • •

IT IS IMPORTANT TO START BUILDING a support network in your new place, starting on day one. Make dinner plans with the person in the next cubicle. Go hang out at a coffee shop and try to strike up a conversation with someone. This isn't to say that you should instantly cut ties with your friends and family from back home. But you shouldn't assume that those people will always be your closest friends, or it will be that much harder to make new ones. It is natural to grow apart from some people when you move. You won't lose the people you are really close to, and they will be glad to see you thriving in your new home.

—*LESLEY*
ATLANTA, GEORGIA

• • • • • • • •

WHEN I MOVED FROM IDAHO to upstate New York, I was lonely for about the first six months. Then one day I realized that I was doing things—jogging, going to the movies, going to the coffeehouse, shopping, and going to the library—without ever talking to the other people at those places. It's hard to make friends if you keep to yourself. So I started striking up casual conversations with people. If someone was sitting alone at the coffeehouse, I'd go over and say hi. Same thing if I saw someone sitting alone at the movies. They didn't all turn into friendships, but a few of them did.

—*CHARLENE WHITTED*
JAMESTOWN, NEW YORK

ALWAYS MAKE NEW FRIENDS; you never know when the old ones are going to head in a different direction. When I first moved to a big city out of college, I went there with my best friend. But after a short period of time, she went back home and I was left alone. I had no choice but to make new friends.

—*MICHELE*
HOLLY, MICHIGAN

* * * * * * * *

66 Use your parents as a sound-ing board as you go through large and important deci-sions. You don't have to listen to their advice, but it helps to be able to talk these things out with someone who's been there. 99

—*T.W.*
YOUNGSTOWN, OHIO

* * * * * * * *

KEEP IN REALLY CLOSE TOUCH with one old friend, and that person can tell everyone everything. I couldn't possibly call 40 people and tell them news—that I had a car accident, or a really good gig, or whatever. If I did that, I would never get anything done and I would resent them all. Then we'd never talk.

—*KAMI*
CAPE COD, MASSACHUSETTS

Looking for Love: Romance (and Loneliness) After College

*A**fter college, everything changes in the world of dating. Even if you don't feel ready for marriage, more emphasis seems to be placed on the romantic future of your dates. Another change: Unlike college, there aren't scheduled events every weekend to help you mingle with dating prospects. In the real world, you've got to find Mr. or Mrs. Right on your own. We asked college grads to give advice on the differences between college and postgrad dating, the search for love (or just a one-night stand), the downsides of dating coworkers, and how to battle loneliness when the email box is empty and the cell phone is silent.*

THE MAIN THING THAT'S DIFFERENT for me and dating is that my opening line—"So, are you in a sorority?"—no longer works.

—*DANE GOLDEN*
SAN FRANCISCO, CALIFORNIA

YOU DON'T FIND LOVE; IT FINDS YOU.

—*ANONYMOUS*
SAN DIEGO, CALIFORNIA

HEAD LINES
Best Advice and Top Tips

- Once you leave school, you have to really put yourself out there to meet new people.
- Use your 20s as a time to date all kinds of people before you settle down.
- Don't rush into a serious relationship—spend some time getting to know yourself first.
- Dating coworkers is asking for trouble.
- Don't linger in a relationship if you know it's not working.

JUST ENJOY THE DATING SCENE. I spent so much time worrying about whether every guy I met was "the one." I didn't just enjoy getting dressed up, putting on makeup, and going out for the evening. I examined and re-examined every word my date said to find out if he loved me and whether he was marriage material. When I finally became exhausted with that process, I just enjoyed dating someone. I changed my expectations and really began to have fun. That's when I met "the one." We got married the following year.

—STEPHANIE
NEW YORK, NEW YORK

Consider

PERSON-TO-PERSON CONTACT IS NECESSARY. Cell phones and instant messaging are a far second to actually being with people face to face.

—LOUIS HAGMAN
SEATTLE, WASHINGTON

HAVE FUN! During college, I was in a long relationship that I came out of in senior year. Through the years following, I realized I had freedom and a lack of consequences to casual encounters. So I had a few more of those.

> —*MATT STONE*
> *SAN FRANCISCO, CALIFORNIA*

• • • • • • • •

DATING IS DIFFERENT OUT OF COLLEGE. A cute guy you meet may just want to hang out for the evening and might never call. In fact, that's likely. Keep an open mind and keep your options open - I guarantee you, everyone else is.

> —*KELLI*
> *ATLANTA, GEORGIA*

• • • • • • • •

IN COLLEGE, YOU HAVE FRATERNITY parties and date functions and you're constantly going out during the school week and on the weekend, so it's easier to meet people. In the "real world," it's definitely harder to meet "quality" people. And for the most part, you can't find out everything about them because your social world is not confined to a school where you know who they dated and their "back story." That always makes it interesting on dates.

> —*CARRIE*
> *ATLANTA, GEORGIA*

Late-late nights! Random hookups! Forgotten phone numbers! There's something magical about dating in your early 20s.

> —*J.A.*
> *ATLANTA, GEORGIA*

POST-COLLEGE DATING

1. **Where Are the Young People?** After you graduate, seemingly everyone in the world ages by 20-30 years. You go to work and you're the youngest by about 25 years. You take an art class to meet people and you're surrounded by retirees complaining of their aching joints. Now, it requires a lot more effort to meet those intelligent, attractive people your age. You may have to search high and low, but they are there.

2. **E-F-F-O-R-T, Find Out What It Means to Me:** In post-college life, you have to put in a little effort in order to sweep the object of your affection off his or her feet. This doesn't mean you need to hemorrhage bundles of money on an evening for two. Cook dinner together. Go to a museum. Climb a mountain. Picnic in the park.

3. **Two's Company, Three (or More) Is a Crowd:** While hanging out with friends as a couple is a lot of fun, romantic one-on-one dating is necessary for building a healthy relationship.

—Sarah Franco

Is it OK to date someone you work with?
There are two rules, and a logical corollary:

1. Never date your bartender.
2. Never date someone you work with.
3. Corollary (because two negatives make a positive): You can date your bartender if you work with her. The idea is that the soap opera is part of the fun of working in a bar.
   —DAREN
   DECATUR, GEORGIA

GUYS, IF YOU ARE LIVING ALONE in an apartment, try to keep it in decent shape. I'm not suggesting you have to vacuum and wash the windows daily, but you have to at least pick up after yourself. About six months after I got my own place, I brought this girl home from a night at the bar. We were getting comfy on the couch, and all was going well until she accidentally slid her hand between the cushion and the couch and touched a piece of week-old, half-eaten pizza. What a mood killer! After that, I became much more cleaning-conscious.

—*B.C.*
HARRISONBURG, VIRGINIA

* * * * * * * *

I MET A CUTE GIRL ONCE IN THE DMV LINE. It was awesome. We had two hours to get to know each other before I asked her out on a date. I guess traffic school could potentially be a good place to meet someone, too—at least you know you have something in common.

—*BILL*
SACRAMENTO, CALIFORNIA

BEST CITIES FOR DATING

1. Austin, TX
2. Colorado Springs, CO
3. San Diego, CA
4. Raleigh/Durham, NC
5. Seattle, WA
6. Charleston, SC
7. Norfolk, VA
8. Ann Arbor, MI
9. Springfield, MA
10. Honolulu, HI

SPENDING TIME ALONE is not the end of the world. Young people today are used to so much visual and audio stimulation from their PlayStations and cell phones that when it's just them and the four walls of their apartment, they don't know what to do with themselves. You should look at that quiet alone time as time to think and plan and reflect. You'll get to know yourself much better and understand who you are and where you are headed. Stop and listen to the little voice inside once in a while.

—*R.D.*
KEEZLETOWN, VIRGINIA

❝Do not ever assume it is the other person's responsibility to handle contraceptives, disease protection, or extra lube. Better to have too much than none, right?❞

—*T.M.*
ATLANTA, GEORGIA

IT'S OK TO TAKE TIME BETWEEN RELATIONSHIPS. Try to understand your emotional triggers during this time; allow yourself time to breathe, but don't hold back if somebody special comes along. I did this recently, and it's made my current relationship a lot deeper.

—*MARK LINDEN O'MEARA*
VANCOUVER, BRITISH COLUMBIA, CANADA

TO LIVE TOGETHER?

I had a few boyfriends after I graduated college. At 25, I met a man I would later move across the country to be with. We lived together for five years. It was a huge growing experience. I loved living with him. But when you're living with someone, you get all the dirt of a marriage (dirty socks on the floor, a sex life you have to work at, and so on) but not all of the rewards – like discussing your shared goals, visions, and dreams. Living together is a strange in-between place where you're still assessing if you want to spend your life with your partner.

Don't fool yourself into thinking living together is a necessary step. If you've been dating a while, chances are you've slept over at your boyfriend's or girlfriend's place, and you've had a window into their living habits. Many people who happily marry have not taken this step and have learned to adjust and live with the person they love.

—ANONYMOUS
TORONTO, ONTARIO, CANADA

YOU HAVE TO BE COMFORTABLE with yourself and realize that sometimes it's better to be alone. There were a lot more men to choose from in college, so when things started going bad with one guy, there was always someone else waiting. After college, it was harder to meet available guys. The older I got, the more "taken" men I met. So when things went bad with one guy, the alternative was being alone. For someone who dated constantly through high school and college like I did, being alone was a hard thing to really get comfortable with. But every woman should have her alone time before committing to marriage and family.

—ANONYMOUS
SAN DIEGO, CALIFORNIA

DANGER: OFFICE DATING

DO NOT HAVE SEX WITH YOUR COWORKERS. This should be printed on every page of this book. *Do not have sex with your coworkers.* Well, unless you are about to get fired. Then bang away.

—*S.H.*
ATLANTA, GEORGIA

• • • • • • • • •

ONCE YOU'RE OUT OF COLLEGE, pretty much anybody is fair game—except coworkers. I've dated a few different colleagues, and all those relationships have done is cause trouble. Normally you go to work to escape a fight, but when you have to see that person there, too, you have nowhere to hide. It ultimately affects your performance because, unfortunately, you can't break up with work.

—*T.J.K.*
WESTMINSTER, CALIFORNIA

• • • • • • • • •

I LEFT A JOB I REALLY LIKED because of an office relationship that turned ugly. I had been dating this coworker, and it turned out he was engaged to someone else. I found out when I heard his friends talking about it in the elevator. He got married, and he became very bizarre with me—breaking into my computer and coming to my house. My boss and a lot of other people got involved, and it just got to a point where I wanted it all to go away. A job opened up somewhere else, so I decided to take it.

—*BETH*
SHAKOPEE, MINNESOTA

• • • • • • • • •

WHEN DATING IN THE WORKPLACE, you have to be a lot more sensitive than you were in the dorms. A lot of places I worked had a "one proposal" rule: If you ask someone out and get shot down, don't bug them again. That's a good rule.

—*ANONYMOUS*
LOS ANGELES, CALIFORNIA

COLLEGE AMOUNTS TO A FOUR-YEAR DATING SERVICE, with potential mates lurking (sometimes literally) around every corner. Once that's over, the options narrow drastically. For many of us, that means coworkers. When you put guys and girls in the same building for any extended period, a few are bound to copulate with each other. It's a situation rife with peril. Sometimes it works. When it doesn't, you just get back to work, clean up the graffiti that's now on your office desk, and move on.

—*JESSE AMMERMAN*
CHICAGO, ILLINOIS

"HE'S SEEN ME NAKED! YIKES!!!" If you don't want to think that about your boss, don't date at work, unless you think you could marry that person. It can make things very awkward in the office. Even if you justify it with, "But he is in a different department; it won't make a difference," just say no. I dated a guy for a couple of months while I was a temp at a company. I thought that it wouldn't matter. Then I got a permanent job at that company and still thought it was OK because he worked on the opposite end of the building. He ended up switching departments and got a promotion and ended up being my boss. Very awkward situation, especially when review time came around.

—*JERALYN*
AUSTIN, TEXAS

DON'T DATE ANYONE WHO LIVES in the same apartment building as you do. That will just cause you both to be uncomfortable after the breakup. I went out with this one guy three or four times, and then I broke it off. He didn't take it too well. Because he knew where I lived, it was hard to avoid him. I was always sitting in my place in the dark so he wouldn't know I was home. Then I always had to look out the window to make sure he wasn't out there before I left. Luckily for me, he moved out about six months after our breakup. But it was a long six months for me.

—*MARYBETH COFNOR*
YOUNGSTOWN, OHIO

" **Always follow your heart. It is never OK to settle. If you settle, you'll end up miserable.** "

—*HEATHER POLLOCK*
ORANGE COUNTY, CALIFORNIA

TAKE THE TIME TO PLAN OUT A DATE. If someone has agreed to go out with you, you should do them the courtesy of planning the evening: where you're going to go, what you're going to do.

—*ANONYMOUS*
LOS ANGELES, CALIFORNIA

DEALING WITH LONELINESS

EVERY YEAR, when August rolls around, I seem to get really lonely. I start thinking about all the good times my friends and I had in college. I call them and reminisce about old times. That seems to take care of it ... until next August!

—*LIBBY WARD*
SPRINGFIELD, MISSOURI

· · · · · · · · ·

I THINK YOUNG PEOPLE confuse loneliness with boredom. Here's the difference: If you feel like you need to talk to someone face to face or on the phone, that's loneliness; if you feel like you need to get out of the apartment and do something, whether or not anybody is available to do it with you, that's boredom. Loneliness can always be cured by picking up the phone. There is always someone to talk to. Boredom is trickier, because sometimes you have to find some money to cure that.

—*CAM THORNTON*
JAMESTOWN, NEW YORK

· · · · · · · · ·

I FOUND THAT I FELT LONELY whenever things in my life were moving fast. You need to slow down and be more attentive to yourself and your surroundings. This can begin by eating more conscientiously, making healthier choices, and taking time to enjoy your food. It might also mean scheduling regular walks or bike rides and stopping to notice some interesting shop or garden along the way. A fast-paced life definitely contributes to feelings of being alone.

—*D.S.*
KENNEDY, NEW YORK

TAKE TIME TO GET TO KNOW YOURSELF. During school, dating was instigated by substantial amounts of alcohol. Most of us wouldn't be getting together in school without those circumstances! After college, I didn't date for a very long time, as I was focused on other things. I haven't regretted that.

—*DARCY BELANGER*
SHERWOOD PARK, ALBERTA, CANADA

SEX BY THE NUMBERS

I WAS WITH ONE WOMAN who followed "The Rules"—who let me kiss her on the first date, but not touch her breasts. On the second date, I could touch her breasts, but not her coochie. On the third, I could touch her coochie, but not have sex. And so I figured next time, I could have sex with her. But it turned out I had to sit through manual and then oral sex before I heard the preferred reply to the condom question.

—*LEE*
BROOKLYN, NEW YORK

• • • • • • • • •

I'VE FOUND THAT THERE is a pretty straightforward sex protocol that is observed in dating in New York, especially among girls I've met on Nerve.com and Jdate.com. Date Number One (if it goes well) is usually the make-out-in-the-bar-or-at-the-subway-platform-before-going-home date. Date Number Two is the I-the-girl-will-come-over-to-your-place-and-make-out-but-I-will-not-get-naked date. Date Number Three is the I-the-girl-will-come-over-get-naked-and-give-you-head-but-not-have-sex-with-you date. Date Number Four is a repeat of Date Number Three, and Date Number Five is usually the date when you have sex.

—*A.F.*
NEW YORK, NEW YORK

IF YOU FEEL LIKE YOU'RE NOT MEETING any new people, go to new places and try new things. There are always more people out there to date. You have to find them or help them find you. Keep an open mind. When you meet someone new, don't be in a hurry to decide if he is right for you; give yourself a chance to get to know him.

—*ANONYMOUS*
CALIFON, NEW JERSEY

" For both guys and girls, dating in college is too easy. Everybody is forced to hang out, whether through classes or other groups. It's like shooting fish in a barrel. Real-world dating is more like deep-sea fishing: You need to put yourself out there farther and cast a strong line. "

—*JESSE AMMERMAN*
CHICAGO, ILLINOIS

DON'T BE AFRAID TO JUMP IN THE DATING POOL and find out about people and yourself. Sort it out, and you'll know what you need to know when the right person comes along.

—*LINDA*
LOS ANGELES, CALIFORNIA

HOW TO PICK UP AT A PARTY

You're not in college any more. But the good news – you'll still be invited to your share of parties. And though keg stands might be less in vogue, real-world mixers are a great place to meet someone to date.

Before you dive in, remember some of the "dos" of picking someone up:

1. DO be impressed by the object of your affection rather than trying to impress him or her with all your stats. People notice when you notice them. No need to ask 20 questions, but do ask a few open-ended and specific questions (rather than yes/no questions), make eye contact and listen. Curiosity is a very attractive quality and a simple way to engage your audience.

2. DO find common ground. What brought you to the party? Chances are you know some people in common in the room. This will help you build connection and trust. When asking the object of your interest questions, figure out some activities, hobbies, or experiences you've shared.

3. DO hang out by the food and drink table when you don't know whom to talk to. Ever notice how people congregate in the kitchen at many house parties? Many people approach this area on their own to refill their cups and grab a bite, and it will be easier to start a conversation when they've stepped away from the other guests. Offer to get a drink for the object of your affection- and if he or she is standing with a friend, extend the invitation.

4. DO see every person you meet as a potential connection. Stay open. Sometimes the people you know the least will help you the most. If you chat with someone interesting who is not single, he or she may know someone to introduce you to. Also, do not assume that the shy person in the corner at a party is boring. Take the opportunity to learn about people in the room before you decide whether or not you are interested.

5. DO initiate conversation. The general rule of networking is to approach someone who is standing on his or her own, or join a conversation with three or more people. In general, it's not a great idea to interrupt two people talking unless you know one of them.

And finally, when approaching someone new, always remember to smile.

—Andrea Syrtash

MEET PEOPLE THROUGH VOLUNTEERING. First of all, helping others makes you feel good, and of course, you're so busy being absorbed in an activity (hopefully with like-minded others) that you are much more likely to relax, be yourself, and you won't have time to experience dating jitters. Do activities that you really like (walking tours, weekend trips, tennis, golf), because if you're happy and interested in what you're doing, you're much more likely to relax and be yourself.

—ALISON BLACKMAN DUNHAM
BROOKLYN, NEW YORK

• • • • • • • •

IF YOU GO ACTIVELY LOOKING for the love of your life you will never find him or her. Most of the time it just happens by accident.

—JOHN BARANYAI
MELBOURNE, AUSTRALIA

Yadda Yadda:

On average, a woman will speak an average of 7,000 words a day; a man, only 2,000.

DATING = *FUN*???

I hate dating. I hate the anxiety, confusion, neurosis, and eventual chaos that may or may not lead to eternal bliss. There's nothing fun about waiting for a phone call or first-date uncertainty... Will he pick you up or do you meet there? Who should pay? Will he kiss you?

Then when it's all over, you replay every comment, gesture, or facial expression to determine its meaning. I'm a girl, and I happily admit that sometimes we girls ruin it for the rest of you. The incessant need to know "What did that mean?" is a killjoy. I don't know how to fix it; I just know how to hate it.

I'm hoping that, eventually, dating will be fun. Maybe the fun part comes after all the angst and effort - once the two of you wade through the mess and start being yourself and just decide to be together. But how do you get there? Is there any alternative to the anxiety and confusion? Nope. It's not a perfect system. But maybe, once I get it right (or rather Mr. Right), it will all seem worth it.

—LAUREL
ATLANTA, GEORGIA

THE THING ABOUT DATING is that it's hardly ever called a date. It's "let's hang out," "let's get together," "let's get some food," or "let's go get some beers." Those are all ways of asking someone out for a date. If someone says, "let's hang out," it's a casual way to ask someone out. Be assertive. Ask people if they want to get together or hang out.

—SYLVIA HOWELL
BERKELEY, CALIFORNIA

THE DANGEROUS THING IS TO FALL IN with people that you wouldn't usually have anything to do with, just because you want friends or love. Right after college, I fell in with this boy who was not good for me, and I think it was because of loneliness. I desperately wanted to connect with someone, have a routine, and share my experiences. I wish I could have turned that experience into an opportunity to appreciate myself, get to know myself, learn to be a friend to myself.

> —E.F.
> HARTFORD, CONNECTICUT

• • • • • • • •

I FOUND THAT IF YOU KEEP a steady stream of girls coming in and out of your life, you never seem to get lonely. And your bathroom will always miraculously get cleaned.

> —J. BERNARD
> CANFIELD, OHIO

• • • • • • • •

I ALWAYS TOOK THE PHILOSOPHY that the more people you meet, the percentage increases that you'll meet someone who you'll really connect with and perhaps have a long-term relationship with.

> —MICHELE
> WALNUT CREEK, CALIFORNIA

• • • • • • • •

IF YOU ARE IN A RELATIONSHIP, do not be afraid if your boyfriend or girlfriend changes. Your 20s are all about changing. You are not going to be the same person as you were in college. Accept it. Don't be nostalgic. Enjoy the growth. Together.

> —AMBREEN HUSSAIN
> NEW YORK, NEW YORK

For a quick confidence boost during a dating drought, peruse the online dating databases to see just how many single people there are out there like you!

> —COURTNEY
> NEW YORK,
> NEW YORK

THE TECHNOLOGY OF DATING

THE INTERNET, IN GENERAL, AND EMAILING, in particular, have been the most revolutionary dating developments. I would be lost without the ability to woo online. The email flirtation, the exchange of words and images, the mingling of souls through correspondence, the sexiness of the suspenseful, delayed, or super-quick response—I owe at least the last three years of nooky to the Internet. Plus, if able, you can cyber-serenade the object of your affection by recording songs and sending them along. The wonder of it all!

> —*LEE*
> *BROOKLYN, NEW YORK*

I SKIM MEN'S PROFILES FOR ANY RED FLAGS, like, "I like women who are open-minded and like to have a good time." To me, this means he wants to find an easy lay with a tongue ring or something. There are plenty of those "read-between-the-lines" things. If he says, "I like independent women" or "50-50 relationships," I read, "Prepare to pay for your half of dinner."

> —*ANONYMOUS*
> *NEW YORK, NEW YORK*

INTERNET DATING IS FUN, but realize that it's a fantasy world. When I was dating someone on the Internet, I could be whoever I wanted. So could he. Then I met someone that I really began to like. Luckily, we were both being truthful with each other. But we could have easily been deceiving the other person. I wasn't very careful, but it turned out OK.

> —*ALICE*
> *POLAND*

DON'T TRY TO DESCRIBE YOUR SOUL MATE in your profile. You want to sound casual, fun, and funny, if you can. No one wants something super-deep. You're just looking at the profile to know if someone has the same interests and might be attractive. After that, you just have to figure it out for yourself. Trying to describe your soul and your soul mate is silly. It's never going to happen that way.

—*ANONYMOUS*
ATHERTON, CALIFORNIA

• • • • • • • • •

WHEN READING PROFILES, go with your instinct. There is no trick to decoding it; it's a combination of what and how they write. Do they seem sincere? Do we have things in common? Do they sound educated? You need to consider these things. But on the other hand, you also have to keep an open mind because sometimes a good person will not necessarily jump off the page.

—*ELLIS*
SEATTLE, WASHINGTON

• • • • • • • • •

ONLINE DATING IS ALL ABOUT VOLUME. It's like dating people in a crowded room. You might hit it off with two out of 50 people. Don't get discouraged. Look at it this way: It's a great way to meet new people. Some of them will become friends or lovers. Others will turn into great stories to share with your friends.

—*D.R.*
ATLANTA, GEORGIA

BE REALISTIC ABOUT OTHER PEOPLE'S expectations. There's nothing wrong with sleeping with someone that you just met if that's what you want and that's all you want. But be aware that it's not like any kind of guarantee of anything else. That's all it is.

—*LEILA*
WASHINGTON, D.C.

. . . .

❝ The best dating advice I ever heard was 'be yourself.' So who else could I be? Tom Cruise? If you can be Tom Cruise, be Tom Cruise. You'll probably have more success. ❞

—*DAVID ARENSON*
JERUSALEM, ISRAEL

. . . .

DON'T GO SOMEPLACE ULTRA-FANCY for a blind date. It's overkill, and seems kind of desperate, I think. The best blind date I ever went on was when this guy took me out to a casual pizza-and-beer place—not tacky, but casual and fun. It made me relaxed, and we ended up hitting it off really well.

—*J.D.*
BALTIMORE, MARYLAND

I HAVE A FRIEND WHO HAS GREAT ADVICE about finding girls: Live with girls. Get one as a room-mate. They are always cleaner, and they bring other girls around. He's had a lot of dates—all her friends.

—*JEREMY FORCÉ*
BOSTON, MASSACHUSETTS

• • • • • • • •

GOING TO A BAR IS A WASTE OF TIME. What are the odds you're going to meet The One at a bar? If you like scuba diving, meet people scuba div-ing. If you like hiking, meet someone there. You're more likely to meet someone who's com-patible while doing something you like.

—*ANONYMOUS*
NEW YORK, NEW YORK

• • • • • • • •

I LOVE EMAIL RELATIONSHIPS. You can be cynical and funny and you get a hint of the true character of a person in email. It's something you don't get with a phone call.

—*LISA*
NORTH CAROLINA

• • • • • • • •

DATING ONLY HAPPENS WHEN you realize you are incredible. The aura of independence is probably the sexiest thing you can emanate. You feel it, you live it, you love it, you believe it. That moment when I felt incredible and happy to be independent is when I had my planner full with Friday night dates.

Also, DATE. Learn from men, and then love one later. Stop trying to fall in love. Start having fun. Do not be afraid of it.

—*AMBREEN HUSSAIN*
NEW YORK, NEW YORK

Women are attracted to the men they love. Men love the women they're attracted to.

—*KIM*
JACKSONVILLE, FLORIDA

7 PLACES TO MEET SOMEONE NICE

The Park. It might sound cliché, but city parks were created to allow people to commune with nature – and each other. Bring a friend, a Frisbee, and a cooler, and be ready to have a conversation with a stranger. Bring a dog, and you have an almost foolproof way to meet other people.

The Coffee Shop. With free wireless available at most coffee shops these days, you'll often find a healthy crowd of non-drunk people there. Even at night. Seating at many of these places almost forces conversation with others. Read the paper, work/play on your laptop – and be ready to talk to others.

A Sporting Event. Run a 5k, join a kickball league, see your town's most popular sports team. Other people will be there, too, ready to have fun.

A Volunteer Event. Nice people do nice things for others. Spend a weekend day volunteering for an organization. You might plant trees or help build a house or clean up a portion of a river. And you will not be alone. Volunteering is a great way to meet other people doing positive things for their community.

An Art Event. We're not talking about one of those high-falutin' art events where you pay a large sum to get in and everyone judges you by how you dress. We're talking about free or low-cost events. Scour your local weekly for readings, art shows, screenings. They're out there, and they attract an interesting crowd.

A Class. Like to learn about cooking? Want to make pottery? Interested in a new foreign language? Take a class. If you meet someone in the class, you can assume at least two things about them: 1) You have at least one similar interest. 2) They are interested in improving themselves, which is an encouraging sign in a new friend.

Church. Granted, if you don't like religion, this might be off-putting. But if you're open to it, you're guaranteed to meet a whole different population of people on Sunday mornings than you would at a bar on Saturday night.

—The Editors

THE DIFFERENCE BETWEEN DATING in the real world and dating in college? There was no dating in college. In college you went out with friends, drank, maybe went home with someone. The next Thursday rolled around, and the cycle repeats. Guys didn't need to actually call girls or make THAT much of an effort. They randomly ran into them on campus or off because everyone just KNEW where to go on any given night. In New York I'm lucky if I go to the same bar twice! Let alone recognize someone I saw at said bar three weeks ago.

—*ROBIN*
NEW YORK, NEW YORK

Don't ever take a first date out for ribs.

—*MIKE*
DENTON, TEXAS

THIS IS MY BEST SIDE

Have someone of the opposite sex look at your online profile. What guys think is great, women think is not essential, or inappropriate, or not critical to finding the right woman. I was involved in online dating, but I wasn't particularly active. While visiting a friend in New York, she asked me how the dating scene was going. I said, "Not so well." She looked at my profile and said, "This sucks."

She revised it and advised me to put up different pictures. I put a surfing shot out there and a picture of me on a dinghy in Laos—I was going to get someone who liked travel and liked to rough it a bit, as opposed to those would want to go to the Ritz-Carlton. Also, I wasn't smiling in one of the previous pictures. Smiling is a good thing. As soon as I updated my profile, I got a hit from the woman who has been my girlfriend for a year.

Get someone to edit your profile for you. It's like writing an essay.

—*DON REIGROD*
SAN FRANCISCO, CALIFORNIA

NO-DUMPING RULES

Is there a good way to dump someone? Probably not, but some ways are better than others. According to my very unscientific study with some friends in my living room one evening, the worst way to deliver the news is via text message (extra points deducted if you have a lazy thumb and use abbreviations: "I cant c u. over").

Breaking up is hard to do. But it helps to be considerate with the basics like time, place and delivery method so you don't add insult to injury. Here are my five "don'ts" of dumping:

1. Timing Is Everything: How many times have I heard someone explain, "I can't break up now. It's a bad time because... (fill in the blank with any event from a friend's wedding to a family reunion)"? There will NEVER been a good or comfortable time to end it with someone you care about, so don't wait for the perfect opportunity. The only exceptions to the timing rule are your date's birthday, a significant holiday like New Year's Eve, or the night before he or she has an important presentation at work.

2. Location, Location, Location! If possible, pick a neutral and quiet place to end your relationship. It may get emotional, so make sure that the dumpee is not driving when you have the conversation and that you're in a place where you both have an opportunity to express yourself without worrying about eyes peering at you. And do not break up at his or her favorite place or restaurant! He or she will never want to go back.

3. The Incredible Disappearing Date: If you've gone out a number of times or have seen each other for a few months, don't suddenly disappear and then rely on your date to get the message that it's over. A close second to disappearing is relaying the message via email or text. If you're going to do that, make sure to include the fact that you would like to have a conversation following your note. Have the courage to end it in person and allow your ex to respond.

4. Hooking Up Will Screw You Up: I'm all for recycling, but not in this case. No booty calls with the person you've broken up with! You're not only making it harder on your ex, who will cling to any glimmer of hope you offer, but you're making it harder on YOURSELF since you'll eventually have to break up all over again when you meet someone new.

5. Mouth Wide Shut: I believe in breakup karma. If you blab to everyone about why you want to end the relationship before you pull the plug, or gossip all over town after you end it, it may come back to haunt you. The dating world is smaller than you think. Unless your ex has done something that you feel you need to alert the masses about (and not just your close friends), keep the details of your relationship private and respect your ex.

—Andrea Syrtash

TAKE TIME TO THINK ABOUT TOPICS you and your date can talk about. I picked topics that would be inspiring to my date and fun to talk about for both of us. If you go in prepared, it'll make her feel important and show that you really care about what interests her. I went out with a girl who was getting her master's in special education. So, I picked topics related to that.

—*W.O.*
SYRACUSE, NEW YORK

• • • • • • • •

I AM LOVING MY INDEPENDENCE. I just got a dog a few months ago and I sometimes feel smothered by that commitment, let alone a six-foot-tall slobbering fool who won't let me sleep the night all the way through. I am enjoying my life solo because once I do get married and have kids, I will be tied down forever.

—*JENNIFER*
ALABAMA

A SENSITIVE GUY'S GUIDE TO LOVE

1) Open yourself up and love. Yeah, it's scary as hell. Yeah, there's a good chance it'll cause you a ton of pain. But it's worth it.
2) Time will heal most all of our wounds, but it doesn't mean you won't have scars. Scars are good.
3) Love is gray - beautiful gray. There is no "right" way. We stumble through life the best we can, loving others the best we can.
4) Be gentle with yourself and with those you love, but make sure to start by being gentle with yourself and your mistakes.

—*COLEMAN SMITH*
ATLANTA, GEORGIA

LIGHTS, CAMERA... ACTION?

THERE'S A THEORY THAT MOVIES MAKE BAD FIRST DATES. Sure, it's an anti-social meeting—you're in the dark and you can't talk to this person sitting next to you whom you've just met. Debunking that myth, I have had good movie first dates. If you've spoken to your date and there's been some banter, or maybe you had time to grab a drink beforehand and there's chemistry, a movie can be fun because it increases the intrigue. A nudge in the dark is sexy, romantic, and if you're able to laugh together, that's great. A movie might give you a sense of his/her humor radar. If it's an interesting movie, you'll have something to talk about at dinner—or at least on the way to dinner. I wouldn't pick just any movie, but if it has some depth, it could give you a good basis for conversation or insight.

—*E.L.S.*
BERKELEY, CALIFORNIA

• • • • • • • •

DON'T GO TO THE MOVIES. The worst first dates of my life have all been movie dates. You don't get to know the person at all, it's unoriginal, and it can be really uncomfortable if there are any sex scenes. Avoid the movies and go somewhere you can talk!

—*M.S.*
NEW YORK, NEW YORK

• • • • • • • •

RENT ONE OF THESE American Film Institute top-rated movies for a date at home. Add microwave popcorn and see what happens!

1. Casablanca (1942)
2. Gone with the Wind (1939)
3. West Side Story (1961)
4. Roman Holiday (1953)
5. An Affair to Remember (1957)
6. The Way We Were (1973)
7. Dr. Zhivago (1965)
8. It's a Wonderful Life (1946)
9. Love Story (1970)
10. City Lights (1931)

I MET A GUY RECENTLY who told me where he worked, so I Googled his name. I saw his company profile and found out some personal information about him, like the sports he played in college. It was too forward for me, because when I went out with him and he introduced different conversations, I knew some of the background already. I felt like a stalker. Better to let things unfold naturally.

—MARY
RENO, NEVADA

· · · · · · · ·

"Use the kiss test. On Date One, sometime during dinner, stare at her and ask yourself, 'Do I want to kiss her?' If yes, keep going and see what happens. If no, it's bad news and get out A.S.A.P."

—AMOL DIXIT
MINNEAPOLIS, MINNESOTA

· · · · · · · ·

I'D KISS A GUY AT THE END OF THE FIRST DATE. After that, it just depends on what I thought about him. Don't have sex if you think it will make him like you: That's something an 18-year-old girl would do. Don't do it if you don't feel like doing it.

—KATE
ATLANTA, GEORGIA

HOW TO STEAL A GIRLFRIEND

STEP ONE: Tell the man she is going out with that you intend to steal her from him. Be prepared for a barrage of threats or even a physical confrontation. The other man will become paranoid and jealous. He will question her daily about her plans before letting her out of his sight. He will scrutinize her attire. ("Why are you wearing that revealing outfit just to go out with the girls?") He will drive her insane.

STEP TWO: Create the impression that you are seeing her when he is not around. Call her at home when he is there and have a casual conversation. If she laughs as she is talking to you, this will increase his jealousy and poor behavior. Be seen walking out of her place of business when he arrives to pick her up or visit her.

STEP THREE: Establish yourself as a sympathetic ear. As he becomes more clingy, make sure she turns to you to complain about his neurotic behavior.

STEP FOUR: Wait. Eventually, his insecurity will become unbearable and she will dump him. Then you can move in and ask her out.

—*DANIEL DUNKLE*
ROCKLAND, MAINE

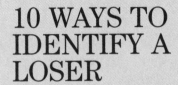

10 WAYS TO IDENTIFY A LOSER

If your man has done any of the following, run:

1. If he asks for a beer at breakfast.

2. If he has to call his mother before staying over.

3. If everything he owns fits in one or two boxes.

4. If he only drives a bicycle.

5. If he used to have a drug problem, but now he has found God.

6. If his last address included "Department of Corrections".

7. If he is married but it is "just not working out".

8. If, when describing him to your friends, you find yourself using the phrase, "But he's a really nice guy."

9. If he takes you to the 7-Eleven for a chili cheese dog.

10. If he asks to borrow money on the first date.

—SHAWN M. GREEN
MELBOURNE, FLORIDA

I WENT TO AN **NBA** GAME FOR A FIRST DATE a little while ago. It was super fun because the game was exciting, so we could talk about the game while we were having a getting-to-know-each-other chat. And there was that mystery, because we would only make occasional eye contact.

—*T.J.*
GRASS VALLEY, CALIFORNIA

• • • • • • • •

TURN OFF THE CELL PHONE. I went on a date just recently with a guy who didn't turn his cell phone off and it kept ringing throughout the meal. It was just his friends checking in and he was like, "Hey, I'm out on a date. What are you doing?" I'm like, hello. Needless to say, we didn't date after that.

—*AMBERLY COY*
SAN DIEGO, CALIFORNIA

• • • • • • • •

I LIKE TO GO TO A BAR ON A FIRST DATE. You can have a few drinks and get to know him. And if you don't like him, you can say, "I'm gonna go over here for a minute." And if you do like him, you can sit there and totally focus on him and you don't even realize what else is going on.

—*CRYSTAL*
BREMEN, GEORGIA

If you're on a first date, watch how much you drink. Catch a buzz, fine. But you're trying to find out who this person is. If you're drunk, that makes it difficult.

—*JOHN PIRIO*
NEW ORLEANS, LOUISIANA

THAT COLOGNE IS SO. . . DIFFERENT

Women are likely to choose mates whose body odor differs from their own natural scents. According to theories proposed in a Swiss study, the collision of odors may somehow create better immune protection for their offspring.

20 DATES FOR UNDER $20

Think of the best dates you've experienced. I'm guessing some of them were memorable moments that didn't cost you a lot of money. The truth about dating is that as long as a date features an activity you and your date enjoy together, there's no need to splurge for every occasion.

Whether you want adventure, romance, outdoor exploration, or cultural exposure, there are plenty of low-cost options to choose from.

Adventurous Dates:

1. Play tourist in your city for a day. Buy a guidebook and discover interesting walking tours.
2. If you and your date enjoy photography, pack your cameras and go on a photography adventure together.
3. Dine at an affordable restaurant offering Eastern cuisine – like Chinese or Indian – and enjoy a cheaper and more exotic meal than your usual date fare.
4. Check out your local paper or the Internet for free events or festivals in your area.
5. Visit your city's famous landmarks that you probably take for granted – or haven't seen since you were a little kid!

Romantic Dates:

1. Hang out at a cozy or charming café for dessert and a drink.
2. Meet for a glass of wine at a wine bar in an interesting area before taking a stroll in the neighborhood.
3. If you've hung out a few times, invite your date over and make a gourmet pizza together.
4. Take a Salsa dance class, which is often cheap or free.
5. Rent a rowboat with your date on a sunny day.

Outdoor Dates:

1. Go on a bike ride or walk that includes a destination offering ice cream or a cold drink.
2. Shoot hoops, play Frisbee, or rollerblade. Sports are great for competitive flirting!
3. If one or both of you have a dog, visit a dog park together.
4. Plan a picnic. Impress your date with a fun dish.
5. Go fly a kite (just don't tell your date that, or he/she may get offended...)

Cultural Dates:

1. Check out your city's indie bands. It's a great way to support local musicians and the cover is cheap.
2. Go see live comedy. Even if it stinks, you'll still laugh.
3. See an old film at a repertory movie house.
4. Attend a lecture or a workshop on a topic that you're both interested in learning more about.
5. Enjoy a gallery or museum together (many galleries even allow you to pay what you can).

—Andrea Syrtash

BE PREPARED

YOU HAVE TO USE PROTECTION, but if you get caught without it, sometimes that can be for the best. Being condom-less, if you refrain from sex, can slow things and give you time to build the relationship before the next opportunity.

—*JESSE WOODRUFF*
WAYNESBORO, VIRGINIA

• • • • • • • •

IF YOU CARRY PROTECTION WITH YOU ON DATES, never keep it in the same place twice. I might put it in my jeans' pocket one time, in my wallet the second, and in my jacket the third. That way, if a girl ever stumbles upon it and accuses you of having bad intentions, you can prove her wrong next time, without being caught off guard.

—*ABIY WONDESSEN*
ETHIOPIA

• • • • • • • •

I ALWAYS HAVE CONDOMS AT HOME, and I keep some in my car. My generation has grown up with them. I don't know anyone who doesn't have them in their nightstand. Nobody likes them. But if you understand the issue, you shouldn't care whether he likes them or not.

—*MEGAN RAMSEY*
PLANO, TEXAS

• • • • • • • •

IT'S THE GUY'S RESPONSIBILITY to have condoms and the girl's responsibility to be on the pill if she doesn't want to get pregnant. When I was dating my old girlfriend and we didn't have a condom, I'd run out to get one because I knew it was up to me. There was one time I stumbled out of her bed at 2 a.m. so I would be prepared in the morning.

—*C.S.*
IOWA CITY, IOWA

THROW THOSE FLANNEL PAJAMA PANTS AWAY! You *never* know where you'll meet a significant other or even (drum roll, please) Mr. or Mrs. Right. One of my best friends met her fiancé while at a convenience store. Do you think her fiancé would have approached her if she had on her favorite flannel pants with socks and sandals? I don't think so.

—*JAMESE JAMES*
DALLAS, TEXAS

• • • • • • • •

"People aren't going to knock on your door and ask to be your date. Put yourself out there. If I think a guy is cute, I talk to him. What do I have to lose? He'll say, 'You're stupid.' And I'll say, 'So are you.'"

—*LEANNE*
ATLANTA, GEORGIA

• • • • • • • •

IF YOU KNOW IT'S NOT WORKING, get out immediately. Once, a guy asked me out to dinner and the waitress took a long time to take our order, so he and I started to talk. We quickly realized we had *nothing* in common. So I said, "You know, it's really early. If we go now, we still have time to meet someone else." It was great: We both parted ways and we were both clearly relieved.

—*KELLY JUSTICE*
RICHMOND, VIRGINIA

Consider

PRIMPING YOUR PROFILE

Dating after college is a whole new ballgame, and so is Facebook. There's a good chance that you are already active on it or other social networking sites, but have you thought about how they can affect your love life? Here's how to make the most of your online profile.

Show Who You Really Are

When you're looking at someone's profile on Facebook, it's easy to forget that there is actually a real person behind it. People are complicated, multifaceted and fascinating, and 99 percent of them never show that on Facebook. Let's take Jim, for example - a runner, a rap fan, and a radiology resident. Jim's entire profile is full of quotes from movies and pictures of him with his fraternity brothers. Not surprisingly, women are not beating his door down, when he's actually an awesome catch! Make sure you don't fall into that trap; show everyone how well rounded you really are.

Interests/Hobbies

Think of your Facebook profile like your own advertisement – list the hobbies and interests that you want to advertise. And be sure you're showing them off the right way. Let's take Lisa, for example. By looking at her profile, you'd think she did nothing but watch TV – the list of shows she likes is a mile long. In actuality, Lisa is an artist and avid rock climber – a lot more interesting and attractive qualities than being a fan of The Bachelor! A little thought and attention to what guys find appealing would make her exponentially more attractive on Facebook.

Pictures

They say a picture is worth a thousand words, but on Facebook it's more like a million. Many of us have seen unflattering snapshots from bachelor and bachelorette parties, for instance. The photos may have been funny at the time, but it's not pretty on Facebook. Unless you relish the idea of being single forever, follow these Facebook photo tips:

- Wear clothes. Beauty is in the eye of the beholder, so please, no bathing suit shots.
- Pictures of you wasted are unattractive. Always. Trust us.
- Fun people are attractive people. Include lots of pictures of you on vacation, with your friends, or doing your favorite hobbies.
- Out with the old. If you break up with someone, lose the pictures or it looks like you're still hung up on your ex.

—Elizabeth Lovett
Angie Mock
Robert Rhu

TAKE THE TIME WHEN YOU'RE YOUNG (early 20s!) to date all kinds of people so you don't feel as curious later on. I went out with someone right after college for seven years. Now, at 30 years old, I'm eager to experience different men before I get married.

—*A.C.*
    TORONTO, ONTARIO, CANADA

• • • • • • • •

DON'T BE TOO QUICK TO FALL IN LOVE. It's a mistake a lot of people make, maybe because being out of school makes them insecure and they want something to hold on to, or maybe because they think it's part of being grown-up. I fell in love with someone. But I also eventually felt like I was missing out on freedom, on dating, on living my life without having to think of the implications for someone else.

—*F.S.*
    CHAPEL HILL, NORTH CAROLINA

• • • • • • • •

DATING DATA

Garden snails court from 15 minutes to six hours. Part of the slow dance includes the snails shooting each other with special snail darts.

DATE PEOPLE YOU'VE SEEN in other relationships, because you learn how they act toward their significant other. After all the different boyfriends I've had in the past few years, it's funny that I ended up with one of my very best friends.

—*CHERI RIOT*
    MISSION VIEJO, CALIFORNIA

• • • • • • • •

I PLAY SOFTBALL AND IT'S A GREAT WAY to meet people, mostly because there's no pretension there. People who play are generally out to have a good time. I've had a few dates that have come out of playing ball.

—*LYNETTE*
    ST. LOUIS, MISSOURI

MORE CHEAP DATE IDEAS

The Classic with a Twist: Dinner and a Movie At *Home*:
With the ever-escalating price of restaurant fare and movie tickets, you will be lucky to escape dinner and a movie for two for under $100. A less expensive, yet more impressive, alternative is to invite your special someone over for a home-cooked meal and your favorite flick. With a little forethought, you can plan a delicious meal for two for no more than $30. Add to that a movie rental for about $5 and you have yourself a fun date that's easy on your wallet.

Take a Hike: Nature has everything the perfect date should have: flowers, ambient music, and – on some days, at least – romantic lighting. As an added bonus, nature tends to be free. Check your state's travel and recreation site for information about public parks and hiking trails best suited for your athletic abilities. Remember to pack your camera, a snack and plenty of water.

You, Me, and Julien Dupré: According to First Lady Michelle Obama, she and President Barack Obama went to the Art Institute of Chicago on their first date. Undoubtedly, President Obama, then a first-year student at Harvard Law, saved some money. Generally, art museums offer free or discounted rates for students. Many museums also offer free general admission one night a week. Some museums offer free admission to all people, all of the time. Whatever the admission price, a trip to a museum promises intriguing and scintillating conversation.

Just Desserts: How often does it happen that you finish an exquisite meal at your favorite restaurant only to discover that you – or your credit card – have no room for the molten chocolate cake or crème caramel? Solve either problem by inviting your date out for dessert instead of a meal. It's just as romantic, it's just as delicious, but it's also considerably less expensive.

—*Sarah Franco*

If you didn't graduate college with a boyfriend, good luck to you. You are now officially a cliché – the single 20-something living in the city looking for love.

—*ROBIN*
  NEW YORK,
  NEW YORK

IN MY EXPERIENCE, dating rules in the real world aren't much different than dating rules in college. I think some of the biggest confusion comes with all of the different ways you can contact someone through technology. What does it mean when he emails you versus posts on your Facebook wall? Or there can be confusion based on technology: I have dated some older guys who may not be into texting (a generational difference, to be sure). If he doesn't respond to my text I freak out, when in reality he's "not into" texting.

—*SHIRA PINSKER*
  WASHINGTON, D.C.

• • • • • • • •

DON'T SETTLE FOR THE COMFORTABLE. I had a serious relationship all though college and two years after. Upon graduation I was full steam ahead and ready to make some money. My boyfriend, on the other hand, was inching his way through his senior year. I moved out of the college town, back to the city, and started my new career. With such different priorities, things got pretty rocky. I saw the writing on the wall long before we actually broke up, but I didn't want to accept it. We finally called things off, and for a while I felt like I had forgotten how to date. It was a scary, lonely, fun, exciting, and depressing time all in one. I was forced to find myself again, and it was liberating.

—*DIANA, MUMMERT*
  CUMMING, GEORGIA

COLD FEET?

In 1950, the average age at which men got married was 22.8; for women, it was 20.3. Today, the average age for men is 27.5 and for women it's 25.6.

ONLINE DATING: WORTH A SHOT?

After ditching a long term, long distance relationship all during college, I decided to try online dating. Having joined *Match.com*, I have become a pro in online dating, after six months of 30+ first dates. Rather than making awkward eye contact across a bar or being hit on by those you deem undesirable, online dating provides a pre-selection process. Is there no initial attraction? Respond "not interested." Are they are a smoker, divorced, or have interests completely opposite from yours? You get a sneak-peek at what's to come in the get-to-know-you process. Although online dating requires putting yourself out there for public consumption (yes, your family, friends, business associates, etc. could potentially see you pouring your soul into your online profile), it is a perfect place to find like-minded individuals. Out of my 30+ dates, I can honestly say I haven't had a bad experience or a truly undesirable date ... even though I'm still as single as can be!

—*ERIN MCCORMICK*
MIDDLEBURY, VERMONT

LET YOUR FRIENDS SET YOU UP on blind dates. They know you, and sometimes they have a sixth sense about what sort of person you could be compatible with. A friend of mine set me up with my future husband after going on a blind date with him herself. She called me the next day and told me that she wanted to give him my number and something in her voice told me to go along with her plan. Normally, I wouldn't have agreed to go out with a complete stranger, but my friend insisted that he was a quality guy and she was right. We hit it off immediately.

—*NICOLE LESSIN*
HELOTES, TEXAS

DATING RULES FOR GUYS

I must have gone on 50 dates before I met my girlfriend. So, I consider myself a mini-expert in the subject. 12 rules to live by:

1. In college, the rule was, don't hook up with someone on the same floor/hallway as you. The same applies in the office: Stay away from your colleagues.

2. Online sites aren't for nerds, but the temptation to only rely on them is bad form. Use them as a supplement. Use them to meet people, but don't forget to get out of the house once in a while.

3. Don't regret the times you let The One get away. The fact is, with over 300 million people in the States, The One is probably more like The 100, The 1000, etc. Be patient, another beauty will come along.

4. Don't be averse to having friends set you up. Even if it goes poorly, know your friends will keep looking for you.

5. On the same note, don't shut the door on someone from your past. Sometimes we overlook people in our past who only needed time to grow up.

6. Don't let the opportunity pass you by without a fight. It doesn't take much to say hi to someone in social setting. Let her – not your brain – decide that you have no chance.

7. Be yourself. If you can't be yourself in front of the girl you want to date, then you have no chance. Self-deprecating humor seems to work.

8. Everyone knows looks are important, but guess what? Chances are, you're no Brad Pitt/Heidi Klum. If you find someone who you click with, ask them out.

9. Don't use the same dating methods you did in college. Binge drinking in the dorm or drunk make-out sessions at the bar don't breed good relationships. Take the girl out. Bowling alleys, improv clubs, and food-crawls are really good, low-cost, successful ways to ensure a good time.

10. To kiss or not to kiss: As a good QB, you have to read the coverage. Is she playing a prevent defense (you have no chance)? Cover 2 (she has some room to let you in, but she's guarded)? Blitz (she's all over you like white on rice)? If it's there on the first date, a small, romantic kiss works.

11. Chivalry still prevails. Just don't use your sword too early.

12. A great way to meet people is just to go out during the day and walk around. Yeah, getting a dog helps, but seriously, most people are normal during the day and easier to talk to if they think you are talking to them to be nice. At night, women turn the switch on and lock the chastity belts.

—RYAN
PHILADELPHIA, PENNSYLVANIA

INTIMACY AND KISSING ARE PERSONAL. You should wait until you trust the other person and you just "can't wait" to take that step.

—*SHANA O'NEIL*
LAS VEGAS, NEVADA

• • • • • • • •

NEVER MAKE DATE NUMBER ONE a dinner date. You don't know this person, so spending $80 is ridiculous. It's not even about "impressing her." First dates should be about conversation over a drink.

—*KEN K.*
SAN FRANCISCO, CALIFORNIA

• • • • • • • •

USE EVERYONE AS A RESOURCE. Networking is NOT just for the professional world. I don't turn down a blind date, introduction or random party invite. You never know who you're going to meet on any night. And make yourself available. In college it was perfectly acceptable to go out with a group of 20 girls in tow. In New York keep it bare bones—I find I talk to/meet the most guys when I go out with a group of three girls at most. Guys do NOT want to have to talk to five girls to get to you, trust me.

—*ROBIN*
NEW YORK, NEW YORK

17

The Inner You: On Health, Spirituality & FUN

A simple truth: There is a finite amount of beer and midnight pizza dinners one body can take before the effects start to show. In other words, part of the fun in college is enjoying relatively good health without even thinking about it. But sooner or later (it's getting sooner by the minute), you will have to work to stay healthy. We talked with other recent grads about how they've learned to juggle a new life with healthy habits and the spiritual changes they undergo as they set out on their own. Read on to find out how to stay happy with yourself, inside and out.

QUIT SMOKING *NOW.* You won't do it later. This is true for cigarettes and marijuana. They can be youthful indiscretions only so long as you're young. After that, they will control your budget and your social life in ways you don't realize.

—ERIKA
TALLAHASSEE, FLORIDA

REMEMBER: KETCHUP AND MUSTARD ARE NOT VEGETABLES.

—J.D.
UNITY, OHIO

HEAD LINES
Best Advice and Top Tips

- Eat right and exercise in your 20s; the habit will go a long way later in life.
- If you are lucky enough to have health insurance, use it.
- Make a list of things that make you happy and post it where you can see it every day.
- Don't give up your spirituality in pursuit of your career.
- Try to maintain a sense of balance within your body and your mind.

PUT SPIRITUALITY FIRST. When I graduated college, I immediately jumped into pursuing my career. I was very materialistic; my main goal in life was to own a BMW by age 30. I jumped from job to job, working first for an author, then becoming a newspaper reporter, then starting my own business as a fitness trainer. Unfortunately, while I was good at everything I tried, I had a lot of trouble finding inner satisfaction with anything. It wasn't until I went on a yoga retreat five years ago and met my spiritual teacher that my life started to change for the better. I now realize that unless you have spiritual satisfaction in your life, no amount of professional success will ever satisfy you.

—*ROBIN*
HARTFORD, CONNECTICUT

WHILE I WAS IN COLLEGE, my mom told me I should start taking multivitamins. I did it just to shut her up, but I was surprised how much better they made me feel. It didn't happen overnight, but over a period of months I realized that I had more energy than before, and that I seemed to get sick less than before, and even my thinking seemed clearer.

—*JASMINE MATRE*
COVINGTON, KENTUCKY

• • • • • • • •

Once or twice a year, take a break.

—*SANDY PRESCOTT*
MEDFORD,
NEW JERSEY

MAKE A LIST OF FIVE TO TEN SMALL THINGS that put a smile on your face and post it where you can see it every day. I used to have a very destructive habit: When I got stressed out, I stopped doing things I knew would make me feel better, like calling a friend, going for a walk, or taking a hot bath. Instead, I'd do negative things, like overeat, lie on the couch, and channel surf, because I was stuck in a downhill spiral of bad feelings. Fortunately, it was an easy habit to break. I made a list of fun things to do. It was an effective reminder that doing even one small thing can send you in a positive direction.

—*SAJIT GREENE*
UTICA, NEW YORK

• • • • • • • •

CHALLENGE YOURSELF to do an activity you would never do. I have done several half-marathons and an MS 150 Bike Race. I am not very fast or quick, but it is definitely something that gives you an awesome high!

—*ERIN BLACK*
PITTSBURGH, PENNSYLVANIA

THE KEY IS BALANCE. I still splurge and enjoy a big bowl of ice cream every now and then. I just make sure that I also exercise a bit more that day. It's unrealistic to try to banish something that you like from your life.

> —*JENNIFER*
> *KANSAS CITY, MISSOURI*

Most of the spiritual experiences I had before I was 30 were drug-induced.

—*PETER STEUR*
BRISBANE,
AUSTRALIA

I'VE STARTED TAKING CLASSES AT THE Y—kickboxing, step aerobics, interval training, and sculpting. It gives you a reason to force yourself to work out. Also, it's a great way to meet fun people. I find myself looking forward to going back just to see how they're doing.

> —*JAYME BOGGIANO*
> *ST. LOUIS, MISSOURI*

STAYING HEALTHY IN YOUR 20S is probably the hardest thing ever. You have just graduated from every chance to really play on a supercompetitive sports team, and you find yourself working all through the day just to crawl home with a desire to go get cocktails. The easiest way to stay healthy would be to join a gym nearby. Also, get into sushi.

> —*JENNI BACKES*
> *SEATTLE, WASHINGTON*

MAKE DEALS WITH YOURSELF. I'd promise myself that if I could sit through an hour-long mass on Sundays, I'd allow myself to go out to the bar on Tuesdays. And the beauty of it was that my parents didn't have to know about the deal. All they knew was that I went to mass on Sunday. It's a good way to start acting like an adult but give yourself a little reward, too.

> —*MIKE POUND*
> *UNITY, OHIO*

I HAVE GOTTEN IN THE HABIT OF GETTING out of bed before work, throwing on my running clothes, and doing three quick miles. Then I come home, put on the coffee, take a hot shower, and have a nice breakfast. I've found that getting the day off to a good, healthy start like that is invaluable. It just gets the day pointed in the right direction, and it creates positive momentum that can last through the whole day.

> —*JALLE LITTLE*
> *INDEPENDENCE, KENTUCKY*

Consider

❝ Just because the girl you brought home from the club later says, 'Oh God,' in the bedroom, that does not constitute having gone to church. Not by a long shot. ❞

> —*TED VALKO*
> *CHURCHILL, OHIO*

FAITH IS A HARD SELL to most 23-year-olds if they don't already have it, and most, even if they grew up in a church, don't have real faith. I went through a long period where I relied on Eastern practices to fill that gap for me—meditation and yoga. It helped. I was able to pay attention to the spiritual without compromising my sense of curiosity. I advocate experimentation at that time of life, exploring different faiths.

> —*F.S.*
> *CHAPEL HILL, NORTH CAROLINA*

IT'S ALL A MATTER OF PERSPECTIVE

PRETEND THIS IS A TV SHOW. No matter what happens, imagine reading in *TV Guide* that this is the plot for our show this week. Like, "Joey misses the bus leaving Chattanooga, and he's stranded there until someone notices." That really happened—the bus took off without me. I just sat on the bus bench until it came back. It took about an hour. The point is, it could be anything, or it could be nothing, but everyone can have his own TV show. It helps you cope with problems better, because nothing seems as serious.

> —*JOEY*
> *CAPE COD, MASSACHUSETTS*

• • • • • • • •

WHENEVER I HAVE A PROBLEM, and it seems really big, and it's really stressing me out, it helps me to look down on it from far away. The phrase in my head is, "Look at it from space." This helps me get along with difficult people in any area, because I think, "This really isn't such a big deal in the grand scheme of things." Instead of looking at a person's angry red face, I look at it from another planet, because it takes all of the personal stuff out of it. It separates you emotionally from what is going on.

> —*KAMI*
> *CAPE COD, MASSACHUSETTS*

I GOT A PERSONAL TRAINER, and in the mornings I meet him at my gym, we go for a run, and we weight-train. I try to work out every day. And I pay him in advance, so if I don't go, I lose money.

> —*ANONYMOUS*
> *LOS ANGELES, CALIFORNIA*

SPIRITUAL PRINCIPLES ARE IMPORTANT, but you can't use them as an excuse to ignore basic human incompatibilities. I'm a very spiritual person. A while back, I was feeling a lot of insecurity, fear, and anxiety in my relationship. I brushed aside these feelings and told myself, "Everything will be OK if only I can learn to forgive," or "God will work everything out in the long run." Basically, I was using the spiritual principles I believed in so firmly to deny what I was feeling on an emotional level. By the time I realized what I was doing, the relationship, along with my peace of mind, had deteriorated.

—*SAJIT GREENE*
UTICA, NEW YORK

• • • • • • • •

PICK UP A NEWSPAPER and look for an interesting event or function. Consider attending as a curious observer rather than with the expectation that it must be fun or the perfect activity for you. See what you can get out of it. I even went to AA meetings just to see what it would be like. Once, I went to a circus and pretended to be working there sweeping up for a little while. You have to be creative.

—*D.S.*
KENNEDY, NEW YORK

I play golf and do yoga. It helps alleviate stress and keeps me more focused at work.

—*GEHONG WANG*
ROCKVILLE,
MARYLAND

WE BELIEVE ... IN ATHEISM?

BETWEEN THE YEARS 1990 AND 2008, the percentage of Americans identifying as Christians has dropped from 86 percent to 76 percent, according to a survey by Trinity College. The number of atheists has nearly doubled since 2001, from 900,000 to 1.6 million.

EVEN IF YOU'RE NOT RELIGIOUS, a rear pew in a beautiful church is a great place to just think things over.

—*N.*
BROOKLYN, NEW YORK

• • • • • • •

66 Don't overestimate the power and allure of the elements. Why has mankind enjoyed the sight of the sunset or sunrise for thousands of years? Because it's cool and elemental. It connects you to your core self. 99

—*MICHAEL*
SAN FRANCISCO, CALIFORNIA

• • • • • • • •

AT LEAST ONCE A YEAR, I go to a different religious service at a different house of worship. It can be a variation of Christianity, Buddhism, Judaism, Islam, whatever. The important thing is that it shows me how other people get in tune with their version of God, and it feels good to do it. For those who are seeking something different from how they were raised, I highly recommend this. One day out of the year is not much, but it's really rewarding.

—*J.A.*
ATLANTA, GEORGIA

BE TRUE TO YOURSELF. I was raised Roman Catholic by two very religious parents. I went to church and Sunday school every single week as a child. As I grew older, I started to realize that there were a lot of things that the church teaches that I didn't really believe. I didn't know how to deal with it, so I just kept on keeping on. I didn't want to rock the boat. But once I got out on my own and started going to church alone on Sundays, it started to seem silly. Here I was spending all this time in a church that was teaching ideas that I didn't agree with. I was afraid to stop going because I knew it would kill my mother. One day I stopped at my parents' house and had a long talk with my mom about religion. To my surprise, she was cool about it. She said I had to follow my heart and that she wouldn't want me to spend the rest of my life living a lie.

—STAN SHENK
HARRISONBURG, VIRGINIA

* * * * * * * *

GROWING UP, WE HAD SHABBAT (Sabbath) dinner every Friday night and celebrated all the holidays in wonderful ways. I now know that traditions are really important and I also realize the extent of the effort that must go in. It's worth it to do these things. Being single in the big city—and not having my family here—I feel a bit uprooted. I don't have an automatic religious context. I notice it. I want to start a Friday night dinner club with my friends, but we still haven't because it takes time.

—JANNA
VANCOUVER, BRITISH COLUMBIA, CANADA

Eat well and go outside. That works for me.

—LOUIS HAGMAN
SEATTLE,
WASHINGTON

GIVING BACK: VOLUNTEERING

You're young. You're capable. And it's the right thing to do. You should spend some of your free time volunteering. Here's what others had to say about it.

VOLUNTEERING IS A GREAT WAY to test-drive a career. I always thought I wanted to be a teacher. Then I volunteered to teach. I realized it was *not* what I wanted to do!

— *TAMIKA BROWN*
ATLANTA, GEORGIA

VOLUNTEERING CAN TEACH YOU NEW BUSINESS SKILLS. When I first started my work with the Make-A-Wish Foundation, I had no experience in accounting or marketing. But I had to dive right in and learn those skills quickly. Service made me a better person and a better businessman.

— *PAT MORRIS*
MIAMI, FLORIDA

VOLUNTEERING HAS ALLOWED ME TO DO THINGS I would have paid money to do. I am a huge soccer fan, and I once was able to volunteer as an assistant press officer for World Cup USA. I acted as an interpreter, trained about 200 volunteers, and even escorted photographers onto the field. My childhood dream was to play in the World Cup, but this was close enough!

— *ANDREW LEONE*
FORT LAUDERDALE, FLORIDA

VOLUNTEERING IS A LOT LIKE WORKING OUT. You may dread the initial going-to-the-gym phase, but if you focus on how good you'll feel afterward, it's way easier to stay motivated.

— *MELISSA BIERI*
NEW YORK, NEW YORK

FOR SINGLE PEOPLE, VOLUNTEERING is a fantastic social bridge. I personally hate small talk, and working together on a project prevents having to engage in it. Service gives you something to do besides sitting around. If you are a shy or anxious person, meeting people this way is far superior to going to bars where you're in a dark room, shouting over loud music, and talking to someone who's probably not sober.

—SANDRA HAMEL
DAVIS, CALIFORNIA

JANE GOODALL, THE RENOWNED PRIMATOLOGIST, gave me some fantastic advice once. I went to see her when I was attending college and completely overwhelmed by all of the world's problems. I wanted to do something about them, but what? I asked her what I could do and she replied: "Just find your piece of it." I think that's excellent advice. Simply narrow the world's problems down to what you can best identify with and work on that one problem. A perfect example of that is my friend who grew up in the welfare system. These days she focuses on welfare issues. She found her piece of it!

—DENISE RIEBMAN
BOSTON, MASSACHUSETTS

IF YOU NEVER HAVE DONE ANY COMMUNITY SERVICE, try volunteering for a political campaign. You will meet people from all walks of life who share your passion. It's also a great starter opportunity since there is a limited time frame. You know when it begins and ends so you won't ever get stuck in it.

—SARA NEEDLEMAN-CARLTON
SEATTLE, WASHINGTON

VOLUNTEERING WON'T EXPOSE YOU JUST TO NEW PEOPLE, but really great ones! I've met some of my best friends through serving, and I even met my boyfriend this way. I believe that the people I meet while volunteering are the cream of the crop—more interesting, more involved, and nicer.

—HEATHER ALEXAKIS
FOREST HILLS, NEW YORK

SERVING OTHERS CAN HELP MEND A BROKEN HEART. Eight years ago, my long-term relationship broke up. When it finally ended, I stayed at home for two months and felt very sorry for myself. I realized I needed to snap out of it. Suddenly, a light went on: I should volunteer! I volunteered at a project that involved doing arts and crafts with abused and neglected kids. Helping these kids really put things in perspective for me: My problems suddenly seemed small in comparison to what they were going through.

—BOB ALDEN
   SAN DIEGO, CALIFORNIA

• • • • • • • •

VOLUNTEER. JUST DO IT. It is like explaining the taste of barbecue to someone who has never tasted it. The experience will explain it better than I ever could.

—JOE MULLIN
   ROUND ROCK, TEXAS

> Find a physical activity you like, and can be consistent at.
>
> —NADIA

I'VE LEARNED THAT EXERCISE truly is a big key to happiness. I'm usually at my happiest when I'm on a regular workout schedule. It's important not only for staying in shape, but for relieving stress built up from work or personal issues while balancing my mind. It's also important to switch my workout so that it doesn't get repetitive and boring. A few visits to a personal trainer are worth it, as they will always find ways to throw some variation into a workout.

—KATIE
   NEW YORK, NEW YORK

• • • • • • • •

I PLAY SOCCER, TENNIS, AND BASKETBALL and get recharged for work this way. In these games, we're allowed to yell at each other, and this helps me release tension from the real world!

—CENIK
   KAZAKHSTAN

IT'S HARD TO KEEP A HEALTHY LIFESTYLE in a big city because there are a ton of bad influences: poor air quality, smokers, drinkers, etc. But I walk a lot, work out at the gym, take vitamins, and don't drink or smoke in order to maintain a healthy lifestyle.

—ANONYMOUS
NEW YORK, NEW YORK

• • • • • • • • •

WORKING OUT AND EATING HEALTHY on a regular basis (i.e., not eating candy and Pop-Tarts for breakfast, lunch and dinner) will keep you feeling good. Also, practice good dental hygiene. It's expensive and painful not to care about your teeth!

—TAI DAVIS
PALATINE, ILLINOIS

• • • • • • • • •

Go to church. It won't kill you.

—FLORA JANICKI
FLORENCE,
KENTUCKY

I AVOID BURNOUT AT WORK by taking at least one kick-ass vacation a year, such as a week in San Francisco or a nine-day trip to Italy. It gives me something to look forward to, and that helps me get through the times when I feel like everything is falling in on me.

—VANESSA MOROGIELLO
WHITEHOUSE STATION, NEW JERSEY

• • • • • • • • •

MY BEST VACATION FROM WORK was when 15 of my closest friends and I flew to St. Louis and we spent the weekend hanging out and going to a Cardinals game. I know that doesn't sound nearly as amazing as going to the Bahamas or to Europe, but when you first start out and you're on a budget, getting all your friends together for a quick weekend trip can be just as fun.

—MARY-MARGARET BRITTON
DALLAS, TEXAS

DURING MY FIRST JOB OUT OF COLLEGE, I joined the Social Club in Chicago, which was a sports-oriented club for people in their 20s and 30s. We played outdoor volleyball and touch football, both of which were a lot of fun. Plus, it was a great way to meet guys!

—*ANONYMOUS*
NEW YORK, NEW YORK

· · · · · · · ·

" Work is an enabler. I do enjoy the work I do. But it gives me a paycheck, which allows me to experience the rest of life. A balanced life, where work does not define you, is the best kind. "

—*ANONYMOUS*

· · · · · · · ·

I AM A TEACHER, AND THE TWO AND A HALF MONTHS I have off over the summer are great for traveling. I've lived in 10 countries, including Spain, Morocco, Israel, Russia, and Turkey. I think it's important to continuously learn, even while you are not at work. I'm always learning and teaching myself new languages. I just try to expose myself to as many different cultures as I can.

—*ANONYMOUS*
BEVERLY HILLS, CALIFORNIA

YOU KNOW YOU'RE WORKING TOO MUCH WHEN ...

... YOU DREAM ABOUT WORK. That's always my sign that I need a breather. When I'm literally rehearsing a big presentation in my sleep, I know I need a day off.

—*KELLY WILKES*
ATLANTA, GEORGIA

... YOU WAKE UP IN THE MIDDLE of the night thinking of all the things you need to do at work. You have to separate work and home or you will go crazy. It is one of the hardest things to do, but it's the most important.

—*LIZ RINEY*
PHILADELPHIA, PENNSYLVANIA

... IT'S DARK WHEN YOU GET TO WORK, and dark when you leave the office.

—*D.B.*
COPPELL, TEXAS

... YOUR NECK ACHES FROM SQUEEZING the phone receiver with your shoulder, your throat is sore from talking, your eyes are watering from staring at the computer monitor, and your backside, from sitting in a desk chair all the time, is as flat as a pancake.

—*M.K.*
BROOKLYN PARK, MINNESOTA

HOW TO PREVENT BURNOUT, AND HOW TO GET OUT OF IT WHEN YOU'RE IN IT

Burnout can sometimes occur when you work too hard for too long, to the point of emotional and physical fatigue. Clients who come to me when they are burned out sometimes feel hopeless and powerless about making a change, cynical, uncreative, and as if they are failing. Every idea they or someone else has is met with "I don't have the energy to do that."

I believe that burnout is a symptom of not feeding your creative side. By creative side, I don't mean only your artistic side, but literally the part of you that can create: create new ideas, create a plan, even create a new job or opportunity. Creativity is like a well of energy. If you've been draining the well and not replenishing it, you are going to burn out.

So, what do you do to prevent burnout or to get out of it? Feed your creative side. Make sure that you are doing things that feel good to you, that feed your soul, that give you energy just by doing them. Creative activities (painting, dancing, writing, photography, and so on) are great, but so are things like taking a long walk on the beach or in nature, working out regularly, or taking a class about something that interests you. None of these things should be done for any reason but the joy of doing them. My favorite easy homework for burned-out clients is to go to one of those pottery-painting places. It's easy to go, sit down, and start painting a mug or a plate, not because it will be beautiful, but solely for the fun and joy of doing it. It puts you in a totally different state, uses a different part of your brain than the part you use for work, and is simply a new experience. Do something that uses your creative side a few times a week for a few weeks, and don't be surprised if the creativity starts flowing again.

—Ricki Frankel

WHEN I'M MOTIVATED IN THE MORNING, I jog to my gym (an easy two miles) and take a yoga class. I get to the office unstressed.

—*ANONYMOUS*
SAN FRANCISCO, CALIFORNIA

• • • • • • • •

ALWAYS MAKE SURE YOU HAVE DAYS OFF. And when you take breaks during your day, try to get away. Instead of sitting in your office for lunch, go away. Even if you just sit in your car, do it so you don't see all the papers on your desk that you have to deal with.

—*AMBERLY COY*
SAN DIEGO, CALIFORNIA

• • • • • • • •

" My father-in-law told me once, 'No one will ever thank you for not taking your vacations.' So I take all my vacations. "

—*BOB G.*
VIRGINIA BEACH, VIRGINIA

• • • • • • • •

I'M A SOCIAL WORKER. There's a lot of stress in my job, so I get massages. I drink. I go out with friends a lot. I see a lot of live music. I shoot pool. I read a lot. I run. I really enjoy my free time; that's how I deal with it.

—*ANONYMOUS*
CINCINNATI, OHIO

I USED TO COMMUTE BY MOTORCYCLE, and let me tell you, by the time I got home, work was the last thing on my mind. Concentrating on riding safely left little room for thinking about work, and the exhilaration of the ride lifted my spirits and reminded me of what I was working for.

—*REGINA*
LOS ANGELES, CALIFORNIA

• • • • • • • •

> I keep sane by traveling often. I travel every two months, and that helps me get by.
>
> —*B.E.*
> *LOS ANGELES, CALIFORNIA*

TAKE A PERSONAL DAY HERE AND THERE. Not all the time, and certainly not when you have work to do or people depending on you to be at work. But if a day comes when you can afford to miss work, take it. Walk through the park, drive to the beach, do something that will make you relaxed and happy. The world won't stop spinning just because you missed a day of work. And on this day of freedom, leave your BlackBerry at home.

—*B.B.*

• • • • • • • •

I USED TO FIND IT VERY DIFFICULT to wind down after work. I would be very tense, and my mind was still at work. Now, I ride my bike to and from work every day. The ride takes about 45 minutes. It really helps to clear my mind and destress my body. By the time I get home, I'm relaxed, clear, and sweaty!

—*J. K.*
SWEDEN

HIT 'SNOOZE'

In its 2009 poll, the National Sleep Foundation found that Americans get an average of only about 6.7 hours of sleep a night during the workweek. A solid eight hours of sleep a night is recommended.

5 TIPS TO STAY MENTALLY AND PHYSICALLY HEALTHY

1. *Exercise.* The first thing to remember: The physical affects the mental. Exercise is not just good for the body; it's great for battling depression, anxiety and stress. Schedule exercise into your weekly routine. Work out, run, play a sport. Just get out and get the lactic acid and endorphins flowing.

2. *Sleep.* That means sleep regularly. Eight hours a night is best. Your body's circadian rhythm demands it. Mess that up and, studies have proven, your thinking deteriorates and you just feel bad. Note: Eight hours of sleep a night does *not* translate to one hour of drunken sleep one night followed by 15 hours of hung-over sleep the next.

3. *Be kind to yourself.* Do the small things that make you happy. Clean out your car. Sit down and read the paper at your favorite bagel shop. Get a manicure. Being kind to yourself helps you feel good about yourself. It sounds simple, but you have to make the effort.

4. *Eat well.* A good breakfast in the morning means a better day of productivity. But lunch and dinner matter, too. Eat lots of fruits, veggies, whole grains and protein. Shy away from fast or processed food. And drink lots of water.

5. *Find your pace.* Sure, you're young and you can still pull all-nighters. But life is a long-distance race, not a sprint. Find a strong pace and stick to it.

—The Editors

HEALTHY - AND CHEAP

We don't need expensive gym memberships ... because the world is our gym! Look at all the depictions of great men like Hercules, Jesus and Poseidon! Do you see how ripped they are? It's safe to say that that Jesus did NOT possess a membership to Cardio Express. Here are just a few things that you can do to get that heart rate going that don't cost a penny.

- Um, go outside? There are tons of things to do outside besides getting the mail: road running, hiking, walking, swimming in local watering holes, biking, Ultimate Frisbie, and Wiffleball. Granted, these are not "classic" exercise activities, but anything that gets your heart rate going and gets you breathing heavy is physical activity. Of course, the amount of calories you burn is dependent upon your intensity, but all the more reason to dive for that volleyball.

- Join a team. Kickball, Dodgeball, Soccer... doesn't matter! Just get out there and do something. Don't know anyone? Worst excuse ever. I mean, at one point you didn't know your best friend. Look how far you've come! Everything is strange and awkward at first, but then it's not. A good place to start looking is just talk to people or check out postings at the YMCA or community center.

- Take the stairs. This is a great workout for your hamstrings, quads and derrière. Plus, you don't have to wait for the elevator and you won't have to risk awkward elevator conversation with your boss about the never-ending construction on your local interstate highway.

- "Fake join" a gym. As a New Englander, I am familiar with the hellish ordeal that Mother Nature bestows upon us every winter. When worst comes to worst and it's simply unfathomable to trek it through the snow, I always resort to a great trick. Many gyms have a "trial period" where you don't entirely sign up, but are usually granted a two-week pass to check out the facility. I'm not saying it's right, but I'm not saying it's wrong.

—AMANDA AUGERI
MIDDLETOWN, CONNECTICUT

STAYING HEALTHY AND EXERCISING in the real world is of utmost importance. After being an active college student, sitting behind a desk all day can be harder than expected. At first, I missed the casual walks between classes, the fresh air. Joining a gym and taking classes is an excellent way to introduce yourself to a new community. Whether finding an exercise partner, a good friend, or someone to date, you never know! It makes you feel good to exercise and extends your social network.

—*ERIN MCCORMICK*
MIDDLEBURY, VERMONT

* * * * * * * *

EXPERIMENT WITH HEALTHY FOODS. When you were living at home, you probably got the same fruits and vegetables from your mother. Moms tend to stick with what works. But don't be afraid to experiment. When I moved out on my own, I went to the produce section of the market and bought all kinds of things that I had never tried before. I didn't even know what most of them were, but I figured if they were produce, they had to be good for me. I found a real love for kiwi, which I had never been exposed to at home.

—*COLIN MCDOUGLE*
CANFIELD, OHIO

* * * * * * * *

THE KEY TO STAYING HEALTHY is to build sports and activity into your life. I really miss working out when I am not able to. Essentially, I have replaced the hard-ass coach I had in high school with a little voice in my head reminding me to work out, to set goals, and to feel good about myself when I succeed.

—*STEPHEN MACKAY*
SOUTH ORANGE, NEW JERSEY

Know that spirituality is different from religion.

—*BRANDI DICOSTANZO*
DALLAS, TEXAS

THE STRESS OF ENTERING THE "REAL WORLD" can lead to some unhealthy habits. It is important to exercise, eat right, and stay on top of your health. I worked full-time while pursuing my Master's degree. In the process I stopped exercising and eating right. I gained 25 pounds and I am only five feet tall. I stopped taking care of myself because I was so overwhelmed and stressed. Since then I have taken better care of myself and I have taken off the weight. I highly recommend having a healthy diet and exercise regime. It will help your overall well-being and help to manage your stress.

—*RACHEL WIECK CUPIT*
NEW ORLEANS, LOUISIANA

• • • • • • • •

YOU NEED TWO THINGS TO STAY IN SHAPE: Someone to work out with, and a sports league or regular pickup league to join. I work out three times a week, but I probably wouldn't do it if I knew my buddy wasn't going to be there, waiting on me. And vice versa. Also, I play basketball on Wednesday nights in a YMCA league. I look forward to it during the week, and it keeps me active and in shape.

—*ALAN*
MEMPHIS, TENNESSEE

• • • • • • • •

I ALWAYS SAY THAT I HAVE GOD IN MY HEART, and that is where I celebrate him. Spirituality is what you make of it. I don't believe in going to church or going through the rituals required by certain religions. In my heart I know what is true, and it is there that my spirituality is prosperous.

—*HEATHER POLLOCK*
ORANGE COUNTY, CALIFORNIA

THE FIRST THING I DO AFTER WORK is go home and change my clothes. That's my literal and figurative transition: Now I'm home, and I'm me.

—*CAROL SCHEUREN*
LINDENWOLD, NEW JERSEY

• • • • • • • •

IF YOU'RE ONE OF THOSE PEOPLE with unused sick days each year, you should see a therapist. I don't care what the company says about sick day policies; they're there if you're really sick, but also if you need to get stuff done around the house, if you want to go to a ball game, if you feel like napping, or if you just hate your boss and need to spend a day throwing your résumé around town. Sick days should be taken advantage of.

—*GERALD*

• • • • • • • •

MY FAVORITE WAY TO RELIEVE STRESS is to go out to dinner with friends. All of my friends are in the same boat; we are all recent graduates who've just entered the "real world." There is nothing more reassuring than comparing stories with each other and realizing we are all trying to figure out the same things about surviving and succeeding in the workforce.

—*MEGAN ELIZABETH KUNTZ*
DALLAS, TEXAS

• • • • • • • •

EXERCISE WILL MAKE YOU FIT AND HAPPY! There's a ton of research on how exercise is more effective against depression than Prozac. I love to wake up earlier and go for a run before work. You'll feel great the whole day!

—*BARAK*
TEL AVIV, ISRAEL

More Wisdom: Good Stuff That Didn't Fit Anywhere Else

When you were living at home and having Mom act as your personal maid and Dad handle money-management duties (or vice versa), you probably heard your parents say one too many times, "After you graduate college and enter the real world, you're going to be in for a rude awakening." It's true. But short of stopping the hands of time or lining up a spot in a nice psychiatric ward, it's impossible to avoid it. Which is why we've gathered just a little more "life advice" from our respondents. Here's wishing you good luck – and welcome to your life!

IF YOU FIND YOURSELF counting among your accomplishments your high score on "Doom," you are not yet living in the real world, and perhaps you should take a break from your computer. There's a whole life out there waiting for you.

—J.A.
ATLANTA, GEORGIA

GET RID OF CABLE! READ A BOOK INSTEAD.

—SHANNON
LAS VEGAS, NEVADA

'fess up to your mistakes instead of making excuses or blaming others.

—MEGAN
  SYRACUSE,
  NEW YORK

APPRECIATE THE THINGS THAT OTHERS DO for you. My boyfriend and best friend really helped me with my first week of work, taking care of my dog and fixing breakfast. Having people you can depend on to help you through transitions, even if it's a friend across the country whom you can call, is one of the most fulfilling ways to success. Just make sure you return the favor when they need it!

> —LACEY CONNELLY
>   CHICAGO, ILLINOIS

• • • • • • • •

LEARN HOW TO BE A GOOD SALESPERSON, without dressing and acting like a salesperson.

> —ZACH
>   DALLAS, TEXAS

• • • • • • • •

I ALWAYS STICK TO THE SAYING, "Doubt means don't." I have become less impulsive in my decision-making. Once you are in the real world you are solely responsible for your decisions.

> —CASEY BOND
>   GRAND RAPIDS, MICHIGAN

• • • • • • • •

TRY NOT TO SWEAT THE SMALL STUFF. If you get in trouble, even so much so that your boss yells at you and you think it's the end of the world, it will pass. Just keep your head down and keep working hard, and everything will eventually go back to normal.

> —SARA WALKER

SUCCESS ISN'T MEASURED by HEMIs or McMansions, bank accounts or bling. Success is measured in the subtlety of life and in your everyday decisions. I'd sing praises to hear that you kept a tree from being cut down or a faucet from dripping. I'd be saddened to hear you live alone in an 8,000-square-foot home 30 miles from work. Keep it simple. And, oh yeah, girls don't like the smell of patchouli.

—ED AKINS II
STATESBORO, GEORGIA

. . . .

" 'Be friendly' is my motto.
I always smile. "

—SANDY PRESCOTT
MEDFORD, NEW JERSEY

. . . .

I RECENTLY TOOK UP PIANO, though I'm not musically inclined by nature. I did this to challenge myself and get out of my comfort zone. When you take up new hobbies that you've never tried and may not even be naturally good at, it helps keep other areas of your life fresh. You're challenging your brain to think in a new way, and when you go back to the real world, things feel newer and more exciting.

—JEFF MALTZ
SAN FRANCISCO, CALIFORNIA

Learn how to spell the word *weird*. I can't tell you how many really smart people write *wierd*.

—ANDREA
TORONTO,
ONTARIO, CANADA

YOU CAN DO IT!

Have patience with yourself. I moved hours from home after college. When I had to go back to my apartment, all I could do was sit on my couch, littered with unpacked bins, and cry. Part of me wanted to just call up the newspaper and say, "Yeah, you know when I accepted this job? I was just kidding." But luckily, I have a good friend who gives me "tough love." She basically explained to me that it's supposed to suck at first when you leave everything you're used to, and that I needed to give it three months.

Well, it's been three months. Not an easy three months, but I've made it, and I'm staying. It's a strange feeling to be so in charge of your own life. I've never been so accountable for my actions. You stop thinking of yourself as just a part of your family and think about what it will be like to start your own branch of the family tree.

There will be good days and bad days. Sometimes you'll be so happy with your decision to start your career, but there will also be the days where you would give anything to rewind your life and go back to your college days. But instead of thinking you already lived the best years of your life, I prefer to think that you have some good years left in you.

—*CHERYL*
PHILADELPHIA, PENNSYLVANIA

CLEANLINESS IS KEY. To avoid messiness, I clean in quick spurts, often. I don't want to put a Sunday aside for cleaning my place, so I Swiffer the floors while I brush my teeth in the morning. I actually like keeping my place in shape.

—BRIAN
NEW YORK, NEW YORK

* * * * * * * *

I THINK THE GREATEST CHALLENGE of living in the "real world"—of living, period—is finding ways to nurture your own sense of freedom and happiness in life, to keep all the pressures from making life feel more like a chore or a burden than the strange gift it really is.

—JOE
BOSTON, MASSACHUSETTS

* * * * * * * *

WRITE YOURSELF A LETTER OF ADVICE NOW, talking about your hopes and worries about the future. Put that letter away in a sock drawer or at the back of your filing cabinet. When you find it, read it.

—J.P.
CHARLOTTESVILLE, VIRGINIA

* * * * * * * *

WATCH THE NEWS MORE and have your own point of view. It's important to do these things as an adult. Be more educated. The news is a good place to start, and you may find connections with people that way.

—MICHAEL ALBERT PAOLI
TORONTO, ONTARIO, CANADA

Hope for everything and expect nothing. That way, when something good happens you appreciate it, and when something bad happens it doesn't get you down.

—H.O.
EVERETT,
WASHINGTON

Never skimp on Q-Tips and toilet paper.

—*JENNIFER*
SEATTLE,
WASHINGTON

JOBS ARE A WAY OF MAKING MONEY and ensuring financial stability so that you can focus on what really matters: your personal life. People work so that their quality of life can be high. Too many people stress out about their job being life changing or whether they are saving the world. I always remind them: *It's just a job.*

—*F.V.*
BERKELEY HEIGHTS, NEW JERSEY

● ● ● ● ● ● ●

" **My mom always says to me, 'Do the very best you can every single time. You never know who's watching you.'** "

—*SARAH DAVID HEYDEMANN*
MONTCLAIR, NEW JERSEY

● ● ● ● ● ● ●

PAYING THE BILLS IS IMPORTANT, but paying attention to what makes you happy will give you the biggest and best payoff. You spend most of your waking hours on the job, so make sure you are doing something that doesn't put your mind, body, or spirit to sleep. Life's too short, and you've got too much to give to this world.

—*SHELLIE R. WARREN*
NASHVILLE, TENNESSEE

> Your time is limited, so don't waste it living someone else's life. Don't be trapped by dogma – which is living with the results of other people's thinking. Don't let the noise of others' opinions drown out your own inner voice. And most important, have the courage to follow your heart and intuition. They somehow already know what you truly want to become.
>
> —*STEVE JOBS,*
> *2005 COMMENCEMENT SPEECH AT STANFORD UNIVERSITY*

TO LIVE THE LIFE YOU WANT, you have to 1) know what you want, and 2) go after what you want. You have to live intentionally, not accidentally. It took me a long time to figure that out.

—*N.*
BROOKLYN, NEW YORK

• • • • • • • •

IF YOU DECIDE TO STAY IN A SMALL TOWN, be nice to everyone. There's always going to be that person who drives you crazy, but you still gotta be nice. In a small town, if you pollute your environment with even one enemy, it can make your life miserable.

—*ANONYMOUS*
CHAPEL HILL, NORTH CAROLINA

• • • • • • • •

JUST REALIZE THAT AS HARD AS THINGS SEEM at first, they'll get better. I've learned that lots of things won't make sense until you look back at them down the road.

—*ANONYMOUS*
NEW YORK, NEW YORK

Whatever path you choose, make sure you have a Plan B.

—*ANONYMOUS*
LOS ANGELES,
CALIFORNIA

CREDITS

Page 9:   http://www.bls.gov/tus/charts/home.htm

Page 10:   Merriam-Webster Dictionary, http://www.merriam-webster.com/
           medical/adult

Page 11:   http://www.huffingtonpost.com/2009/05/17/ten-best-commence-
           ment-spe_n_204427.html

Page 24:   U.S. Department of State.

Page 29:   www.EurailPass.com.

Page 37:   http://www.forbes.com/2009/05/14/adult-kids-moving-home-
           forbeswoman-time-family.html, "Hi, Mom! I'm ... Back!"
           Forbes.com, May 14, 2009

Page 43:   The Wall Street Journal, "The Next Youth Magnet Cities,"
           September 30, 2009
           http://online.wsj.com/article/SB2000142405274870378720457444291
           2720525316.html

Page 46:   http://www.kiplinger.com/magazine/archives/2008/07/2008-bestci-
           ties-to-live-work-play.html

Page 56:   "11 Essential Purchases for Your Apartment," Jennifer Lai,
           About.com

Page 56:   http://www.mayflower.com/moving/government-military/movingtips/
           facts-about-moving.htm

Page 84:   "Amherst Grads Shun Wall Street, Save World as $45,500 Teachers,"
           Bloomberg, June 23, 2009

Page 99:   "Jobs That Will Disappear," May 20, 2006
           http://www.forbes.com/2006/05/20/cx_hc_06work_disappear_jobs_
           slide.html?partner=msnedit

Page 150: "Give Thanks, Get the Job" - http://hotjobs.yahoo.com/career-arti-
           cles-recruiter_roundtable_thank_you_notes-218

Page 152: Adapted from "Job Rejection Letter Sample," About.com
           http://jobsearch.about.com/od/morejobletters/a/rejectajob.htm

Page 176: CareerBuilder.com
           http://www.careerbuilder.com/share/aboutus/pressreleasesdetail.as
           px?id=pr481&sd=2/10/2009&ed=12/31/2009

Page 182: HappyWorker.com, http://www.happyworker.com/bossman/surveys

Page 202: "Ask Annie: Must I Buy My Boss a Pricey Holiday Gift?"
           http://money.cnn.com/2006/11/21/news/economy/gifts.at.work.fortune/
           index.htm

Page 208: http://justinhartman.com/2008/03/03/interesting-email-facts/

Page 209: Just what do you mean http://www.businessweek.com/magazine/
           content/06_49/b4012096.htm?chan=search

Page 212: http://www.theregister.co.uk/2005/04/22/email_destroys_iq/

Page 230: http://grad-schools.usnews.rankingsandreviews.com/best-graduate-
           schools/top-business-schools/rankings

Page 240: Grad School Humor – About.com
           http://gradschool.about.com/od/gradstudenthumor/Grad_Student_
           Humor.htm

Page 240: http://www.nytimes.com/2009/03/07/arts/07grad.html 'Humanties Ph.D's Anticipating Hard Times," The New York Times, March 7, 2009

Page 253: WeightLossforAll.com http://www.weightlossforall.com/mcdonaldscalories-list.htm
Diet Bites http://www.dietbites.com/calories/calories-in-pizza.html

Page 263: NYTimes.com, June 14, 2009
http://roomfordebate.blogs.nytimes.com/2009/06/14/how-much-student-debt-is-too-much

Page 276: http://www.soyouwanna.com/site/toptens/expensivecities/expensivecities.html

Page 329: http://www.bestplaces.net/docs/studies/DatingCities.aspx

Page 375: American Religious Identification Survey 2008, Trinity College, http://www.americanreligionsurvey-aris.org/

Page 386: "Why we're sleeping less," March 6, 2009
http://www.cnn.com/2009/HEALTH/03/04/sleep.stress.economy/index.html

ANOTHER GREAT RESOURCE FOR GRADUATES!

Start Here: Getting Your Financial Life on Track is the guide to fulfilling your dreams. It's a study of tactics: concrete plans and procedures for getting what you want, specifically in the realm of money.

- How to Pay Your Bills on Time
- Your Credit Score—And What to Do about It
- Couples and Money: Outsmarting Conflict
- Is It Time to Buy a House?
- And More!

To purchase a copy, please visit the AIER Bookstore: www.aier.org/bookstore.

THANKS

Thanks to our intrepid "headhunters" for going out to find so many respondents from around the country with interesting advice to share:

Jamie Allen, Chief Headhunter

Gloria Averbuch	Lisa Jaffe Hubbell	William Ramsey
Jennifer Batog	Natasha Lambropoulos	Kazz Regelman
Jennifer Blaise	Linda Lincoln	Besha Rodell
Helen Bond	Robin Lofton	Stacey Shannon
Jennifer Bright Reich	Ken McCarthy	Jody Shenn
Sally Burns	Carly Milne	Graciela Sholander
Nicole Colangelo-Lessin	Lindsay Nash	Staci Siegel
Scott Deckman	John Nemo	Marie Suszynski
Sara Faiwell	Christina Orlovsky	Andrea Syrtash
Connie Farrow	Andrea Parker	Matt Villano
Jayne Leigh Hallock	Adam Pollock	Jade Walker
Carrie Havranek	Lisa Powell	Sara Walker
Shannon Hurd	Pete Ramirez	Patricia Woods

Thanks to our assistant, Miri Greidi, for her yeoman's work at keeping us all organized. The real credit for this book, of course, goes to all the people whose experiences and collective wisdom make up this guide. There are too many of you to thank individually, but you know who you are.

CHECK OUT THESE OTHER BOOKS FROM HUNDREDS OF HEADS®

**HOW TO
SURVIVE
A MOVE**
(256 pages, $13.95)
ISBN 0-9746292-5-1

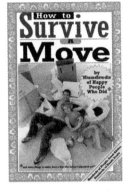

Useful suggestions and entertaining stories from hundreds of people who have moved in every possible direction across the country. The tips in this book will ease the task of planning, packing and enduring a move.

"After 14 moves in 34 years, I thought I knew everything about how to move. But I was wrong - I could have used this book at every stage of my life in moving."

—Caren Masem
  Greensboro, NC

"Whether you're moving in, moving out, or moving up, you're sure to find just the advice you need in How to Survive a Move."

—Dallas Morning News

**BE THE
CHANGE!
CHANGE
THE WORLD.
CHANGE
YOURSELF.**
(336 pages, $14.95)
ISBN-10: 1-933512-00-8
ISBN-13: 978-1933512-00-6

By intertwining practical advice on service and volunteerism with real-life stories of personal transformation, this book is the perfect companion for people who want to be inspired and informed and to take action to change their lives and their world.
Edited by Michelle Nunn, Co-founder and CEO of Hands On Network.

"This is a wonderful and inspiring book."

—Walter Isaacson CEO, Aspen Institute

"This is a book that could change your life ... It's almost magic and it could happen to everyone. Go!"

—Jim Lehrer, anchor, PBS' NewsHour with Jim Lehrer

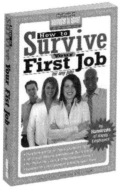

Hundreds of gainfully employed, recently out of college, young people offer the best tips, stories, and advice on how to survive your job. Learn the best strategies for landing a first job, launching a career, and succeeding (or just hanging in there) at work. Get great tips on dealing with difficult bosses, odd coworkers, sub-optimal environments and tasks, and climbing (or slipping down) the corporate ladder.

Special Editors: Ricki Frankel, Executive and Career Coach, and Master Coach for the Leadership Coaching Course at Stanford's Graduate School of Business; and Angela Reddock, attorney and workplace consultant.

HOW TO SURVIVE YOUR FIRST JOB OR ANY JOB...by Hundreds of Happy Employees (268 pages, $14.95)

ISBN-10: 1-933512-07-5
ISBN-13: 978-1933-512-07-5

The best straight-from-the-trenches tips on dating, from hundreds of happy singles, and some who tied the knot.

"Whether you are single or not, *How to Survive Dating* will have you rolling with laughter …. The book contains hundreds of pearls of wisdom …. This isn't your ordinary dating book."
—TRUE ROMANCE

A 'top 10' dating book.
—ABOUT.COM

HOW TO SURVIVE DATING...by Hundreds of Happy Singles Who Did (and some things to avoid, from a few broken hearts who didn't) (248 pages, $12.95)

ISBN-10: 0-9746292-1-9
ISBN-13: 978-0974-62921-6

About the Contributors

AIER: For over 75 years the American Institute for Economic Research (AIER) has offered unbiased research to the general public. AIER research is conducted by eminent economists and scholars and provides timely and incisive analysis of contemporary issues. AIER has been featured nationally in such publications as the Wall Street Journal, Money.com, CNN, Investor's Business Daily, The Christian Science Monitor, USA Today, Miami Herald and on Fox Business News TV shows.

MARIO CARANNANTE is an independent financial advisor who operates out of Blue Bell, Pennsylvania but serves clients who reside throughout the country. He assists in many areas of financial planning, including: saving, budgeting, investing, insurance, retirement planning and business planning. He volunteers his time providing financial advice to college students in his area. Mario is a graduate of Kutztown University. You can email him at Mario_Carannante@ipgroup.info.

SHANNON DUFF holds a BA and an MBA from Yale University, and works as a private advisor for applicants to college, graduate school, internship, and jobs. Through her work, Shannon is dedicated to helping students to find the right fit in a school or job, teaching valuable lifelong self-marketing skills all the while. Her previous experience working as an admissions reader for Yale's Undergraduate Admissions Office enables Shannon to bring firsthand perspective to today's admissions landscape. Before working as an educational consultant, Shannon worked as an associate at Lehman Brothers. She was active in recruiting throughout her four years on Wall Street, giving her a unique perspective on what employers are looking for in both interns and full-time hires.

SARAH FRANCO graduated from Middlebury College in May 2008 with a B.A. in Religion. Since then, she has worked as the Research Consultant for the Project on Creativity & Innovation in the Liberal Arts at her alma mater. She is currently pursuing a Master of Education, specializing in Higher Education Administration, at Northeastern University's College of Professional Studies.

KATE HUNTER earned a Master's of Education in Student Affairs in Higher Education at Kutztown University and a Bachelor's Degree in Psychology from Moravian College. Kate is currently employed as the Director of Career Services & Internship at DeSales University in Center Valley, Pennsylvania. In addition to her role in Career Services, Kate also co-coordinates the Senior Success Series and serves as a lecturer in the Psychology Department.

Whether it's art reviews, corporate communications, or her latest project, *Your Little Black Facebook*, **ELIZABETH LOVETT** infuses her artistic and creative background into everything. Her international background spanning London, Southeast Asia, and the deep South gives her a unique vantage point from which she observes emerging social trends. Lovett currently lives in Atlanta with her equally adventurous husband and much less adventurous beagle.

ANGIE MOCK's varied career has taken her from CPA, to CEO of a hotel management company, to communications consultant, to relationship expert and co-author of *Your Little Black Facebook*. The common theme throughout her career has been her interest in people and their interactions: her colleagues, her friends and family, and the world at large. She has been interviewed by several media outlets on this subject, and she's always learning more. She lives with her husband and three children in San Antonio, Texas.

Dr. R.D. NORTON is a senior fellow and research advisor at the American Institute for Economic Research. He is the author or editor of a dozen books on economics and finance and holds a Ph.D. from Princeton University. He was formerly Executive Director of the Eastern Economic Association and an economics professor at the University of Texas at Dallas, Mount Holyoke College, and Bryant University, where he had an endowed chair in business economics.

ANGELA J. REDDOCK, ESQ., an attorney and workplace consultant, is the founding and managing partner of the Reddock Law Group, headquartered in Los Angeles, California. Reddock specializes in all aspects of employment and labor law, including litigation, advice and counseling, and workplace training programs. She has advised corporate executives, in-house counsel, and human resource professionals on a variety of employment and labor law matters. Reddock earned her J.D. from UCLA School of Law. She has twice been named a Rising Star in employment and labor law in the Southern California edition of *Super Lawyers* magazine.

People and their stories hold no end of fascination for **ROBERT RHU**. A professional speaker and co-author of *Your Little Black Facebook* by day, after hours his focus shifts to his music. An accomplished singer/songwriter, Rhu's music is a vehicle for connecting with audiences and telling his story. Rhu currently resides in Boulder, Colorado, where he wakes up every morning, looks at the mountains and is happy to be there.

ANDREA SYRTASH is a dating expert, author and the host of "ON Dating," produced by NBC Digital Studios. She is a regular advice columnist for Yahoo! and The Huffington Post, and has shared advice in various media outlets including "The Today Show," NPR and USA Today. Andrea was the Special Editor for two Hundreds of Heads titles: *How to Survive the Real World* (2006) and *How to Survive Your In-Laws* (2007). She is currently working on her third book, a dating advice title. For more, please visit www.andreasyrtash.com.

ABOUT THE SPECIAL EDITOR

NADIA BILCHIK is the author of *The Little Book of Big Networking Ideas: A Guide to Expert Networking.* She also serves as a television news anchor, author, keynote speaker, media trainer, and communications consultant. In her consulting work, Nadia delivers workshops and keynote addresses around the world on interpersonal communication, networking, presentation skills and professional presence to companies like CNN, Cartoon Network, Equifax, Women in Cable Telecommunications, TruTV, Coca-Cola, Home Depot, and Delta.

Over the course of her broadcasting career, Nadia has hosted feature programs for CNN International, and anchored the CNN Airport Network. She has interviewed world-renowned politicians, celebrities and musicians, including Nelson Mandela, George Clooney, Matt Damon, Jennifer Lopez, and Slash. She was also a prime-time anchor and special assignment reporter for MNET Television, the leading South African network.

Nadia received a Licentiate in Speech and Drama from Trinity College, London, and a B.A. in Drama and English from the University of Cape Town, South Africa. Early in her career, she had parts in nine feature films. She died in all of them.

ABOUT RICKI FRANKEL

RICKI FRANKEL is an executive coach specializing in career and leadership development. She is particular passionate about helping her clients navigate skillfully and gracefully through career and life transitions. She is also a Master Coach and adjunct staff for several leadership courses at Stanford's Graduate School of Business. Ricki has an MBA from Wharton and a BA from Dartmouth College.